APPARENT NARRATIVE AS THEMATIC METAPHOR

The Organization of THE FAERIE QUEENE

BY
JAN KAREL
KOUWENHOVEN

ἔρχεται ὥρα καὶ νῦν ἐστιν

CLARENDON PRESS · OXFORD
1983

Oxford University Press, Walton Street, Oxford OX2 6DP
London Glasgow New York Toronto
Delhi Bombay Calcutta Madras Karachi
Kuala Lumpur Singapore Hong Kong Tokyo
Nairobi Dar es Salaam Cape Town
Melbourne Auckland
and associated companies in
Beirut Berlin Ibadan Mexico City Nicosia

Oxford is a trade mark of Oxford University Press

Published in the United States
by Oxford University Press, New York

British Library Cataloguing in Publication Data
Kouwenhoven, Jan Karel
Apparent narrative as thematic metaphor: the organization of The Faerie Queene.
1. Spenser, Edmund. Faerie Queene
I. Title
821'.3 PR2358
ISBN 0-19-812819-3

Library of Congress Cataloging in Publication Data
Kouwenhoven, Jan Karel, 1951–
Apparent narrative as thematic metaphor.
Revision of thesis (Ph.D.)—University of Edinburgh, 1981.
Bibliography: p.
Includes index.
1. Spenser, Edmund, 1552?–1599. Faerie queene.
2. Spenser, Edmund, 1552?–1599—Allegory and symbolism.
I. Title.
PR2358.K68 1983 821'.3 83-15009
ISBN 0-19-812819-3

Typeset by Joshua Associates, Oxford
Printed in Great Britain
at the University Press, Oxford

to my Renaissance tutees

(*Edinburgh, Autumn Term 1980*)

Cathrin Burton
Kenneth Dixon
Isabelle Nurser
Alexandra Watson

Elizabeth Heinsohn
Eileen Nicoll
Peter Norman
Christianne Rostant

that they may live with the eternity of my fame

PREFACE

This book is a revised version of my doctoral thesis with the same title (University of Edinburgh, 1981). It re-examines Spenser's Letter to Ralegh, so often ignored or even maligned, to find that it makes sense, both internally and with reference to his poem, on two conditions. One is that we grasp the poet's conceptual argument, according to which morality manifests redemption in Christ and so constitutes the earthly anticipation of heavenly glory. The other is that, for once, we take him literally when he calls his work a continued allegory. Existing criticism, while generally accepting the poem's allegorical status, persists in treating its fiction as narrative. Spenser makes such treatment logically impossible. He invites it only to expose the stories' illusoriness, thus directing the reader to take them as symbols, not *exempla.* Literally the whole poem falls to pieces, which are united exclusively in virtue of their allegorical meaning. This unity is given. Yet interpretation has to struggle endlessly to work it out: it reveals itself only intermittently, in flashes. Salvation, too, is given. Yet morality has to battle continuously to work it out, being only an elusive intimation of immortality. The poem's mode enacts its theme.

Two institutions deserve my gratitude for financial assistance. The University of Edinburgh granted me a studentship covering the period from October 1976 till December 1977, which enabled me to start the project. The Netherlands Organization for the Advancement of Pure Research (Z.W.O.) employed me from January 1978 till December 1979, by which time the dissertation was receiving its penultimate draft. Less easily measurable is the assistance of my three supervisors: Professor Alastair Fowler, who took the lion's share; Dr Jonquil Bevan, who volunteered to take his place when he was on sabbatical leave; and Professor A. L. Vos, who monitored the Dutch connection. I do thank them all; and Professor Fowler in particular for suggesting a good many of the passages that needed to be rethought or rephrased for publication. I have derived much comfort and stimulation from discussions with Mr Richard Hamilton, Dr Michael Leslie, and my dedicatees.

Edinburgh,
December 1982

CONTENTS

One

GROUNDWORK

I What is Wrong with *The Faerie Queene*?

Spenser's *magnum opus* eludes its readers, or even loses them altogether. To most lovers of English literature their national epic is peripheral. It fails to register. This is not because of its unfinished state: for a fragment the work is strikingly complete in itself. The trouble lies in its apparent indeterminacy, both semantic and structural. One feels as though condemned to an interpreters' Hades, groping vainly for meanings or clasping nebulous tautologies. The poem persistently frustrates one's need for self-authenticating rightness and so mortifies one's libido. One also faces its 'labyrinthine unsearchability', to use Fowler's phrase. Sale, less glamorously, calls it 'theoretically endless', noting how 'it never "gets anywhere" '.[1] The unsettling effect of the work *qua* story is too profound to be traced to Spenser's use of interwoven narrative, much though that in itself flouts both the argued prejudices of doctrinaire neo-classicists and the implicit assumptions of those reared on naturalistic novels. *Entrelacement* dislocates readers only to raise and, eventually, fulfil expectations of home-coming, as in Ariosto.[2] Nor is it that Spenser, in self-defeating rivalry with Ariosto's complexity, leaves suspended too many strands to be remembered; let alone that he loses control of them himself. (His inconsistencies, when not 'obviously' slips of the pen, prompt specific explanations, such as Bennett's evolutionary theory.[3]) It is, rather, that the internal coherence of his strands seems insubstantial. Not only does he not imitate the zest and bravura with which Ariosto abandons, picks up, and gathers in the threads: when one joins constituent scenes for him, more often than not the hinge turns out to be a mere 'and then', without any content. Take the story of Belphœbe. Neither the first Belphœbe episode (II. iii), nor the second (III. v), is manifestly 'to be continued'. Nor does the vantage point of the third (IV. vii–viii) reveal a unified story with an intelligible development. This inconsequentiality does not result from *dispositio*; which, on the contrary, conceals it to some extent. It obtains equally between consecutive episodes belonging to a single strand. Thus the Red Cross Knight's meeting with Archimago does not truly follow on from his defeat of Error, which reads like a self-contained mini-story in spite of being 'continued' immediately (I. i).

As an attempt to identify the stumbling-block in *The Faerie Queene* this will probably command the assent of those who have given it up. As an indictment, however, it begs the question. If the poem's indeterminacy is as pervasive as here alleged, it must be, in philosophical terms, a property rather than an accident. Hence it cannot be adduced to justify neglect as if it were a flaw in conception or execution. The deserters are trapped. So far the work's champions have not alerted them to their condition. This may be because they know that embarrassment alone will not send them flocking back. But it may also be because they believe that in the last resort the poem's indeterminacy requires not an answer, which they could not provide themselves, but a taste; about which, as the proverb says, there is no disputing. They have, of course, noticed the poet's own recognition that 'the discourse . . . may happily seeme tedious and confused' and his awareness of 'how doubtfully all Allegories may be construed' (L 132–3, 1[4]). However, they have missed the earnestness both of his self-accusation and of his desire that the semblance should be removed and the doubt resolved. They take him to be making tactical overstatements, to win an audience by suggesting his modesty and its cleverness. And they may well be perfectly honest in this attitude. No doubt long familiarity with the poem and critical sophistication reduce the impact of its elusiveness; or, to speak from their point of view, the present diagnosis is exaggerated and crude. *The Faerie Queene* unreadable, with its superb rhetoric and versification, and its wealth of powerful description? The allegory inaccessible, when everywhere this mode is coming into its own again, after the romantic-symbolist eclipse, and extended introductions to its function in Spenser abound?[5] The narrative trackless, when it is schematically contained, almost as in Dante, in Books devoted to distinct virtues and full of small-scale patterning; intricate, as in Busirane's tapestry (III. xi) and the wedding of Thames and Medway (IV. xi),[6] or even straightforward, as in the processions of the Seven Deadly Sins (I. iv) and the Twelve Months (VII. vii)? Compared with the discourse of, say, Deguileville or Langland, is Spenser's not a model of naturally progressing narrative, as allegories go? True, some perplexity remains; whence the growing consensus that Spenser cannot have cared much for plot.[7] But surely genre dictates an air of mystery? Not only the poem's ostensible subject matter, knightly quests, but also such features as absence of motivation, lack of suspense, and supernaturalism are proper to romance. Inconsequentiality characterizes dreams, too; and although the poem is not formally a dream vision, we might make the most of the analogy, with Hough, who hints at a subliminal import.[8] Alternatively, we might regard the fiction as myth, in the sense defined by C. S. Lewis. He writes—though perhaps not with *The Faerie Queene* in mind—of 'the persistent tendency of humanity to provide myths with allegorical explanations. And after all allegories have been tried, the myth itself continues to feel more important than they.'[9] Could it not be that Spenser is one of our great visionary poets, in direct communication with the world of archetypes?

With such considerations the champions dodge the issue. The question is not whether allegory in general enjoys critical favour but whether Spenser's allegory makes sense. The prolix disquisitions on 'how it works' do succeed in making the poem seem inexhaustible. But their very indecisiveness and divergence act as deterrents. Occasionally we will be assured that 'the need for narrative coherence may conflict with the need for consistency of thought' or that 'illogicalities inevitably arise in situations where absolutes and relatives jostle one another'. Do we really deserve to be branded 'naïve' if such assertions make us restive?[10] Are we not bound to infer that our guides are lost, quite like ourselves? Again, *The Faerie Queene*, however comparatively smooth, remains inherently baffling. Nor, incidentally, can it be taken for granted that Spenser improves on his predecessors: they may not aim at the result he 'almost' achieves in the first place.

The generic mysteriousness of romance is cold comfort. Finally, Spenser's fiction does not strike most of us as too meaningful for words; it seems meaningless, rather. Elusiveness is not necessarily numinous. Attempts to induce spurious awe will soon look ridiculous. Some may be momentarily carried away by the riotous cult of the unfathomable now practised in certain quarters. But few are genuinely convinced even by Lewis's relatively sober conclusion, over forty years ago, that the poetry 'has really tapped sources not easily accessible to discursive thought'.[11] (The conclusion itself feels more important than its intention, namely as an ironic circumlocution meaning, quite rightly, that the poetry is silly beyond description.) In short, any defence of *The Faerie Queene* along the lines indicated above is futile. Though the cowardly deserters are trapped, so are the seasoned champions. They have made a virtue of necessity; they have not redeemed the poem.

But this is blanket condemnation, inevitably unfair and probably counter-productive. Why not seek common ground and stress that most critics admit, if only obliquely, to an uncertain grasp at least of the poem's overall design? After all, nobody follows Upton in blithely crediting the work, in the face of the evidence, with unity of action through Arthur.[12] Hardly anybody shares Lewis's blind faith in the ways of romance: 'It has been the fate of the *Faerie Queene* to be attacked where it is strongest. The plan, the story, the invention are triumphant. If they have faults, they are such faults as never deterred any reader except those who dislike romance and would not be allured to read it by any perfections.'[13] Instead we all admire Hurd's sensible discussion of the poem 'under the idea not of a classical but Gothic composition', finding ourselves drawn towards yet reluctant to accept his conclusion that

> as an allegorical poem, the method of the *Faerie Queene* is governed by the justness of the moral: as a narrative poem it is conducted on the ideas and usages of chivalry. In either view, if taken by itself, the plan is defensible. But from the union of the two designs there arises a perplexity and confusion, which is the proper, and only considerable, defect of this extraordinary poem.[14]

To dispel uneasiness about the poem's overall design in

particular seems to have been Spenser's main concern in the Letter to Ralegh, which directs the reader 'to the wel-head of the History; that from thence gathering the whole intention of the conceit, [he] may as in a handfull gripe al the discourse' (L 130–2). The poet beams confidence in the unity of his creation. Ironically, his effort at illumination has itself proved an embarrassment—when it is heeded at all, that is: some critics, emancipated from the 'intentional fallacy', treat it in cavalier fashion or ignore it altogether, to indulge in the most bewildering varieties of exegesis;[15] which, needless to say, do not reveal the poem's 'fore-conceit'.[16] Most critics, however, are prepared to welcome the Letter as a promising guide, only to find that it does not tally with the poem. Thus Arthur, discussed at length as though he were its dominating character, appears only incidentally. And the account of the origin of the knights' adventures is, where it can be checked against the poem, repeatedly at odds with it in fact or by implication.[17] Besides, there are quite a few puzzles not directly concerning plot. So the Letter seems to disqualify itself. Convinced that the discrepancies are real, critics agree that their business is with the poem as it stands; naturally, since even staunch intentionalists could not allow authorial comments to overrule the evidence of the work.

Nevertheless, many have given thought to the problem. For some it loses much of its acuteness on considering that the Letter is a postscript rather than a preface in the 1590 edition of *The Faerie Queene* (Books I–III) and, what is more, does not reappear in the 1596 edition (Books I–VI).[18] Surely, though, accuracy is not a function of relative prominence. And Spenser's withdrawal of the Letter can be construed in more than one way. It need not be a silent admission of its inadequacy. Perhaps he no longer considered it necessary. Perhaps he felt disinclined to recast or expand what is really an introduction to Books I–III in particular. Perhaps the Letter's absence is simply an oversight, or else a reflection of altered external circumstances: the addressee, Ralegh, after his secret marriage to Elizabeth Throckmorton had aroused the Queen's displeasure, never regained the position of favourite courtier that he had enjoyed before 1590.[19] Spenser may have felt that it would be indelicate for his *Faerie*

Queene, dedicated as it is to his sovereign, to advertise its association with Ralegh.[20] Alternatively, he may no longer have cared to posture as an obedient servant. (Ralegh ordered the Letter, if we are to take the poet at his word: 'Being so by you commanded', L 5.) Had the Queen not acknowledged Spenser's poetic tribute to her after the appearance of its first instalment? The Dedicatory Sonnets to Elizabeth's statesmen, too, are absent from the 1596 edition. All this remains, of course, speculation. But it does prove one thing: the mere fact that the Letter was not republished does not imply that it must be at odds with the poem of 1590—or, for that matter, with that of 1596, whose first half is, but for an additional stanza in I. xi and the different ending to Book III, substantially identical. In any case, to play down the status of the Letter is not to explain why it misrepresents the poem.

Among those who have attempted such an explanation two tendencies can be observed. Some take the discrepancies at their face value and dismiss the Letter as all but irrelevant. Owen and Lewis, each in his different way, are exponents of this tendency. Owen believes that the Letter 'describes a version of *The Faerie Queene* which Spenser planned in 1590 but never wrote'. His essay certainly expounds some of the difficulties which the Letter raises with admirable lucidity. Yet his argument is too narrow to dictate its conclusion. For one thing, the Letter would be the only piece of evidence that in 1590 Spenser wished to depart from his original plan. Owen offers no suggestions as to why he should, all of a sudden, have become dissatisfied with his work as it stood. For another thing, if the new scheme is as muddled as Owen would have it, can it really be distinguished confidently from the one it is allegedly meant to replace? And then, why did Spenser publish it, if 'he did not find time in the haste of printing, proof-reading, and the like' to adjust his poem?[21] C. S. Lewis takes a different line. As he sees it, the narrative is to be conceived of not, rhetorically, as the embodiment of a definite, consistent, and elaborate plan but, romantically, as an organic growth, whose design lends itself only to rough-and-ready rationalization.[22] On this view discrepancies between the poem and any schematic account of it are simply in the nature of things. Thus any reason for anxiety seems removed at one stroke. But Lewis's argument does not explain any one of the discrepancies individually: it is vacuous. This becomes painfully manifest when one turns to his point-by-point denunciation of the Letter in a later study. It is one thing to hold that the mysteries of the creative process are not easily caught in sober expository prose. It is quite another thing to pass this off as the explanation for a Letter bristling with glaringly counter-factual statements. Its tone and structure certainly do not suggest a writer fumbling for safe generalizations. In truth Lewis's conception of the poem's genesis is no more than an assumption; and a thoroughly anachronistic one at that. His picture of Spenser the poet as an inspired *vates*, uttering profundities that can be fully apprehended only 'on the tripod', is clearly dear to his heart. But does it rest on anything more solid than his animus against humanist poetics?[23]

Arguments to prove the Letter irrelevant carry little conviction. They go against common sense and look like special pleading. That is why other critics prefer to think of it as *essentially* valid. They attribute the discrepancies to the Letter's general purpose, in light of which they may be considered immaterial. According to Hamilton, its account of the knights' adventures is 'deliberately formalized': Spenser himself says that they are '"severally [that is, differently] handled and discoursed". But in a preface . . . he need not describe . . . how they are differently handled.'[24] 'Severally' does not mean 'differently', though: it means 'in one-to-one distribution', as Owen points out.[25] Tuve's important study of medieval 'Allegory of Vices and Virtues' goes a long way towards explaining Arthur as *conceptually* central to *The Faerie Queene.*[26] But, curiously enough, she will not see that in the narrative Arthur's role is 'puzzlingly minor'. Nor do the other discrepancies really register. To her Spenser's poem is representative of the medieval tradition of Arthurian romance. Its 'fore-conceit', so far from being a unique scheme, is almost trite: 'We must recognize how conventional and unfortuitous his design is, and how likely it is that such a framework was assumed long before the precise statement of it.'[27] The Letter, for all its specific inaccuracies, conveys the type adequately enough. But surely to ease the problem in this way is to create a new one: if *The Faerie Queene* falls so obviously into place, a Letter purporting to 'give great light to the reader' must be oddly superfluous. As it happens, the Letter does not define the poem *vis-à-vis* medieval romance at all. Instead it aligns it with Renaissance romance-epic (Ariosto, Tasso), which it treats on a par with classical epic (Homer, Virgil; see L 17–25). Moreover, as an account of that genre it agrees perfectly with humanist theory of epic, as has been usefully shown by Nelson.[28] Not that this necessarily invalidates Tuve's position: the theory in question does not involve structure. Perhaps, indeed, Nelson takes unfair advantage of this so as to avoid coming to grips with the specific discrepancies unnoticed. But then, who does explain why they are there? The idea that the Letter's essential purpose naturally entails carelessness over minor details, if that is what they are, is by no means inherently compelling.

The Letter, then, like the poem, has its deserters and its champions. And again both parties are trapped. Thus we find our predicament confirmed instead of resolved. Yet this is, paradoxically, encouraging. Prompted to embrace our confusion, we sense salvation at hand. In this Chapter I shall try to articulate the solution, which Spenser states *sotto voce* in the Letter, and to show how it bridges the gap between Letter and poem. Such an attempt more or less presumes correspondence. However, I have no time for procedural scruples. Though the validity of the Letter depends on whether it agrees with the poem, it is there to illuminate it, not to be justified by it. After centuries of interpretative failure let us not disdain authorial assistance.

II One Meaning

Preoccupation with the Letter's apparent inaccuracies has obscured a more fundamental incongruity: the information it provides, whether correct or not, does not answer the *kind* of questions the poem raises. It does nothing to relieve uncertainty about 'how the allegory works'. Instead it says what the allegory means. And it does this so summarily as to make itself useless, or so it would seem, for anything but the most superficial interpretation. 'In that Faery Queene I meane glory'; 'in the person of Prince Arthure I sette forth magnificence'; 'the knight of the Redcrosse, in whome I expresse Holynes'; 'Sir Guyon, in whome I sette forth Temperaunce'; 'Britomartis a Lady knight, in whome I picture Chastity' (L 49–68). All this is hardly revealing. Nor, surely, does it qualify as a specimen of the type of reading *The Faerie Queene* requires. For it subsumes where the poem expands, running, even in its unfinished form, to over four hundred closely printed pages. Allegorical reading cannot consist in sticking on labels such as these. Conversely, more than half of the Letter is devoted to an outline of the poem's narrative framework. Yet, in spite of the maze-like fiction, the need for this does not make itself felt. What the Letter has to say about Arthur's story (L 43–9) can easily be gleaned from the poem (I. ix. 1–15). And while the Letter's circumstantial account of the origin of the titular knights' adventures at the Faery Queen's annual feast (L 77–124) does give information not contained in what we have of the poem, it does not unify the narrative but merely complements it rather irrelevantly. The one major point, that the knights have started out from Faery Court, emerges clearly enough from the poem itself. The reader's detailed knowledge of events at Faery Court, which recedes beyond his horizon no matter where he immerses himself in the poem, contributes nothing to his grasp of the fiction.

What are we to make of an explanatory document that is so stupendously uninformative? I propose that the function of the Letter's narrative component has been radically misunderstood. It is not a plot summary. Spenser directs us to 'the wel-head of the History' so that we may 'from thence gather . . . the whole intention of the conceit'; not 'the whole course of events': its extremely limited scope could not possibly enable us so to 'gripe *al* the discourse' (L 130–2). 'Conceit' reminds us that *The Faerie Queene*, which the Letter's second half discusses in terms of story, is really, as its first half states at once, 'a continued Allegory, or darke *conceit*' (L 3). The 'wel-head' is not a guide to the vehicle of the allegory (the 'History') but a metaphorical definition of its tenor (the 'intention'). Though (ostensibly) *part* of the 'History', it defines 'the *whole* intention'; which implies that *all* parts of the 'History' have the same 'intention'. This, in its turn, implies that there is no autonomous 'History': the poem is a collection of synonymous allegorical set pieces masquerading as narrative. The fiction *qua* story is an insubstantial pageant, a mosaic of vehicles for metaphors skilfully contrived and arranged so as to create the illusion of narrative, but in reality disconnected.

On the face of it Spenser's adoption of the role of 'Historiographer' (L 78) precludes such a revolutionary adjustment. Does it really, though? 'But because the beginning of the whole worke seemeth abrupte and as depending upon other antecedents, it needs that ye know the occasion of these three knights severall adventures.' (L 68–71.) This certainly suggests narrative discourse. Yet the sentence is cleverly non-committal. 'Seemeth' and 'as depending' do not allow us to decide that the appearance of abruptness and dependence is true. Nor does the logic of the sentence as a whole: the account of the adventures' origin might be intended to reveal that the appearance is illusory, rather than to supply a narrative context. After all, it provides no truly *con*-textual support, as we have just seen. And because of the poem's pervasive inconsequentiality the abruptness of its opening does not stand out and so arouses no curiosity about 'thinges forepaste' anyway. Moreover, Spenser distinguishes the 'Poet historical' from the 'Historiographer' by saying that the former, in abandoning the method of the latter, who 'discourseth of affayres orderly as they were donne, accounting as well the times as the actions', 'maketh a pleasing Analysis of all' (L 73–7). What could the word 'analysis', used here of poetry itself, mean if not, in accordance with its etymology, the 'unloosing' of the temporal and causal chain basic to narrative proper?[29] And how could the reconversion of such analytic poetry into sequential history be anything but a pseudo-procedure?

The narrative component of the Letter to Ralegh merely pretends to be a key to the poem's fiction as such. It is in fact a complementary metaphor for a work which, as the closing paragraph so unmistakably implies, means one and the same thing throughout. But can this implication be taken seriously? Are we to believe that Spenser was a monomaniac, or a colossal bore? This objection presupposes, wrongly, that what makes his work interesting is that it offers opportunities for construing a multifarious allegorical significance. Consider the riddle, which rhetoricians commonly classify with allegory[30] and which must be particularly close to Spenser's variety, the 'darke conceit'. The point of a riddle is not its solution but the transfiguration into intelligibility of the riddle itself, the elated recognition of how every puzzling element finds its *raison d'être* in the solution. Similarly with Spenser's allegory. The point is not the tenor for its own sake but the 'revelation' of the vehicle as irradiated by the tenor. Proper reading is conditional upon but not oriented towards discovery of meaning. To interpret *The Faerie Queene* is not to extrapolate meanings but to see how its single meaning informs and sustains it in its every detail. It is in this light, and in this light only, that one can endorse Hamilton's insistence on what he calls, not very felicitously, 'the primacy of the literal level'.[31] It will now be appreciated why the poet turns a deaf ear to the clamour for methods of decoding. If there were guide-lines for the solution of riddles, there would not be riddles.

So a *Faerie Queene* with a single tenor is by no means an unimaginable monstrosity. But now another difficulty presents itself. Are Spenser's statements about what the allegory means, which at the beginning of this Section we took almost unquestioningly for broad generalizations, not at odds with singleness of meaning even when interpreted as tightly fitting definitions? Surely glory, magnificence, holiness, temperance, chastity, to say nothing of the virtues of Books IV–XII, are manifestly different things? The Letter answers that they are only in the sense of being different aspects of one and the same thing. ('Aspect' is used strictly here, and throughout. For one notion to be an aspect of another means that the former *is* the latter, seen from a particular angle.) There are two stages in Spenser's argument. First he says that 'in that Faery Queene I meane glory in my generall intention'. After a digression to point out that 'in [his] particular' both she and Belphœbe 'shadow' Queen Elizabeth, he goes on to say that 'in the person of Prince

Arthure I sette forth magnificence *in particular*'. This, despite the final words, clearly defines the *general* intention of Arthur; for 'magnificence' is on a par with 'glory', as an abstract noun, not with 'our soveraine the Queene'. Hence magnificence must be a particular aspect of glory. Secondly, Spenser says that magnificence, in its turn, is '(according to Aristotle and the rest) . . . the perfection of all the [virtues], and conteineth in it them all'. (L 49–61.)

Unfortunately, though the presence of some such argument can easily be detected, its logic cannot. For all Spenser's casualness the equivalence of glory and magnificence is certainly not self-evident. Besides, as a comprehensive term for all the virtues added together magnificence is a mere *flatus vocis*, so that no particular virtue could be truly an aspect of it. Nor is this conception of magnificence at all obvious and familiar. The poet's reference to 'Aristotle and the rest', presumably thrown in as a reassuring allusion to a commonplace of ethics, only makes confusion worse confounded. Aristotle, for one, does not use magnificence in this sense. Or could it be that this final difficulty, at least, is unreal? As Lewis observes, in the poem, too,

> there is no trait of *megaloprepeia* (Magnificence) in [Arthur's] character, no slightest indication that he is a large spender. But there is probably a confusion of terms here, due to some bad Latin translation you were using. What you mean is Magnanimity, not Magnificence; *megalopsychia*, not *megaloprepeia*. The crown of all the virtues is for Aristotle a right Pride or Magnanimity, which deserves and claims the highest honour.[32]

At first sight this looks plausible enough. As an overarching virtue magnanimity resembles Spenser's magnificence, while its relation to honour parallels that of magnificence to glory. But does this justify Lewis's confidence that Spenser means magnanimity if, as he himself recognizes, Arthur 'has only as much resemblance to the Aristotelian *megalopsychos* as any good knight was bound to have'? Anyway, further reflection dissolves even the correspondence that does seem substantial. For Spenser's scheme of magnificence as an inclusive virtue to be traced convincingly to the *Nicomachean Ethics*, this treatise ought to be, structurally, a discussion of the several virtues as constituent elements of magnanimity. It is not.

In addition, the philosopher's alleged catch-all ought to derive its content from virtues at least similar to the poet's. It does not, as Lewis is well aware.[33] He has precipitated his 'sympathetic' reading of the Letter on the assumption that it need not significantly fit the poem or even with the deliberate intent to find fuel for his rage against the document. Instead of accepting such an insidious vindication we conclude that, if it had not been for Spenser's reference to 'Aristotle and the rest', his argument would never have suggested the Aristotelian tradition at all.

But this conclusion may seem premature. How about Spenser's statement, earlier on in the Letter, that 'I labour to pourtraict in Arthure, before he was king, the image of a brave knight, perfected in the twelve private morall vertues, *as Aristotle hath devised*' (L 26–8)? This is another notorious crux, though: Aristotle's *Ethics* does not present a scheme of twelve virtues. Nor do neo-Aristotelian treatises Spenser could have consulted; supposing his reference warrants citation of such as analogues. For instance, Francesco Piccolomini, in his *Universa Philosophia de Moribus*, which Hankins claims to have been the poet's major source, argues that Aristotle ought to have named either ten or twelve virtues, rather than eleven, and frowns particularly at the omission of holiness. Yet he does not adopt the improved scheme himself. Burgersdyck, early in the seventeenth century, does; but even so the result, Aristotle's eleven virtues supplemented by piety, is a far cry from Spenser's scheme.[34] The problem has been solved by Mills, who perceives that 'as Aristotle hath devised' modifies not 'the twelve private morall vertues' but 'pourtraict'. 'Spenser's claim . . . is that Aristotle devised a method of portrayal rather than a list of twelve virtues. Thus regarded, his allusion is not to the *Nicomachean Ethics* or its elucidators, but to the *Poetics*.' After all, the context of the poet's statement is a discussion of epic in relation to its moral purpose, not of moral theory *per se.* Ironically, Mills proceeds at once to create a difficulty capable of a similar solution. '*Perfected* in the twelve private morall vertues' seems to him irreconcilable with Aristotle's stipulation that a poetic character should not be perfect. So he argues that Spenser alludes to the *Poetics* as understood in the influential commentary of Averroes, who regards poetry as 'the art of praise and blame, and therefore exemplary and paradigmatic in its presentation of virtue and vice'.[35] But it cannot be taken for granted that poets sharing this view are bound to devise perfect characters. Nor does the mere fact that Aristotle himself does not see poetry as an instrument for moral education explain his stipulation. Perhaps, indeed, it applies to characters in tragedy only, as Tasso would have it.[36] Be that as it may, Spenser's allusion to the *Poetics* justifies theoretically not Arthur's perfection but the decision to achieve 'the *generall* end . . . of all the booke [which] is to fashion a gentleman or noble person in vertuous and gentle discipline' (L 8–10) by means of a *particular* fiction, about Arthur. For Aristotle contends that, while, like history, concrete and specific,

> Poetry is *philosophoteron* and *spoudaioteron*, that is to say, it is more philosophical and more studiously serious than history. His reason is, because poesy dealeth with *katholou*, that is to say, with the universal consideration, and the history with *kathekaston*, the particular.[37]

Spenser worries about the disparity between end and means. Having already invoked the practice of his epic predecessors, he shows next that he follows them on good authority; and then goes on to acknowledge and placate those to whom 'this Methode will seeme displeasaunt, which had rather have good discipline delivered plainly in way of precepts, or sermoned at large' (L 32–4). He never wanders.

So Spenser's second reference to Aristotle cannot be taken as an allusion to that philosopher's *Ethics* on the strength of the first. Tuve would go further. If only critics had not been blinded by these references, she thinks, they would have seen that in the Middle Ages a conception of magnificence as the virtue 'by which we designate all the other virtues if perfected' was precisely the commonplace that Spenser's casualness implies. She marshals an impressive array of analogues, headed by a telling quotation from Caxton's version of the *Somme le roi* of Frère Lorens, and demonstrates how this conception goes back to Cicero and Macrobius. Admittedly, 'Aristotle and the rest' becomes awkward as a result. Nor is her explanation entirely ingenuous. It may be true that 'the uncontaminated, warranted-truly-Greek Aristotle that a modern student tries to isolate and read was neither a possibility nor a desirable possibility to Spenser'.[38] One would not begrudge the poet a vague gesture. But he cannot quite afford to be positively incorrect. As a matter of fact, his reference is hardly suggestive of medieval traditions. Or if it is—for there was a strand of medieval thought in which Aristotle figured as 'il maestro di color che sanno' (Dante)—it evokes Aquinas. And about him Tuve is conspicuously silent; of necessity, since he, as befits the disciple, leans towards his master's definition of magnificence.[39] The decisive flaw in her argument lies elsewhere, though. Compared with that of Lewis it does seem a major advance. For the medieval works she cites treat magnificence not simply as the crowning virtue rather as Aristotle does magnanimity. They also Christianize its content, thus providing a better perspective for its relation, in Spenser, to glory; which is hardly Aristotle's purely secular honour. However, the overall structure of these works is not determined by magnificence as an inclusive virtue any more than that of Aristotle's treatise reflects the comprehensive scope he appears to attribute to magnanimity. Nor is this surprising. Magnificence as Tuve defines it on the basis of Lorens, 'Christian Perseverance, perfecting the virtue by carrying it through to the end',[40] is not an inclusive virtue at all, in spite of what alternative formulations such as the one quoted previously may suggest: it is, on her own showing, a 'pars' of fortitude. By contrast, magnificence as Spenser defines it is inescapably inclusive. His statement that 'in the whole course I mention the deedes of Arthure applyable to that vertue, which I write of in that booke' (L 61–3) can only mean that Arthur represents holiness in Book I, temperance in Book II, and so on. If, despite its 'applicability', magnificence were a separate virtue, one would have to envisage a *Faerie Queene* in which Arthur not only rescues his peers in their Books but also performs a quest like theirs in a Book all his own, abandoning his orientation towards Gloriana. Perish the thought! Luckily the Letter rules this out: it assigns 'xii. other knights' (L 63–4), not eleven, to a poem due to consist of twelve Books (L 78–9, 82; and compare the title-page). Tuve's tradition does not inform Spenser's programme; even its magnificence is not strictly an aspect of glory. Anyway, perseverance does not characterize the Arthur of the poem any more than does magnanimity. True, he perseveres in his search for the Faery Queen. But his comparatively brief and widely scattered episodes are hardly calculated to bring this home; especially since this search is not their subject. Nor, with his lightning victories, does he persevere in the titular knights' virtues anywhere near as convincingly as these knights themselves, with their protracted adventures, culminating in the accomplishment of their tasks.

III The Conceptual Rationale

Spenser's magnificence corresponds neither to the common medieval understanding of that virtue nor to the Aristotelian conception of it, or even of magnanimity. Is there a precedent at all for using this term to designate a virtue that is comprehensive, substantial, and equivalent to glory? And what are we to make of 'Aristotle and the rest'? Besides, does the poet not contradict himself? If magnificence signifies merely all the virtues taken together, if it 'conteineth in it them all' without adding to them, how could it be 'the perfection of all the rest' as well (L 60–1)? But here we must exonerate Spenser. It is our query that is self-contradictory, presupposing, as it does, that virtues, to be perfect in themselves, need to be crowned by a different one. Our interpretation of 'perfect' requires adjustment. For this word is ambiguous. It has invariably been assumed that it means 'in the state of complete excellence; free from any flaw or imperfection of quality; faultless'. But it can also mean 'in the state proper to anything when completed; complete; having all the essential elements, qualities, or characteristics; not deficient in any particular' and 'completely corresponding to a definition, pattern, or description'.[41] Instead of ultimate degree of accomplishment the word may convey complete embodiment of essence: something is perfect, *τέλειος*, when it answers fully to its final cause, its *τέλος* (as Aristotle would say). Spenser uses it in that sense. Magnificence, as 'the perfection of all the rest', is not a crowning virtue remedying 'the insufficiencies of individual virtues'[42] but another word for each of these virtues when 'perfect'. Now observe the corollary of this: the individual virtues do not *add up* to magnificence. It is not an aggregate but includes all the others as aspects of itself. In other words, it is not a mere name but has all the substance of any of its aspects. They *unfold* it, and it *infolds* them. (Let me enter a caveat here. Spenserians will be familiar with these terms from Wind's discussion of Neoplatonic triads.[43] Nowhere in this book, however, do they have a Platonic connotation. Nor is there any reason why they should. St. Paul is, technically, unfolding when he says: 'But the fruit of the spirit is love, joy, peace, longsuffering, gentlenesse, goodnesse, faith, / Meekenesse, temperance' (singular subject and verb; asyndeton). Conversely, he is infolding when he says: 'For this, Thou shalt not commit adulterie, Thou shalt not kill, Thou shalt not steale, Thou shalt not beare false witnesse, Thou shalt not covet: and if there be any other commandement, it is briefly comprehended in this saying, namely, Thou shalt love thy neighbour as thy selfe.'[44] Who would infer from this that he sat at the feet of Academics?)

So magnificence, as the 'perfection' of the virtues, is simply true, all-round virtuousness. It is a general notion, meaningful even before its meaning has been specified and irrespective of whether it can be specified exhaustively; not an expedient to top up a finite set of virtues conceived of as separate entities. And, understood correctly, it does indeed name an idea to be found in 'Aristotle and the rest':

> Die Stoa führt einen aristotelischen Satz weiter, wenn sie betont, τέλειος sei nur der, der alle sittlichen Fähigkeiten ἀρετάς besitze, u τελεία sei eine Tat nur, wenn sie allen ἀρεταί gemäß geschähe, also alle in ihr zusammenwirkten.[45]

The Letter states that magnificence '(according to Aristotle and the rest) . . . is the perfection of all the rest'. This means not that Aristotle defines magnificence as the perfection of all the virtues—which would be untrue. It means that what Spenser calls magnificence is moral perfection as understood by Aristotle. (For 'according to' as 'in accordance with' compare L 56–7.) Clearly this general idea of moral perfection can be unfolded in various ways. In this respect Aristotle and the Stoics freely diverge. So does Spenser. The Letter does not burden us with the impossible task of squeezing his virtues into the Aristotelian mould. The poet's off-hand manner squares with the commonplace nature of his understanding of moral perfection. The fact that he calls it magnificence need not be equally a matter of course. Considering, on the one hand, critical failure to cite a precedent and, on the other hand, the poet's casualness in presenting magnificence as an aspect of glory, we should try to grasp that equation first and allow for the possibility that the other is peculiar to Spenser.

Few critics discuss Spenser's glory. Even Tuve, with her keen interest in concepts and their relationships, says little on the subject, perhaps in the conviction that it needs no clarification. Those who do deal with it, however, run straight into trouble: in the poem glory is both earthly and heavenly. Thus Hankins at first associates it with honour, stressing that 'while heaven and union with God may be considered the ultimate objective, they are not the immediate objective of the quests in *The Faerie Queene*'. Yet later on we find him quoting St. Paul, to conclude that 'it is this shimmering vision of an ultimate glory from the virtuous performance of the daily task that provides the theme of *The Faerie Queene*'.[46] He does not make any attempt to resolve the paradox. C. S. Lewis does. 'Earthly glory would never have moved us but by being a shadow or *idolon* of the Divine Glory, in which we are called to participate. . . . It is in the very nature of the Platonic quest and the Eros religion that the soul cannot know her true aim till she has achieved it.' On this reading Arthur's pursuit of Florimell (III. i, iv) will fall into place, he thinks; for he is, rightly, anxious to acquit the Prince of inconstancy. But then, the lines

> Oft did he wish, that Lady faire mote bee
> His Faery Queene, for whom he did complaine,
> Or that his Faery Queene were such, as shee
>
> (iv. 54)

do not quite 'parallel . . . the repeated (and always disappointed) belief of the Trojans in *Aeneid*, III, that they have already found the *mansuram urbem*'. They do not imply that Arthur ever mistook Florimell for Gloriana. On the contrary, they confirm that he has known Gloriana for his true aim all along. Since, nevertheless, he does not repent of his wishful thinking, Florimell must be an aspect rather than a shadow of Gloriana. Lewis is much given to high-handed solutions. To impose them he will suitably 'correct' problems not just in the loathed Letter but even in the beloved poem.[47] The value of what he says lies in the way he says it. Speaking in the first person plural, he aligns the reader with Arthur; hinting that we, too, are committed to a perpetual search for a 'Faerie Queene', during which we are to catch only tantalizing glimpses of glory. Let us be 'perfect', though, true to type, and make sure of our bearings.

For this purpose, it must be admitted, the Letter's equation of magnificence and glory looks singularly unpromising. Apart from being a mystery, it would appear to be overruled by the poem, which, with Gloriana throughout beyond Arthur's ken, conveys distinctness rather than equivalence. It seems far more plausible to suppose that magnificence relates to glory as effort to reward—especially since that way we can, oddly enough, give the Letter some credit, after all: we all know, if only from hearsay, that the effort in question, virtue, is its own reward. Just because this reward is somewhat intangible, the poem may well present it as heavenly earthly glory. It certainly bears out our supposition in so far as Arthur embraces every chance of action for its own sake, not with a view to winning Gloriana. That he happens to befriend knights who turn out to be her emissaries neatly suggests the reality as well as the elusive and involuntary character of the reward: he finds himself being oriented towards her. However, as this formulation should remind us, Arthur conducts a deliberate search for Gloriana *as well.* To accommodate this fact we need something like Fowler's vision of 'cosmic rhythm'.[48] But this is invalidated by its Neoplatonism, which blurs Spenser's ethics in a haze of metaphysics. Platonic gradualism, according to which a variously imperfect world of appearances approximates closely or distantly, as the case may be, a perfect other-world of Ideas, is radically incompatible both with the Letter, which outlines an image of sublunar moral perfection, and with the poem, which could hardly be more earthy in its delineation of virtue triumphantly pitted against vice. Nothing remains but to clutch at the equation of magnificence and glory in despair. Mercifully, its rationale is not far to seek, as the poet's casualness implies. We shall find it in that most popular of Elizabethan books, the New Testament.

The biblical meaning of 'glory' is 'manifestation of God's essence'.[49] Often the word is used with particular reference to the resurrection life. Thus Peter, writing about Christ, says that 'God . . . raised him from the dead, and gave him glorie'.[50] Similarly Paul, defining the body's transmutation, says: 'It is sowen in dishonour, and is raised in glorie.'[51] However, the resurrection life is 'nothing but' the consummation in Eternity of God's *full* identification with Man in Time, through Christ.[52] In Time, therefore, God's glory exists, paradoxically, 'already—not yet'. Hence Paul can exhort his brethren in Christ to 'glorifie God in your bodie'; that is, to witness to His presence 'in earthen vessels'.[53] Now the New Testament also uses 'magnify' for 'glorify' in this sense. Thus: 'As all wayes, so now Christ shal be magnified in my bodie, whether it be by life or by death.'[54] Spenser's statement that the Faery Queen represents glory and Arthur magnificence in particular means that his poem is about the temporal manifestation of God. Granted, the noun 'magnificence' does not occur in the New Testament in the relevant sense. But, as we shall see, the poet has excellent reasons for allowing himself this discrepancy, which in any case is purely formal.

But does magnificence as glory equal magnificence as perfection of all the virtues? It does; or rather, the latter is strictly an aspect of the former. Man's intended end (τέλος) is to embody God's glory: he has been created in the image of God. ('Image' in this context is εἰκών, not εἴδωλον. As Kittel observes, commenting on II Corinthians 3: 18, 'diese Ebenbildlichkeit . . . ist . . . identisch mit der δόξα'.[55]) Since Christ is God incarnate, Man in Christ is perfect. Paul sees it as the purpose of his ministry to 'present everie man perfect (τέλειον) in Christ Jesus'.[56] And since Man in Christ is, by definition, inspired directly by the Spirit of God, he does His will as a matter of course: he is, among other things, morally perfect. (This means that his disposition is virtuous, not that his performance is faultless. It never can be, in a fallen world.) What clinches the identity of the two meanings of magnificence is that Scripture, so far from reserving the notion of perfection, as one might expect, for Man's ultimate glory, associates it emphatically with his 'provisional' state. To give the most telling example, it is at his ignominious death on the cross that Jesus exclaims: 'It is finished' (τετέλεσται). The marginal gloss, catching the root of the verb, comments that 'Mans salvacion is *perfected* by the onelie sacrifice of Christ'.[57] Resurrection does not compensate for life imperfect through death: it vindicates eternally life perfect in obedience unto death.

Seen in its proper, biblical, perspective the Letter's conceptual argument becomes entirely coherent. It possesses an authority made inapparent only through the implicitness of this perspective. It may well be asked why the poet was not more explicit. One cannot invoke the ideal contemporary reader, naturally on the right wavelength, since he would have been more familiar than we are not just with the Bible but also with Aristotelian, Ciceronian, and medieval ethics. His predicament was, if anything, more acute than ours and less apt to be fatal merely because, like ourselves conceiving Spenser in his own image, he would not have assumed authorial carelessness as readily as we do. One must conclude that the argument is meant to throw any reader. In view of the Letter's declared purpose this will seem even more improbable than the idea of confusion on Spenser's part. But it is not really. For he does not strictly prevent illumination, as we now know. Rather, he puts our logic and tenacity to the test; as he does again later on when posturing as 'Historiographer'. The Letter is all the more 'perfect' as an introduction for giving a bitter-sweet foretaste of the poem's deliberate mystification, which allows its indubitable light to be only 'doubtfully . . . construed' (L 1). By the same token, in more obviously sharing than resolving the poem's apparent indeterminacy, the Letter also seems to belie its introductory status. Accordingly Spenser makes this preface a postscript in 1590, due to disappear in 1596. But this paradoxical placement, as though in recognition of the Letter's complete uselessness, in fact serves to equate 'fore' and 'after' and so to intimate the unprogressive, non-narrative status of the fiction in between. Its assertion that the poet 'thrusteth into the middest' (L 74–5) deprives his 'pleasing Analysis' of the temporal dimension it pretends to advertise.

Awareness of the Letter's significance prompts the admission that it could be true to the poem and, indeed, that sooner or later we shall have to trust it implicity: conclusive verification would require nothing less than interpreting each and every one of the poem's countless episodes, most of which do not themselves guide us to any sure understanding. Still, at this early stage we may indulge our scepticism a little. Let us take some 'clear' samples from the poem and see whether they support the Letter. Here is one of Guyon's rapturous descriptions of the Faery Queen:

> In her the richesse of all heavenly grace
> In chiefe degree are heaped up on hye:
> And all that else this worlds enclosure bace
> Hath great or glorious in mortall eye,
> Adornes the person of her Majestie;
> That men beholding so great excellence,
> And rare perfection in mortalitie,
> Do her adore with sacred reverence,
> As th'Idole of her makers great magnificence.
>
> (II. ii. 41.)

Idol, not icon. Yet there is nothing 'shadowy' about this solidly ideal Gloriana. But then, Guyon is not philosophizing *à la* Lewis; let alone flouting God's jealous commandment that 'sacred reverence' shall be paid to Him only. Gloriana is *Spenser's* idol, or allegory: a literary image without substance; that is, without intrinsic meaning. (In the preceding Canto the poet conveys the emblematic nature of the fiction in a similar way, through Guyon's comment on the sad spectacle of Mordant and Amavia: 'Behold the image of mortalitie' (i. 57). We shall discover later why Book II denies its narrative with such emphasis.) Nor does Guyon remain content to spell out Gloriana's fictional status: he could not have expressed her meaning more meticulously if we had bribed him to make a case for the Letter's conceptual argument. He establishes her identity with God. Next, to ensure that she stands for God's glory as His full commitment to Man in Time, he calls her everything 'glorious in mortall eye'; 'all heavenly grace' in 'this worlds enclosure bace'; in short, 'perfection in mortalitie'. Moreover, he equates this glory explicitly with magnificence. This makes sense within the stanza's context: 'the *richesse* of all heavenly grace' betoken 'her makers great magnificence', God's Aristotelian *megaloprepeia*, so to say[58]—and, if one may suspect a sly authorial boast, Spenser's huge artistic investment in his *Faerie Queene.* But the equation seems calculated to identify Gloriana with Arthur. Finally, to forestall the objection that elsewhere the poem does not bear out their identity, he differentiates them as opposite aspects of a single notion. Gloriana, he says, represents God's riches 'heaped up on hye'; a phrase suggesting concentration and elevated unattainability, unmistakable qualities of the monarch so elusively at the heart of her enormous realm. Arthur, by contrast, represents magnificence proper, the scattering of those same riches; enacted impressively in the free aid he lends his peers with due panache throughout so as to encompass his lady's realm with a precious chain of 'great doing'. But in the divine economy to spend virtue *is* to hoard glory 'already—not yet': Timothy's flock are to 'be riche in good workes . . . / Laying up in store for them selves a good fundation against the time to come, that they may obteine eternal life'.[59]

As a justification of the Letter's conceptual argument this is hard to beat. Nor does the poem contain other stanzas of equal range and clarity. Sometimes, though, a passage dark in itself will positively flare up as soon as one thinks of the norm and thus lend more than it borrows. Consider Nature's cryptic verdict, in the Mutabilitie Cantos:

all things stedfastnes doe hate
And changed be: yet being rightly wayd
They are not changed from their first estate;
But by their change their being doe dilate:
And turning to themselves at length againe,
Doe worke their owne perfection so by fate.

(VII. vii. 58.)

According to Hamilton 'change is interpreted in Aristotelian terms as a becoming. Yet "first estate" suggests also the Platonic notion: the end of growth is "turning" or returning to original perfection. (The Pauline notion of sowing a natural body to raise a spiritual body . . . is absent because Nature answers Mutabilitie in her own terms.)'[60] Such pseudo-commentary refutes itself. If Hamilton's reason excludes the Pauline notion, it excludes the Platonic notion too; happily, since this does not agree with the Aristotelian notion. Besides, the verdict is obviously false 'in her own terms', whether Mutabilitie's or Nature's: most things do *not* 'turn to themselves' in Time. It is true precisely because 'Natur's selfe did vanish, whither no man wist' (59). And then, glossing change as 'growth' trivializes the issue. The text associates it with decay. Even Jove admits that 'Time . . . doth . . . all disseise / Of being' (48). Perhaps 'dilate' has given rise to this error. The word means 'expand', to be sure; that is, 'unfold', not 'approximate progressively'. And here it also has its obsolete meanings, 'extend in time' and 'delay'.[61] Nature does not contend that things become perfect through change, on the assumption that change is providentially guided.[62] She asserts that they prove themselves in the midst of (destructive) change. They 'worke their owne perfection', she says; not 'work towards'. Even as they change they realize in advance their changelessness 'at length'. Fowler does not really see this; although he has enough historical sense not to commit the poet to 'growth'. 'Mutability, which generations of poets had taken as a subject of complaint, was for Spenser something quite different: a creative process, almost a subject of encomium', he writes; to conclude that '*The Faerie Queen* as a whole could be said to hymn creation in process, rather than created nature'.[63] How splendid, as testimony to the work's marked *Diesseitigkeit*; and how sensible, in not associating dull stability with *Jenseits*, which is, after all, a subject of encomium too. Yet surely creation in process and created nature are one and the same thing? There simply is no static nature. There *was*, before the Fall. The dichotomy can be maintained, but it would imply that Spenser hymns the Fall for its own sake. Could anybody stretch the idea of *felix culpa* that far? We need to respond, with Fowler, to the favourable view of change. However, we must not overlook that it finds expression in the Legend of Constancy. This makes for a paradox; one that resolves itself immediately thanks to the concurrent reminder that the Cantos are not cosmological fable but, like the rest of *The Faerie Queene*, moral allegory. 'Rightly wayd' means not only 'properly considered (weighed)' but also 'in the way of righteousness' (and so 'in Christ, Who is the Way'[64]). As the metaphor suggests, virtue, in all its aspects, is 'on the move'. Our passage concerns one of these aspects, constancy, which anticipates, in motion, 'stedfast rest . . . Upon the pillours of Eternity' (viii. 2).

These samples are exceptional in their spontaneous translucence. To say that they are typical in the exactness with which they correspond to the prescribed rationale would be a mere profession of faith. Yet they do inspire such faith. And we shall need it; for we are taking arms in an apparently desperate cause. Let us raise our standard here, with a polemical affirmation of Spenser's theme, earthly glory: the temporal manifestation of God, that is; not secular honour. This theme hinges on Christian doctrine where it is subtly but crucially at variance with Platonism, namely in its conception of Time. Both Christians and Platonists call Time the mirror image of Eternity. But they use the analogy to mean different things. To Platonists Time is Eternity's eternal insubstantial reflection. While in his body Man lingers among phantoms, in his soul he ascends to the Ideas, his ultimate haven:

> Life, like a dome of many-coloured glass,
> Stains the white radiance of Eternity,
> Until Death tramples it to fragments.[65]

To Christians Time is Eternity temporarily seeing itself only indirectly. Man is not caught behind the looking-glass but standing in front of it. He consults it, though of necessity; knowing not only the unreality of the image itself but also its reality as a likeness (whether good, bad, or indifferent). The same point can be made in other ways. Platonists escape from Time to Eternity. Christians invade Time with Eternity. The former discard Time as a total loss, pinning their hopes on Eternity for damages. The latter redeem Time[66] for Eternity, buying it up with the riches of Christ. Their quasi-Platonic longing for transcendence indicates 'merely' that this redemption still awaits consummation. Fighting a good fight, they are already assured of the 'crowne of righteousnes', the 'incorruptible crowne of glorie', which still eludes them.[67]

It is this paradoxical identity of self-fulfilling virtue and eschatological expectancy that informs Arthur's continual yearning for Gloriana even as he comes fully into his own in his knightly exploits. To secular humanism, satisfied that these exploits illustrate its own grimly high-minded conception of virtue as its own reward, this 'unwarranted' yearning will be an affront. Not so to Christianity, which, on the contrary, legitimizes it. Seeing virtue as nothing but the return of grace received, it caters still further to human weakness in nevertheless crediting the desire for something in return, its crystallization as eternal glory. In the Sermon on the Mount Jesus repeatedly follows his moral injunctions with the promise that 'thy Father that seeth in secret, he wil rewarde thee openly'—'in the day when all things shalbe reveiled', as the marginal gloss explains.[68] Here we may usefully dismiss Woodhouse's epoch-making lecture on 'Nature and Grace in *The Faerie Queene*' as a red herring. 'The question is not whether the natural virtues can be ratified by religion before being transcended by it (for all of them can), but whether in the particular instance the motivation and the sanctions of the virtue are from nature or from grace.' Quite so. Spenser presents *all* his virtues as issuing from and heading towards God's identification with Man. Nor is this an unlikely procedure in a poem intended to 'fashion' moral integration. Playing off nature and grace against each other, creating tension and resolving it through synthesis, would not have served nearly so well. Indeed, it would have been impossible: grace is not an antithesis to nature's thesis but a new dispensation 'already—not yet' supplanting an old one that has become flawed (on the Catholic view) or depraved (on the Protestant view). They are not susceptible of synthesis. Neither are Hooker's and Calvin's views of their relation; for these are mutually exclusive. If, as Woodhouse would have it, 'Spenser tries to do justice to the facts of human experience which support these two rival views', we must not expect a resolution.[69] Carol Kaske would agree. Fortunately, her view of *The Faerie Queene* as genuinely pluralistic is as unnecessary as it is preposterous.[70] How can she have failed to see that the poem celebrates, in Una, truth's singleness?

Spenser's view of virtue as self-rewarding cosmic traffic, then, so far from marrying Platonism and secular morality, both of which it apparently resembles, excludes both. It is radically Christian; and it enables us to specify his Christianity. Virtue inspired and validated *sola gratia, sola fide*, is a battle-cry of the Reformation. Therefore, with virtue so conceived for its sole theme, *The Faerie Queene* is not an epic more or less recognizably written by a Protestant, as most critics would say, but a Protestant epic *tout court.* More specifically still, it has a distinctly Calvinist flavour.[71] Organized around virtue as glory, it evinces both the notorious zeal for righteous conduct and the theocentric position of the Genevan reformer, to whom 'the first purpose of the creation is to embody the fact of God', with 'election . . . purely a matter of grace *ad solam Dei gloriam*'. Focusing virtue's glory as assured expectation, it echoes the keynote of Calvin's thought, suggested by Torrance's dictum that 'if Luther's was the theology of faith and Bucer's that of charity, Calvin's is that of hope'.[72] We need not hesitate to attribute such 'narrowness' to such an unprovincial poet, a Londoner taught at Cambridge, conversant with bishops and courtiers. Calvinism was the ruling ideology of Elizabethan England, which read the Geneva Bible more than any other version[73] and found itself, if perhaps willy-nilly, championing Genevan partisans abroad through its military interventions in France and the Netherlands (duly commemorated in the poem). Spenser's convictions are at home in a national epic. They are all the more so for sustaining a fiction which, in its obvious affiliations with medieval and Italian Renaissance literature, professes its Catholicism: the incongruity is that of the Church of England, whose externals similarly 'belie' its doctrine; as much to the satisfaction of its royal head as to the exasperation of the presbyterians among her subjects. Fittingly Spenser shares the stance of his dedicatee; though one suspects that he exceeds her in religious fervour. Seen in this light his poem rivals *Of the Laws of Ecclesiastical Polity.* Both are monumental salutes to the Establishment, enshrining with comparable grandeur different conceptions of its status. Over against Hooker's reasoned moderation, which argues for Anglicanism as a richly comprehensive third option, we have Spenser's enthusiastic poise, which envisions it as one manifestation of the Church Catholic regaining its bearings. It would be absurd to say that the divisiveness of English Christianity can be traced to deficient understanding of *The Faerie Queene.* It would be a good deal less absurd to say that they are a major and a minor instance of the same spiritual blindness.

IV The Fictional Mode

Spenser's fiction looks like narrative. For all its looseness it does not, on the whole, *invite* interpretation in accordance with his 'fore-conceit'. Its true status is obvious only *a priori.* Concrete demonstration will require a strenuous and prolonged effort, which could, in the circumstances, be mistaken for zeal in blinkers. To forestall the charge of critical wilfulness let us recapitulate and do some random sampling first. The Letter to Ralegh presents *The Faerie Queene* as an allegory with a multifarious vehicle thoughout irradiated 'already—not yet' by its triune tenor, glory—magnificence —(any) virtue. The relation between vehicle and tenor, puzzles as epiphanies, parallels that between the tenor's components, trials as mercies: mode enacts theme. Self-righteous interpreters labour in vain. The poem's meaning is given. Through grace its readers are atoned with their Father that sees in secret; having to wait till Doomsday to be illuminated openly. In the meantime nothing could steady our vision more than the knowledge that *The Faerie Queene,* apparent narrative, is really a glorified moral treatise. A rare piece of 'biographical' evidence confirms this. Lodowick Bryskett reports, in his *Discourse of Civil Life,* how, during a gathering of friends in Ireland, he had urged the poet to give a systematic exposition of moral philosophy. Spenser declined on the grounds that he had 'alreedy undertaken a work tending to the same effect, which is in *heroical verse* under the title of a *Faerie Queene* to represent all the moral vertues'.[74] This implies that his meaning is abstract. Accordingly the Letter defines the Faery Queen, Arthur, Red Cross, Guyon, and Britomart as concepts. These characters are not more or less glorious, magnificent, holy, temperate, and chaste persons but personifications of 'perfect' virtues. So they do not exemplify what they represent: they symbolize it. For as concepts they cannot go into the making of real stories. The categories of the world of stories (place, time, causation, interaction, personality, moral stature, and so on) simply do not apply to concepts.

To abandon the poem as narrative is to offer a sacrifice—a meaningful one. Spenser leads us to cherish the illusion of genuine temporal sequence. Our frustrated response symbolizes Man's reluctance to accept that he cannot redeem life within Time. The tragedy of this failure need not be played down. It can be embraced realistically in the assurance that in Man God redeems Time itself. Similarly we need not dissemble our agony over the poem's death as narrative. We can give rein to our grief in the consoling awareness of its allegorical glory. Let us make sure, though, that we do not, in the luxury of mourning, misconceive our loss. Transforming persons into personifications sounds reductive. But the reduction is insubstantial, since we adjust our perception without changing its objects. Nor should we think of these as 'mere' personifications. For they are not devitalized persons who, oriented conceptually, lack human impact and preclude emotional response. Quite the contrary. They are concepts coming 'alive' as pseudo-persons for the very purpose of engaging us emotionally as well as intellectually. Usually, of course, Spenser's characters do not prompt the kind of empathy characters in novels commonly do, as any reader who presses a proto-novelistic approach must recognize to his distress. But there is no reason why they should, in a poem not generically akin to the novel. The comparison should be with abstract discourse. An example: even such a decidedly flat character as Archimago is, simply through being introduced, with powerful rhetoric, as 'that cunning Architect of cancred guile' (II. i. 1), far more effective in mobilizing the reader against the deceptiveness of appearances, which is what he stands for, than any purely philosophical discussion of the subject could ever be.[75] 'So much more profitable and gratious is doctrine by ensample, then by rule.' (L 41–2.) Spenser's sentiment, a truism epitomizing the humanist view of poetry, applies *a fortiori* to allegory.[76]

'Ensample' does indeed mean 'historical fiction' generally, including allegorical fiction, as opposed to 'rule' or 'precept'; not 'literal *exemplum*' as opposed to 'metaphor for virtue'.[77] Spenser is not going back on his promise of 'continued Allegory'. Anyway, who could say in all honesty that his fiction manifestly *exemplifies* particular virtues? Let us take our cue from Lewis's observation, already quoted, that Arthur 'has only as much resemblance to the Aristotelian *megalopsychos* as any good knight was bound to have' and from our subsequent discovery that he does not behave like a paragon of perseverance either. We may generalize: neither he nor the titular heroes exemplify anything more specific than knightly action. Although there is nothing incongruous about the idea of military adventures being conducted in a holy, temperate, just, courteous, and even, at a pinch, chaste, or friendly manner, those of Spenser's knights just do not correspond to this idea. Their literal behaviour *per se* does not differentiate them morally for us. We label them on the basis of non-literal features of their exploits. For instance, we associate Red Cross with holiness not because killing dragons should be a saintly occupation but because the poet, or the tradition he follows, has moulded the dragon into a symbol of unholiness. We should also consider that inculcating the virtues *as practised by knights* would be an altogether pointless limitation of scope. Spenser may have written for an audience of knights; but hardly for the type that engages in dragon-slaying and the like.

Are we labouring the obvious? If so, why has the obvious conclusion not been drawn, namely that the fiction must be symbolic rather than exemplary? Why has Spenser not been credited with modal consistency? Why do critics prefer to steer an impossible middle course, allegorizing on and off in a most arbitrary fashion and tortuously reincorporating the meanings they come up with into the fiction; thus salvaging a story that Spenser certainly did not write and could not reasonably expect to be reconstructed? Why, for instance, do they not realize that vanquishing Error (with a capital E) just is not the sort of thing that can be done by a particular knight at a particular stage of a particular adventure; in short, that Red Cross cannot be a person?[78] To rescue the story one would have to assume that Error does not mean Error but a particular error committed by Red Cross. Now Red Cross does not commit any such error; or if he does the poet does not tell us about it. For his entry into the Wandering Wood does not qualify. Taking shelter from a thunderstorm in a forest is not erroneous: it is very sensible. Similarly, decapitating a monster is in no way truthful. We should take the knight not as an individual making a slip and promptly rectifying his mistake but as a personification. Red Cross goes into the Wandering Wood and confronts Error to signify Man on this side of Eternity naturally prone to error. The Wood and its denizens are particular fictions symbolizing the temporal condition generally as it tends to mislead people into falsehood. Red Cross also defeats Error to signify Man in Christ, Who is the Truth[79] (highlighted in Una, who, naturally, still goes veiled and enjoins faith; see I. i. 4, 19). The episode expresses emblematically one aspect of salvation in Time, 'already—not yet'. It is not a fragment from an imaginary biography stylized for the purpose of moral instruction. It *ought* to read 'like a self-contained mini-story', as we put it at the beginning of this Chapter. And Spenser certainly marks it off:

> So forward on his way (with God to frend)
> He passed forth, and new adventure sought;
> Long way he travelled, before he heard of ought.
>
> (28.)

Two stanzas later we find the knight satisfying his eager curiosity about 'straunge adventures'. This is hardly suggestive of a purposeful quest with a clearly envisaged goal. (It *is*, strictly, compatible with it. One could decide that Red Cross need not move on to his set task at once; just as one could decide that he does literally commit an error, in the Latin sense of the word. For a reason which we shall discover later Book I 'upholds' its narrative even as it denies it. Particularly suggestive of sequence are the several summaries of previous episodes, by the Dwarf (vii. 26), Una (vii. 43–51), and Red Cross himself (xii. 15). But illusions are none the less illusory for being strong.) In much the same way, though not always so blatantly, the poet (virtually) atomizes the story of Red Cross throughout. As Nelson says, 'if plot is soul, the poem cannot escape damnation'.[80] Most strikingly, the knight's later adventures do not really lead up to his battle with the Dragon any more than does his confrontation with Error. (It is fascinating to see Kaske, in her study of this battle, hovering on the brink of the non-narrative abyss.[81]) The assumption that, nevertheless, they all prepare Red Cross for his final encounter, shared by most critics, involves interiorization of his outward actions: a translation into inner events, the psychological rationale for whose sequence we would have to think up. Let us forbear.

But are some, at least, of the poem's atoms not themselves literally significant stories? For instance, are the actions of Paridell and Malbecco (III. x) not truly (cautionary) *exempla* of unchastity and jealousy? This objection presupposes, incorrectly, that characters enacting what they represent must be people. Nobody would hesitate to label the Seven Deadly Sins (I. iv. 16–35) 'personifications'. Yet they all commit the sins they stand for (thus making their contribution to the 'inconclusiveness' of Book I's inconsequentiality). True, they are each confined to three stanzas. Lacking scope to develop their inclinations, they make for pictures rather than stories. Paridell and Malbecco, by contrast, enact what seems to be a realistic fabliau. Still, the strength of appearances (certainly worth noting) cannot decide the issue. What does is Spenser's final transformation of the man Malbecco into the personification Jealousy (III. x. 60). Since such a transformation is logically impossible, Malbecco, and therefore the other characters in his episode too, must be personifications all along. We can concede nothing more than that, with their names far less unequivocally status-revealing than those of the Sins, they do sustain the illusion of progressing story till the last minute. (Book III has its own peculiar way of denying its narrative.)

Guyon's adventure at the Bower of Bliss (II. xii) similarly

fails to meet the requirements of an *exemplum*, admittedly dressed up allegorically, of (sexual) temperance put to the test. Many critics, reading literally, have been aghast at Guyon's destruction of so enchantingly beautiful a place; and rightly so.[82] Convinced though we are that the knight is up against real evil, his action jars, especially since we must accept Brooke's splendid refutation of C. S. Lewis's still influential view of the Bower as an evil antitype of the Garden of Adonis (III. vi): Art versus Nature, sterile versus generative sex.[83] The passage heightens the suspicion of some, raised by the allegorical mode generally, that the poet is schizophrenic, committed to morality and sensuousness alike without the ability to reconcile them. But they have missed the logical cruces hidden beneath the psychological dilemma. 'The tempest of [Guyon's] wrathfulnesse' (II. xii. 83) is the very opposite of a crowning demonstration of temperance, which one would expect to find at the climax of Book II. Conversely, stanza 51 makes the luscious Bower that provokes his rage a *locus* of temperance:

Thereto the Heavens alwayes Joviall,
  Lookt on them lovely, still in stedfast state,
  Ne suffred storme nor frost on them to fall,
  Their tender buds or leaves to violate,
  Nor scorching heat, *nor* cold *intemperate*
  T'afflict the creatures, which therein did dwell,
  But the milde aire with season *moderate*
  Gently *attempred*, and disposed so well,
That still it breathed forth sweet spirit and holesome smell.

The wanton enchantress and her realm symbolize the lure of intemperance as Man's nostalgia for the *natural* temperance of Eden, where he enjoyed ἀ-κρασία in the sense of freedom from any need for self-control: the bliss forfeited irrevocably through the Fall. Art does not literally vitiate the Bower. It signals allegorically that Nature's Paradise is no longer. So does Acrasia *qua* witch. (One notes that she does not literally bewitch, bestialize, her prime victim, Verdant.) *Moral* temperance, which preserves bare life in the wrack, brings home more forcibly than any other aspect of virtue that to inherit God's grace is to acknowledge and appropriate

God's curse. Hence Guyon's wrath. To upgrade an expletive, Acrasia is goddamn lovely. Nor does she exemplify immoderate lust. She is having an orgasm, at once the most liberating and the most fleeting of Man's physical pleasures and so unsurpassable as a symbol for unfallen Nature as it beckons and recedes. We should trust the fiction, instead of cheapening it into a pastiche of pornography. At the same time we should 'unstory' it and realize that it is not about sex. Acrasia complements 'Excesse' unspecified, who sits, with etymological propriety, under the Bower's porch (55–7), to mean that entering her dream-land is ex-ceeding, going beyond, reality.[84]

Spenser's allegory demands from its readers not emotional restraint but logical discipline. Many critics talk casually of Arthur seeking glory instead of Gloriana, or else discuss his search so vaguely that they can be taken to mean either.[85] Obfuscation of this sort, however understandable, has to be denounced vigorously. In the poem Arthur seeks Gloriana. This needs to be interpreted, of course. But you cannot interpret Gloriana without interpreting Arthur as well; unless you suppose that Arthur himself regards his geographical search as a purely symbolic expression of his spiritual longings—an unbelievable supposition, which the information he grants inquisitive interlocutors (I. ix. 1–15) does not necessitate at all; quite the contrary. Alternatively you might consider Arthur to be seeking both glory and Gloriana; were it not that her name rules out this dissociation of the concept and the woman. She is an 'idol', a symbolic construct. And so is he. Nor is his meeting with Prays-desire (II. ix. 36–9) evidence to the contrary.[86] In the fiction she is a character, like Gloriana; not Arthur's aspiration inside his head. You cannot treat Prays-desire as a personification, which she undoubtedly is, without treating Arthur likewise: people do not converse with symbols. That she answers Arthur's censure with the retort that he is like herself merely confirms that they are *equivalent* personifications. They both embody the same aspiration inside *Alma's* head; and she has as little personal appeal as anybody in the poem. If you want to read *The Faerie Queene* as story, you must respect the fiction as Spenser wrote it. To interpret it you must conceptualize it *whole.* Tinkering with the narrative is out.

Examples such as these boost one's confidence that Spenser's fiction is fundamentally and continuously allegorical. Consequently the view that the Letter attaches undue importance to Arthur ceases to impress. Narrative prominence cannot be a criterion where narrative is illusory. Arthur is *conceptually* dominant, in that he stands for all the virtues. The appearance of a minor role results from Spenser's decision to farm out the several aspects of magnificence to 'xii. other knights', a decision taken, as he says, 'for the more variety of the history'; that is, for the sake of achieving a richly diversified pseudo-narrative (L 63–4). Thus we can explain a discrepancy which we could not explain by invoking Arthur's 'perfection' in comparison with the titular heroes he has to assist. For the widespread misinterpretation of the word[87] fails to make narrative sense. Arthur does not complete the knights' adventures: they tackle their ultimate antagonists unaided by him.[88] Nor does he fulfil their moral potential. Flawed characters are not perfected by somebody else's ethical superiority. How could Arthur overcome Red Cross's pride for him if Red Cross cannot overcome it himself? Or what comfort would there be for Red Cross in the thought that Arthur can defeat his own pride? As a matter of fact Arthur does neither: he slays Orgoglio. We must not tamper with the story by spiritualizing the Prince into a sudden influx of God's grace; as though Spenser thought of Red Cross as, generally speaking, able to cope quite happily under his own steam and needing divine support only in an emergency. For that matter, it is arbitrary to assume that dallying with Duessa exposes the vulnerability of Red Cross's morality more powerfully than do straying in the Wandering Wood or fainting before Despair. Arthur does not really rescue the knights: he substitutes for them; or rather, they substitute for him elsewhere. What he is left with constitutes a fictional pattern symbolic of magnificence *in particular*, in its dual identity (as of Gombrich's rabbit-duck figure): glory beginning to collect itself even as it depletes itself in sheer generosity. Structurally *The Faerie Queene* thrives on the evaporation of its narrative.

V Gloriana and Arthur

It has never, I think, been mooted that we should reject Spenser's title for his work. It is certainly a deliberate choice (L 2). Yet the discrepancy between the major role the Letter ascribes to Arthur and his apparently minor role in the poem is paralleled *ad absurdum* in the Faery Queen's virtual absence from a work named for her. Why have critics not taken exception? Probably because the Faery Queen 'shadows' Elizabeth. If the poem celebrates its dedicatee, it is proper that its title should advertise this somehow. Now the appearances of all the other characters with whom Elizabeth is, or may be, associated, such as Belphœbe, Una, Britomart, Mercilla, are strictly localized. Those of the Faery Queen, while far less prominent and always by way of flashback, are far more evenly distributed. This makes her the obvious candidate for an eponymous heroine. Although this theory does not explain why the poet does not support his important complimentary reference with a correspondingly substantial narrative,[89] critics might argue that the incongruity is typical: the poem's historical allegory seems to be extraneous generally, as though Spenser had felt obliged to incorporate it in spite of himself, with predictably mindless results.[90] The excitement of ferreting out allusions soon gives way to the sobering realization that, as an indirect account of Elizabeth's reign, the poem is random in its selection of events, insensitive to their relative importance, and disconcertingly simple-minded in its presentation of them. If you are interested in real history, with all its tensions and complexities, *The Faerie Queene* is just about the last book you should consult. Even a pointedly detailed passage such as the Mercilla episode (V. ix), which alludes definitely to the trial of Mary Queen of Scots, distorts rather than parallels history: Spenser virtually glosses over the crucial event, Mary's execution. Of course, encomiastic literature observes style and decorum; not to falsify, though, but to focus on what it singles out for praise, shorn of all irrelevancies. Spenser's poem turns its back on history in the very act of referring to it. Take Gloriana. It is just as well we have the poet's word for it that she stands for his sovereign (L 50–2). For she is the opposite of a striking likeness: Elizabeth reduced to queen, virgin, and inspirer of heroic action. No wonder that the historical allegory tends to be written off as a half-hearted attempt to bring the poem into line with epic practice and with the fashionable cult of the Virgin Queen; or even to be denounced as an incipient disease: 'Spenser was the instrument of a detestable policy in Ireland, and in his fifth book the wickedness he had shared begins to corrupt his imagination.'[91]

But can this argument be countenanced? Is it plausible that the poet should have compromised the moral and aesthetic integrity of his work by a purely adventitious element? Does the very dullness of the historical allegory as commonly conceived of not suggest that this conception might be inadequate? In view of its theme, the redemption of Time, the poem's averted immersion in history seems too appropriate to be ignored. And the role of the Faery Queen turns out to be all-embracing when measured properly, in terms of conceptual range rather than of narrative prominence. Her absent presence symbolizes (virtue as) hidden glory. Critics assume that the historical allegory is a distinct layer of meaning, which ought, but fails, to be interesting in itself. But as a continued metaphor with a single tenor *The Faerie Queene* possesses no such additional layer of meaning. There simply is no historical allegory, in the accepted sense of the phrase. The poem alludes to history as a complementary vehicle for its single meaning. And it does so in two different ways, already adumbrated. Sometimes the fiction parallels history in reverse, as it were. The trial of Duessa is a case in point. From a comparison with the trial of Mary, Mercilla emerges as mercy overruled by justice and Elizabeth as justice overruling mercy. It follows not only that the former cannot mean the latter but also that neither exemplifies mercy. Instead they are synonymous allegories of mercy as an aspect of justice (and so of virtue undifferentiated), distinct in their equivalence in much the same way as Arthur and Gloriana.[92] At other times, as in the case of the Faery Queen, the fiction genuinely parallels history but without clinching its reference. Not inappropriately Spenser uses the verb 'shadow'; in a context implying that this is not the only kind of historical allusion. For he says that Elizabeth 'beareth two persons, the one of a most royall Queene or Empresse, the other of a most vertuous and beautifull Lady', which are shadowed in Gloriana and Belphœbe (L 53–6). Since this dichotomy, reflecting the common sixteenth-century conception of the king's two bodies,[93] is exhaustive, one may infer that other characters associated with Elizabeth do not shadow her. Considering the compatibility of fiction and history, 'shadow' might equal 'mean, however vaguely'. The Letter hints, with a characteristic semblance of casualness, that it does not. 'In that Faery Queene I *meane* glory in my generall intention, but in my particular I *conceive* the most excellent and glorious person of our soveraine the Queene.' (L 49–52.) The poet does not say 'in my particular *intention*'; apparently to avoid repetition, in fact to avoid contradicting himself: the Queen is a particular 'dark conceit', or shadow. Like Gloriana, she stands for glory in the biblical sense. And this symbolic meaning is embodied not in her personality or her political career but precisely in those few features identifiable even in her shadow. Thus the majesty of her office, earthly kingship, represents the glory of the citizens of God's Kingdom, who reign uncertainly in anticipation of their everlasting reign.[94] Similarly, virginity represents 'already—not yet' the freedom from generation and death that the faithful shall enjoy. The parity of Elizabeth and Gloriana gives a breath-taking immediacy to the theme of *The Faerie Queene*, reminding its contemporary readers that their hope of glory, rekindled by the fiction, finds its concrete historical symbol and seal in their very own monarch. A more realistic portrait of Elizabeth as a person and a politician, which would certainly have been of greater intrinsic interest, would just as certainly have been a disastrous misfit: two-pronged *lèse-majesté*. This 'high' interpretation seems preferable to that of Cain, who holds that Spenser treats Elizabeth, initially at least, as goddess and mediatrix—an unlikely heresy. Also, it forestalls his notion that in the later Books Spenser, disappointingly, relapses from humanist idealism into medieval Augustinianism, thus wrecking his poem as encomium.[95]

Gloriana is not a person loosely connected with some vaguely exalted state and, in addition, a perfunctory courtesy in Elizabeth's direction; she is the coincidence of two sharply contoured shadows of exactly definable glory. Even her sex has the required symbolic anchorage: 'The woman is the glorie of the man.'[96] Her city, Cleopolis, falls into place as a complementary metaphor. We might emphasize, with Kaske, the contrast Red Cross discerns between it and the New Jerusalem:

> Till now, said then the knight, I weened well,
> That great Cleopolis, where I have beene,
> In which that fairest Faerie Queene doth dwell,
> The fairest Citie was, that might be seene;
> And that bright towre all built of christall cleene,
> Panthea, seemd the brightest thing that was:
> But now by proofe all otherwise I weene;
> For this great Citie that does far surpas,
> And this bright Angels towre quite dims that towre of glas.
>
> (I. x. 58.)[97]

Alternatively, we might concentrate, with Cain, on the Hermit's rejoinder, in which Gloriana's city is nevertheless related to heaven:

> Yet is Cleopolis for earthly frame,
> The fairest peece, that eye beholden can:
> And well beseemes all knights of noble name,
> That covet in th'immortall booke of fame
> To be eternized, that same to haunt,
> And doen their service to that soveraigne Dame,
> That glorie does to them for guerdon graunt:
> For she is heavenly borne, and heaven may justly vaunt.
>
> (59.)[98]

But why not respect the text, do both, and steer safely between the Scylla of pluralism and the Charybdis of Platonism? We easily could, if only we were to renounce the habit of intermittent allegorization. It is not as though Red Cross faces two distinct and, as Kaske sees it, incompatible ways of life, action and contemplation. The episode does not mean, literally, that Red Cross should continue to pursue fame instead of gazing at the New Jerusalem. This city is a biblical metaphor for Eternity, the resurrection life. Now 'kein Aug' hat je gespürt, kein Ohr hat je gehört solche Freude'.[99] As yet Spenser must do without 'that Sabaoths sight' (VII. viii. 2). You can see it only as a symbolic vision, 'in the spirit', with St. John in the Apocalypse. Yet Red Cross sees physically what presupposes Nature's annihilation. So he cannot be a person having to make his 'choice of life'. As an aspect of virtue he has no option. Logic dictates the prohibition of the Hermit Contemplation (63), so oddly out of character, it would seem; just as it dictates the paradoxical position of the Hermit himself: whereas John is conveniently carried on to the mountain to inspect the heavenly city from close quarters,[100] Red Cross and Contemplation alike strain to see it from 'far off', neither climbing the 'little path, that was both steepe and long' (55). Distant perception of the solid New Jerusalem equals conscious residence in the elusive Cleopolis. The two cities are opposite aspects of glory in Time. Cleopolis is not secular. Its tower, so far from alluding to the pagan Pantheon,[101] makes it 'wholly God's'. Nor is the fame to be found there a pagan value, as Kaske would have it. Gloriana's knights are not persons thirsting for worldly honour. They are virtues; and thus, metaphorically, God's κλέος or *fama*: the indirect, wayward, manifestation of His presence in humanity.

'A man is known by the company he keeps.' The saw becomes an axiom with personifications such as Arthur. We have already glimpsed him in conversation with Prays-desire. In the Bible 'praise' usually signifies not a human tribute to a human performance but a divinely prompted rehearsal of the *magnalia Dei.*[102] It refers to speech acts as the proclamatory aspect of, not as distinct from, God's gracious involvement with Man. Hence 'praise' is a focused synonym of 'magnify' and 'glorify'.[103] One begins to see why Arthur and Prays-desire emerge equivalent from their little altercation. Spenser's comment following her name, 'that *by well doing* sought to honour to aspire' (II. ix. 39), explains her alignment with Arthur as against Gloriana. But why this particular focus, praise? Why Prays-*desire*? And whence the dispute? To answer these questions we need to remember that Arthur meets her under the rubric of temperance. As such magnificence sustains a doomed existence, the after-taste of Paradise Lost rather than the fore-taste of Paradise Regained, witness Guyon's razing of the Bower. *Qua* temperance God's salvation remains dumb in spite of itself. It *is* Shamefastnesse, who 'answerd nought' (43). The poet describes Prays-desire as follows:

> In a long purple pall, whose skirt with gold
> Was fretted all about, she was arayd;
> And in her hand a Poplar braunch did hold.
>
> (37.)

For Brooks-Davies 'her purple and gold signify social position and hence, again, desire for glory (according to Ripa, 202 Honour or Glory (*Honore*) is dressed in purple because it is the royal colour and sign of the highest honour)'.[104] But the attributes of achieved social honour do not tally with Prays-desire's frustration (38). Anyway, the citation of Ripa hardly identifies Prays-desire as *Honore*, since they have in common only the wearing of purple.[105] The damsel demands the biblical intepretation. She is clothed in a pall. The *Oxford English Dictionary* quotes Spenser's lines as an instance of the general meaning, 'robe, cloak, mantle'. However, the specific meaning, 'robe or mantle put upon the sovereign at coronation', is more to the point.[106] When Christ was crowned, with a crown of thorns, by Pilate's soldiers, 'they put on him a purple garment'.[107] Temperate Man reigns with Christ in His Passion, mortifying the passions. (Appropriately, a pall is also 'a cloth, usually of black, purple, or white velvet, spread over a coffin, hearse, or tomb'.[108]) The rustless gold of Eternity shows only marginally: the skirt 'fretted all about' (contrast Florimell's 'garments all . . . of beaten gold', III. i. 15). As for the poplar, Brooks-Davies rightly sees it as an emblem of Hercules. It associates Arthur with this 'type of heroic virtue',[109] as do his twelvefold exertions. But there is more to it than that. When Hercules crowned himself with poplar leaves, on going down to Hades for his twelfth labour (or, alternatively, on returning from it), his sweat made one side of the leaves pale, while the other remained dark.[110] Temperance is magnificence victoriously struggling down in Hell (evidently so in the Cave of Mammon episode, II. vii). There virtue cannot see the laurel with which glory will crown it but only a poplar branch, the promise of a reward stained by effort and painfully evoking the condition that requires it.

Arthur has other associates with tell-tale names: his squire Timias and his tutor Timon. The usual derivations, though, from *τίμιος* (honoured) and *τιμή* (honour), are not sufficiently exact. 'Timias', when traced to the adjective, is anomalous in its last vowel, for a man. One posits a nominal form, *τιμία*; which does not exist. What does exist is the privative *ἀ-τιμία*: St. Paul uses it in antithesis to *δόξα*, as we have seen.[111] The squire's name means heavenly glory, which does indeed exist deprived of itself, submerged in Time, the English resonance of his name. 'Timon', the present participle of *τιμάω*, a variant of *δοξάζω* in the New Testament,[112] means Time glorifying (God); that is, cultivating glory, the offspring of Eternity, as virtue. Hence Timon is Arthur's foster-father. He is, emphatically, old (i. ix. 4); and Arthur receives a 'long education' (L 44), 'all his dayes' (I. ix. 4)—a specification which does not really make literal sense. Virtue is co-extensive with Time; in other words, both quasi-endless yet even so dying into or being educated, 'led out', into Eternity. In the 1590 edition Timon receives a second name, Cleon, only five stanzas later. Although the accompanying list of Faults Escaped already removes the inconsistency, 'Cleon' is hardly a misnomer, being the present participle of *κλέω* or *κλείω*, 'spread the *fama* of . . .'. The poet's pretended slip consolidates Timon's status of personification, as well as rounding out its meaning.[113]

Arthur's own name is not obviously symbolic. Literally it seems almost perverse, though. As C. S. Lewis taunts, 'you say *I chose the historye of king Arthure.* But you didn't. There is no Uther in your poem, no Mordred, no Guinevere, no Launcelot, no wars with the Saxons. It was not the history of Arthur you chose, but the bare name.'[114] To some the poet's choice becomes meaningful when related to his work as a celebration of his Queen in terms of the Tudor myth, according to which Elizabeth descends from Arthur. And, to be sure, Spenser protests that 'thy name O soveraine Queene, thy realme and race, / From this renowmed Prince derived arre' (II. x. 4). But when it comes to the crunch, he traces her back to Britomart and Artegall instead (III. iii. 26–49). His own explanation is that he chose Arthur 'as most fitte for the excellency of his person, being made famous by many mens former workes, and also furthest from the daunger of envy, and suspition of present time' (L 14–17). Such considerations, however, are not specific enough to rule out any hero other than Arthur; while they account in no way for the total lack of correspondence between Spenser's Arthur and the figure familiar from the medieval chronicles and romances. But then, in saying that he chose the history of *king* Arthur Spenser cannot possibly mean that he is going to *retell* that story, for he announces that his own story concerns Arthur 'before he was king' (L 26–7). He means that the history of king Arthur symbolizes his conception of virtue so well that he has decided to call its personification 'Arthur'. As an allegorist he leaves it to his readers to discover the symbolic relation. He can do so confidently because the major features of king Arthur's story are well known, 'being made famous by many mens former workes'. (The Letter's reference to Arthur's variously rehearsed fame and his tendency to obliterate 'present time' is itself allegorical, signifying multifarious yet Time-transcending virtue.)

One of these features is Arthur's dual kingship (*quondam rexque futurus*). Not only did he create the age of prototypical Britondom but he will return to establish it for good. This fits magnificence to a nicety: virtue's full splendour, both historical and legendary in that, dispersing itself in Time, it eludes empirical verification; but expected to return as eternal glory. The features Lewis mentions complement the symbolism. As for Uther, he is best remembered for begetting Arthur out of wedlock on 'the Lady Igrayne' (L 45–6) when Merlin's magic has transformed him into the likeness of her husband Gorlois. Virtue, similarly, springs from God's supernatural identification with Man in Christ. Uther's title, Pendragon, means 'head of an army'; that is, Lord of Hosts, or God. (The dragon was the standard of a cohort.[115]) Like Father, like Son. In Christian theology the latter reveals the former.[116] Accordingly

Spenser's Arthur literalizes Uther's title (in Book I, be it noted):

> His haughtie helmet, horrid all with gold,
> Both glorious brightnesse, and great terrour bred;
> For all the crest a *Dragon* did enfold.
>
> (vii. 31.)

This is the ancient serpent, Satan, 'already—not yet' conquered in Christ and so inspiring vain yet real fear, like the Dragon defeated by Red Cross (xii. 9–11). As for Mordred, Guinevere, Launcelot, and the Saxons, these names conjure up treachery at Arthur's court while he is fighting his wars abroad and his downfall as a result. Virtue, similarly, finds itself betrayed by Time, the condition of mortality. Accordingly Spenser's Arthur dies, in spite of his magical armour (vii. 36). And there is a further point. In the medieval tradition given currency by Geoffrey of Monmouth, Arthur and the Britons ultimately hail from Troy. This tradition explains why the most notable city of Spenser's Britain is called Troynovant.[117] But it does not justify literally the poet's assertion that 'Troynovant was built of old Troyes ashes cold' (III. ix. 38). This requires allegorical interpretation. 'New Troy' equals the New Adam, who is indeed the gracious reconstruction of the natural Old Adam, not a substitute. As an unmistakable allusion to London Troynovant must be Arthur's capital. It is therefore truly remarkable that the poem never once associates the Prince with the city where he is manifestly destined to reign. He seems to be heading for Cleopolis *instead.* This distinction is, of course, as insubstantial as that between Cleopolis and the New Jerusalem. But it is deeply significant all the same. Magnificence, Spenser means to say, so far from rushing to the scene of its coronation as glory ahead of Time, goes out of its way to spread the manifold rumour of this event, virtue in its several aspects. And so does the poem itself; obviously inspired by the divine Muses (VI Proem 2–3) as virtue is by grace, since without their aid 'ad nos vix tenuis famae perlabitur aura'.[118]

The preceding argument may seem flimsy, because the 'connection' between Arthur and Troynovant can only be inferred. It will look more persuasive when we detect Arthur's rather less implicit association with Hector, the mainstay of falling Troy, and Aeneas, the epitome of Rome, another New Troy (III. ix. 44) *in statu nascendi*. Infolded, the classical heroes symbolize virtue as life out of death. And so they do in their own right, merged as they are with their foremost enemies. *The Faerie Queene* begins 'Lo I the man', advertising itself as the British *Aeneid*. One expects that its central character will be another Aeneas. Spenser obliges. Arthur's helmet, with its plume and its dragon that 'seem'd to throw / From flaming mouth bright sparkles fierie red' (I. vii. 31–2), recalls the 'terribilem cristis galeam flammasque vomentem', part of the new armour Venus presents to her son. It is forged, under Vulcan's supervision, by 'Aetnaei Cyclopes' in 'antra Aetnaea'. Arthur's sword had been 'in flames of Aetna wrought apart' by Merlin (II. viii. 20). However, helmet and sword recall with even greater force those of Aeneas' irreconcilable antagonist Turnus, who almost succeeds in bringing down the Trojans' Latin settlement and is not slain until the very end of the epic. His 'triplici crinita iuba galea alta *Chimaeram* / sustinet, Aetnaeos efflantem faucibus ignis': a dragon-like monster. And his sword 'ignipotens deus ipse . . . / fecerat et Stygia candentem tinxerat unda', just as Arthur's sword had been 'dipped in the bitter wave / Of hellish Styx' by Merlin. The British hero contains polar opposites. He stands for virtue as its own enemy, victorious *in extremis*.[119]

Since Turnus is 'alius Achilles',[120] one expects that Arthur will be another Achilles as well as another Hector. Again Spenser obliges. The 'glorious brightnesse' of his helmet makes him κορυθαιόλος, an epithet peculiar to Hector (apart from *Iliad* XX. 38). 'Upon the top of all his loftie crest, / A bunch of haires . . . Did shake' (I. vii. 32), as on Hector's helmet: one remembers how it frightens the little Astyanax, to the amusement of his parents—a touching moment of relief and renewal of motivation amidst the pressures and horrors of war.[121] The helmet of St. Paul's *miles christianus* is 'salvation' or, more particularly, 'the hope of salvation'.[122] No wonder Arthur's plume 'seem'd to daunce for jollity'. But the poet qualifies this note, too un-Homeric to be true. The plume also resembles 'an Almond tree', the white hair of old age,[123] symbolizing Time as it undermines life. Nor should we forget that, whereas Aeneas kills Turnus, Hector is killed by Achilles. Virtue's victory *in extremis* involves its defeat as virtue. Arthur's armour identifies him even more pointedly with Achilles than with Hector. It is the Greek's crest that has hairs waving in a dance-like movement (περισσείοντο). When he draws near to Hector, the bronze protecting his body flashes 'like the gleam . . . of the sun as he riseth', just as Arthur's 'glitterand armour' shines like 'Phœbus brightest ray' (29). And the precious stone on Arthur's baldric, sparkling 'like Hesperus emongst the lesser lights' (30), recalls Achilles' fatal spear, scintillating 'as a star goeth forth amid stars in the darkness of night, the star of evening, that is set in heaven as the fairest of all'.[124] Does Hector triumph in his downfall at all? Like virtue, he does proleptically: he wears Achilles' old armour in token of his defeat of Patroclos, Achilles' *alter ego.* So does Arthur. His baldric shining 'like twinkling stars' (29) reminds one of Achilles' 'corselet . . . spangled with stars (ἀστερόεντα)', which Patroclos puts on. And he does not carry his own spear (37), just as Patroclos goes without that of his friend. More decisively, Spenser intensifies the sun-like quality of Arthur *qua* Achilles to the point of suggesting his identity with Apollo, the god who will slay Achilles, as the dying Hector anticipates.[125] His transference of the 'Hesperus' simile has a corresponding significance. It implies that Arthur's jewel will be the death of him. 'Shapt like a Ladies head' (30), however, it is clearly an amulet representing the Faery Queen, who stands for glory unto death as the promise of glory beyond death. Similarly, in the hands of Timias the fatal spear becomes precious (τίμιος): 'O death, where is thy sting!'[126]

With Arthur's gem shining like the evening star, its visual effect must be negligible in the light of his sun-like armour. But the comparison verges on the bathetic even if we shut our eyes to its context. Although Hesperus does outshine the other stars, it hardly shines *amongst* them: it soon gives way to them, vanishing altogether. This does not matter in Homer, whose simile conveys not so much the spear's superiority as 'nightfall' for Troy. It does in Spenser, who highlights the stone's comparative splendour. Incongruities such as these are not to be passed by, or else denounced. They are meant to disturb our literalist slumbers. The description as it were 'phases' the response to this admonition of St. Paul's: 'The night is past, & the day is at hand: let us therefore cast away the workes of darkenes, and let us put on the armour of light.'[127] In Arthur we see Man thus armed reaching his zenith of glory. Yet this glory is even so but a bright star that ushers in the night of Time, whose darkness admits only a baldric of 'lesser lights', glory unfolded into its several aspects. Spenser's literal nonsense makes allegorical sense; here with all-encompassing implications. For the description sums up the entire poem. It contains the twelve knights' multifarious adventures: a zodiac of virtue; Gloriana's occasional appearance in flashback: an evening star of glory briefly above the horizon with its reflected light; and Arthur's passage through all the Legends: 'the Sunne of righteousnes',[128] kindling the evening star, rising and setting in each sign of the zodiac to blaze the night sky into temporary invisibility in its perpetual revolutions.

If Arthur rotates through *The Faerie Queene*, his story must be illusory. Level-headed examination of its 'stages' will confirm this. It might seem that his search for Gloriana has been triggered off by the dream in which she reveals herself to him. This experience cannot be merely a dream, however, in view of the 'pressed gras where she had lyen' (I. ix. 15). To Lewis it seems one 'to which the contrast . . . between dream and waking does not strictly apply', namely 'the soul's new-kindled raptures at its first meeting with a transcendental or at least incorporeal object of love'.[129] This is precisely wrong, because Arthur definitely dreams and just as definitely wakes up. He does not wonder:

> Was it a vision, or a waking dream?
> Fled is that music:—Do I wake or sleep?[130]

Now an experience at once dreamt and real can hardly be an experience. A further illogicality settles the matter. Gloriana's love for Arthur is to appear only 'when just time expired'. Yet Spenser hints unmistakably that they make love. She lies down 'by [his] side', exposing 'her daintie limbes', and makes 'most goodly glee and lovely blandishment', as only a woman inviting entry to seal her commitment would (13–14). What does she withhold, giving herself? 'Just time' refers not to a certain period of time but to Time justified in Christ, or what the New Testament calls 'the fulness of time',[131] to be revealed when Time 'expires', ceases to be. Until then God's already unbounded love for Man shows itself at one remove even when at its most apparent. That is why Arthur conveys his fulfilment through reticence rather than explicitness; and enjoys it in the form of a quasi-nocturnal visitation rather than a daylight vision. As a Venus Gloriana remains an 'evening star'. The heavy imprints of the ethereal Faery Queen on the grass and on Arthur's memory are not evidence of some transcendental event but complementary metaphors for a particularly manifest aspect of generally elusive glory. So the dream, being an allegory, cannot give rise to the search. Their relationship must be of a different kind. Fowler takes deep soundings when he says that Arthur's 'waking experience extends his dream, as he pursues in life the ego-ideal he dreamt. To change the figure, he goes on to enact the epic Gloriana recited to him in his vision.'[132] But such figurative language confuses more than it clarifies. The narrative needs to be given up unambiguously.

Arthur's search itself soon betrays its allegorical status. We have already noted in passing that Spenser does not really describe it. Apart from the dream and the pursuit of Florimell Arthur's story consists of martial exploits, usually in support of the titular heroes. Of his search proper we never see anything more than that he resumes it, to disappear from the fiction (except in Book IV).[133] This is easily explained: since his knightly feats symbolize noonday virtue, they must be qualified by a crepuscular view. That is all. They cannot be events taking place during a search. So considered, they could only be so many interruptions impeding its progress. Yet Arthur, despite his preoccupation with Gloriana, clearly does not feel that he is being side-tracked all the time. On the contrary, he eagerly embraces every opportunity to show his mettle. At one point he even turns up positively 'seeking adventures', as though he had forgotten about his love (IV. vii. 42). It is only literally absurd that he sets out, with the specific purpose of finding Gloriana, 'throughly instructed' by Timon (L 48–9), his tutor in military skills, who counsels against love (I. ix. 9). Exploits and search are not phases in a career but aspects of an extended metaphor. Even time references do not imply sequence. In Book I Arthur has been seeking for 'nine monethes' (ix. 15), the period of gestation, aptly symbolic of magnificence in Time about to be delivered as glory in Eternity.[134] In Book II we hear of a twelve months' search (ix. 7 and 38), as though three months had elapsed since the meeting with Red Cross. However, in the 1590 edition these stanzas mention seven and three years, contradicting each other[135]—one more pretended slip to signal the unreality of the story. For the silent 'correction' of 1596 could hardly betoken a complete transformation of the fictional mode. (The second edition does heighten the poem's spurious credibility as narrative with some consistency. The change mentioned here has the same smoothing effect as the substitution of 'Timon' for 'Cleon' (I. ix. 9) mentioned earlier on. And so, more powerfully than any incidental alteration, does the withdrawal of the patently 'incorrect' Letter, which defines the work explicitly as a continued allegory. That Book I does not positively preclude literal interpretation of its time reference whereas Book II does illustrates once again the difference in their attitude towards the fiction.)

Some critics hold that the projected Twelve-Book *Faerie Queene* was to have culminated in the wedding of Arthur and Gloriana.[136] This assumption, if true, would destroy our thesis. And it is undoubtedly compelling: an Arthur perpetually frustrated would be unacceptably demoralizing. Still, it is entirely groundless. The Letter to Ralegh, which does contain information about Book XII, does not even hint at a marriage. Nor does Arthur get appreciably closer to Gloriana as the narrative progresses. Already in Book II he has 'walkt round about the world', like the sun, 'yet no where can her find'; and Prays-desire rubs it in (ix. 7, 38). More conclusively, perhaps, the Proem to

Book I, summarizing the action of the poem as a whole, speaks of

> fairest Tanaquill,
> Whom that most noble Briton Prince so long
> Sought through the world, and suffered so much ill,
> That I must rue his undeserved wrong.
>
> (2.)

Not a whisper of a happy ending here! Besides, *The Faerie Queene* models itself on the *Aeneid.* Both are about New Troy a-building. Arthur's helmet and sword make him another Aeneas. Gloriana, central yet elusive, proves another Lavinia. Virgil keeps her inconspicuous but introduces her, in retrospect, at the very heart of his epic, reporting how, during a ceremony at the altar, her hair had caught fire—an omen whose interpretation epitomizes Gloriana's role:

> namque fore *inlustrem fama* fatisque canebant
> ipsam, sed populo *magnum portendere bellum.*[137]

The flames of the holy ritual, a counterpart to the biblical fire of heaven, burning yet not consuming,[138] surround her head like a 'glory'. Now the Latin poet as it were truncates his work, in that he stops short at the death of Turnus and fails to narrate the union of Aeneas and Lavinia for which it paves the way. Spenser must follow suit. (This argument would not have seemed tendentious to Renaissance readers, familiar with 'the so-called Thirteenth book, a supplement describing the marriage of Aeneas and Lavinia and Aeneas's apotheosis, written by the Italian humanist, Maphaeus Vegius' and often published with Virgil's text.[139]) Like Virgil, Spenser does imply a marriage—and, indeed, an apotheosis; not as events beyond his narrative scope, though. After all, Gloriana is quintessentially a virgin. She presides over an Order of Maidenhead. Also, she could not sacrifice her virginity for the joy of sex without ceasing to 'shadow' Elizabeth. Arthur's consummated dream leaves her, mysteriously but unquestionably, intact. It cancels itself out precisely because of her unabashed advances, so untypical of the Queen; as does his search, which presupposes her sexual availability.[140] The Prince's exploits *are* the fulfilment of his love, tacitly, beyond the horizon, like his dream as he tells it: magnificence *is* glory 'already—not yet'.

Arthur has no story. The story he appears to have does focus what he stands for, all-round virtue, as 'e-ducation': again and again he is led out of the poem. But it is not the story of an education. Spenser knows that moral growth does not mean acquiring the virtues in a row. He never relates Arthur's performance in any one Book to what he might be supposed to have learnt previously. Indeed, Arthur manifestly does not learn at all: he is master throughout. Nor does he set the reader examples in all the virtues *seriatim*—what a repellent, unedifying monster he would be if he did. Whatever the rationale of the Books' sequence, it is not temporal.[141] We are well rid of Arthur's story. Not only his invariable readiness to assist his peers but also his unquestioning pursuit of his mistress is too mechanical to appeal as narrative. He seems immune to the passing of time. Never does he wonder uneasily whether Gloriana might not be a 'deceiving elf', tempting him out into 'faery lands forlorn'.[142] Even his ignorance of the way leaves him unperturbed. His zest does not evidently increase when he hears others reminiscing about Faery Court. And he certainly does not press them to guide him thither, in compensation for his efforts on their behalf. Let us be honest and refrain from disingenuous or heady theorizing to save the tale at all costs. For instance, let us not turn Arthur into a 'daemonic agent'.[143] Fletcher's lurid conception of allegory may apply to, say, 'The Rime of the Ancient Mariner'; that is, to the 'immanent' symbolism Coleridge so perceptively distinguishes from allegory proper.[144] Arthur acts compulsively because he is a personification tethered to a concept.

If Arthur has no story, Spenser's work, *qua* Arthuriad, cannot be an epic. C. S. Lewis assails the Letter's suggestion to the contrary with divine fury: 'Or take your invoking the precedents of Homer, Virgil, and Tasso. This implies that *The Faerie Queene* is an epic. But it isn't. An epic represents some great event that made a change in the world historically, whereas your poem, while it is full of events of a kind, is in another sense motionless.'[145] The poet would have smiled assent. But then, he does not imply that his work is an epic as Lewis defines it. This definition hardly fits Ariosto, to say nothing of Xenophon, whom Spenser mentions among his models (as Lewis forgets in his passion). Moreover, it is virtually irrelevant to all his models as interpreted by him (in the Letter) and, for that matter, by Renaissance humanists generally.[146] Nor does he ever use the word 'epic'. Instead he speaks of 'Poets historicall'; that is, makers of fiction (L 17, 71–2, and compare 11–12). Spenser would also have agreed that, *qua* series of Legends, his work is 'static and repetitive', lacking the 'dynamic and developing structure' of epic.[147] In Section III we already discovered in what sense the poem 'thrusteth into the middest' (L 74–5). As the next Section will show, his promise that Book XII was to have provided a flashback to the Faery Queen's annual feast (L 78–80) is similarly a matter of keeping up epic appearances. We should certainly continue to refer to *The Faerie Queene* as an epic; but only because that generic term adequately suggests both the importance to which it aspires and most, though not all, of its relevant analogues, as 'romance' does not.

VI The Titular Knights and the Annual Feast

Since Arthur has no story, the adventures of the titular knights, with which his intersect, cannot be stories either. However, this bare inference, though logically incontrovertible, does not persuade, because in the knights' case the illusion of narrative is undeniably stronger. The truth about the fiction can be certainly known, but hardly ever can it be easily perceived. Just as the knights are grace abounding tested all the Time as virtue embattled and imperilled, so the reader of their Legends has his *a priori* understanding of their conceptual rationale challenged throughout as an active faith. We are to 'work out' the gift of salvation with fear and trembling.[148]

One truly explosive argument is that the knights' quests are pageants *as well*: an impossibility. Schulze suggested long ago that 'Spenser's use of the Faerie Queene's annual twelve days' feast to motivate the action of his great poem . . . may well be a reflection of certain chivalric practices of the

[Elizabethan] age rather than a mere reversion to the feast of the romances'.[149] Taking up this point, Frances Yates has urged the need for research into the connection between *The Faerie Queene* and Elizabeth's Accession Day Tilts in particular.[150] It would seem that the poem was thoroughly modern in its very neo-medievalism, not 'already a little out of date when it first appeared' (a description characterizing its author rather than its object).[151] Now the idea that the knights' adventures are pageants staged in honour of Gloriana has considerable explanatory power. Thus the fact that she does not figure in them except, retrospectively, as their initiator makes sense if they are a spectacle to her, as courtiers' tournaments were to Elizabeth, after she had authorized her champions formally at the outset. It also becomes clear why the knights never guide Arthur to Gloriana: the world of pageantry in which he enacts an imaginary search is discontinuous with the real world from which she watches. Actually, Red Cross once refers to Guyon's adventure as the 'pageant' which 'next ensewes' (II. i. 33); implying that his own has the same status. And E. K., in his commentary on 'June', in *The Shepheardes Calender*, slightly misquotes II. iii. 25 (1) from what he calls the poet's 'Pageaunts'. Many of the exploits that could not conceivably happen, such as killing Error, could well be staged. Besides, the adventures are obviously not strung together by chance, notwithstanding the plentiful references to it. They are bound to come full circle. One feels that there is no possibility of any knight, even Calidore, abandoning his task, or dying by accident. There is a scenario. Quite a few episodes are, in fact, unmistakably pageants or organized performances of some other type, such as the procession of the Seven Deadly Sins (I. iv), the Mask of Cupid (III. xii), and the wedding of Thames and Medway (IV. xi). These would fit much more comfortably into large-scale pageants than into genuine adventures.

As pageants the knights' adventures *constitute* the Faery Queen's feast: they do not merely find their origins there. The Letter, so far from forcing us to distinguish the feast proper from the adventures, implicitly encourages us to equate them. For as Historiographer Spenser is conspicuously silent about what else the feast could be. The most natural assumption, a banquet,[152] is subtly qualified by the poem. The two major 'feasts' embedded in *The Faerie Queene*, Satyrane's (IV. ii. 26, v. 6) and Marinell's (V. iii. 2, 3), are tournaments. Only the latter includes banquets, which Spenser leaves rather emphatically undescribed; just as on the occasion of the minor 'feast' to mark Red Cross's victory, which is a banquet, he had exclaimed: 'What needs of daintie dishes to devize.' One gathers that his 'narrow leaves' (*sic*—I. xii. 14) will not accommodate any descriptions of festive meals. And then, the departure of twelve paragons of knighthood one after the other hardly fits the idea of a feast in the first place: you do not celebrate by leaving the party. True, the poet's statement that 'the *occasions* of the xii. several adventures' happen at the feast (L 80–1) could imply that the adventures themselves do not. But it could also imply that the adventures are occasions; which, as pageants, they certainly would be. The equation has much to recommend it. For one thing, without it one could not begin to counter the damaging complaint that 'an account of the feast at any length (and the attention given to the matter in the letter suggests that the account when it does appear will be more than trivial), placed in [Book XII] . . . would inevitably break the back of [that] book . . . and thus destroy the symmetry of the scheme'.[153] Spenser says that in Book XII 'I *devise that* the Faery Queene kept her Annual feaste' (L 79–80); not 'tell how'. It was to have revealed, or rather hinted obscurely[154] and no doubt briefly, that the entire poem *is* the account, indeed more than trivial, of that feast. Only a revelation of such scope would need to be anticipated in an introductory Letter. For another thing, the equation enables us to solve the awkward discrepancy between the time schemes of the Letter and the poem. How can the adventures begin on consecutive days, as the Letter surely implies (L 80, 83, 110, 116),[155] if in the poem, which has the knights handing over to each other at their completion, they take months? They can only if they are pageants, whose performance takes a day each while the action represented in them is imagined to take months. Also, Arthur, as the recurring figure in a set of pageants at Faery Court, would be the centre of *magnificence* in the sense of splendid court entertainment.[156] One infers that Spenser's 'magnificences' are the wedding celebration of Arthur and Gloriana; and, *qua* poetry, their epithalamion.

To show that the knights' adventures are pageants is not to show that they are pseudo-stories. On the contrary, it is to rehabilitate them as real stories, telling what happens at an imaginary feast. But then, there are formidable arguments militating against their status of pageants. Apart from the Red Cross Knight's farewell to Guyon nothing suggests that the knights are consciously actors. Despite our sense of a scenario we do not feel that they are masqueing, going through the motions of a prescribed ritual. They oppose their enemies and pursue their aspirations with the intensity and commitment that go with inescapable exposure to the human predicament. They cannot opt out of their roles. Besides, though the frame of the pageantry world fictionalizes Arthur's properly erotic designs upon his bride, they are even so hardly suitable for a public show put up specially for her. Anyway, there is no evidence of her presence all along as a spectator. The possibility that Spenser would have revealed it at the very end of the poem cannot be seriously entertained: such a gesture would unmask the knights after all and thus quite gratuitously annihilate the poem's moral urgency so carefully maintained throughout. In short, the knights' adventures are as truly genuine quests as they are pageants. Hence they cannot possibly be real stories. They are indeed *insubstantial* pageants. 'Quest', 'pageant', and 'feast' do not really specify narrative; they are overall metaphors. Apparently virtue is glory 'not yet', and thus 'quest'; secretly it is glory 'already', and thus 'pageantry' at elusive Cleopolis. Because it is both, Gloriana's feast takes place annually, year in year out, perennially, as long as Time lasts—like the sun's journey through the zodiac. Only when Time expires will it be concluded by a banquet, the marriage supper of the Lamb,[157] which lies beyond Spenser's thematic range. Elizabeth's recurrent Accession Day Tilts, as it were Time's unfolding of her motto *semper eadem*,[158] are history's coincident allegory. That they were not Coronation Day Tilts shows the hand of Providence.

Now for our next demonstration that the titular knights

do not have stories. The appearance that they do derives from the idea, reinforced notably by the Letter, that each has a single task, accomplished in between a departure from and a return to Faery Court. This mould, so far from being obviously exploded by the sheer incoherence of the narratives, seems rather to regiment them sequentially in spite of it. Yet this same mould also hints that the knights rotate, like Arthur; especially because their returns are invariably anticlimactic. Red Cross must go back to undertake new tasks (I. xii. 18) and so forsake the bliss of Una unveiled. Guyon finds himself haring after the Gloriana-like Florimell. Artegall is summoned back prematurely (V. xii. 27), to be reviled by Envy and Detraction. And Calidore's triumph over the Blattant Beast culminates in its escape, to play havoc with *The Faerie Queene* itself (VI. xii. 38, 41). In short, Gloriana's court appears in a distinctly inglorious light. This is more than a little at odds with the raptures of Guyon and Red Cross in reminiscing about their Queen and Cleopolis and with Arthur's expectation, implied by his unremitting search, of undiluted felicity and utter fulfilment. To attempt a synthesis of these two valuations would be futile: in their stark contrast they rule each other out. Faery Court is not a place but an allegory, of glory 'already—not yet'. Hence it cannot be left and revisited. 'Departure' and 'return' are symbols, conveying the hidden authenticity of glory in Time: the knights belong where they cannot apparently be. Like Arthur they shine as virtue, to be dimmed as glory. If the attitude of Red Cross is not untypical (L 83–8, 98–100), they 'abandon' Gloriana as eagerly as Arthur 'interrupts' his search for her. They find themselves, their τέλος, Arthur, in the midst of their struggles. The mould of their adventures does not really mend their incoherence, after all.

This is not to say, though, that in dismantling the knights' stories we ought to make ourselves unresponsive to their illusory charms. These should be interpreted, rather. Thus the dream-like quality of the quests, which so impresses Hough, defines them as the counterpart of Arthur's vision. It does *not* define Spenser as a dreamer with a subconscious surfacing in his poem. Again, the appearance that Arthur and the knights have contrary orientations, towards and away from

Gloriana, is not without significance. Only we should not glibly impose a Neoplatonic *choresis*; as does Fowler, who sees the knights' missions as *emanatio*, their quests as *conversio*, and Arthur's search as *remeatio*.[159] The prince would certainly represent *remeatio* better than his peers, for he aspires to Gloriana while they simply return to her because they have finished their jobs. However, he does not *return*. On Fowler's view of the knights as sub-characters of Arthur he returns on their behalf, as it were. But how can they be his sub-characters, being so differently preoccupied? They are in that he waives his own preoccupation with Gloriana—so that there is no true *remeatio* at all. They are also in that he shares their alleged *emanatio* and *conversio*, moving as he does to Gloriana *from* Gloriana, via martial exploits. The distinction between missions and quests is too precarious to sustain the relevant part of the Platonic scheme. The quests proper are only seemingly turning-points. They remind the reader of the knights' starting-point without reversing the orientation of the knights themselves. *The Faerie Queene* presents not a triadic but a dyadic journey; one that is far more emphatically outward-bound than homeward-bound. Whereas the cosmic rhythm of the Platonists stresses the glory of its origin and goal, Spenser concentrates throughout on glorifying the divine flow at its lowest reaches. He can do so because his God does more than emanate: He is in Christ Emmanuel, with us in person. Arthur's centripetal e-ducation hardly gathers in the knights' centrifugal in-ducements to their tasks. On the contrary, they virtually prevent it. The entire poem constitutes an explicit call 'to virtue'. The inconspicuousness of its contrary orientation 'to glory' is as important as its reality. At the beginning of Book VI the poet subtly warns us that its Legend, and by implication all the other Legends of Faery *Court*, 'of [which] it seemes, men Courtesie doe call' (i. 1), are

> nought but forgerie,
> Fashion'd to please the eies *of them, that pas,*
> *Which see not perfect things but in a glas*
>
> (Proem 5)

—that is, of transient creatures, who see perfection in

mortality, in reverse. We are not to be deceived by 'that glasse so gay' but to remind ourselves that 'we all beholde *as in a mirrour* the glorie of the Lord with open face, and we are changed into the same image, from glorie to glorie, as by the Spirit of the Lord'.[160] Virtue is nothing but the visible counter-current, unto death, of its secret Pauline sweep, 'from glory to glory', unto life everlasting. Knowing that, we can follow its lead as unreservedly as does the poem, without any sense of getting trapped in its apparently vicious circles.

To complete our incrimination of the knights' stories let us return to the Letter's narrative component and take its awkwardness and inaccuracy as such for what they are, explosive clues. As we saw in Section II, the account of the adventures' origins is superfluous. With respect to Red Cross, to be sure, there are no positive discrepancies to prevent us from regarding it as a genuine prelude dovetailing into the narrative of Book I (L 83–109). However, as Bennett acutely observes, *qua* prelude it 'belongs at the beginning of the narrative. Its chief function, that of creating suspense as to the knight's ability, is destroyed if the story is not told until after the knight has proved his worth. Either Spenser's plan to put this part of his story at the end of the poem was a serious error in narrative technique or the introductory scene was an afterthought.'[161] It is both and neither: it serves as an allegorical definition of the Book's theme, devised specifically for the Letter and, as the absurdity of its allocation implies, not meant for inclusion in the poem at all. The same goes for the origins of the other knights' adventures. Owen remarks that 'there appears to be no precedent either in practice or in theory for placing the preliminaries to an epic action in the last book'.[162] The prescriptive force, to humanists, of generic properties entails that Spenser cannot have envisaged such an unprecedented move. Anyway, the poem, which mentions the quests' festive origin only in connection with Guyon, belies the feast Book XII was allegedly to have narrated by making it a one-day rather than a twelve-day event (II. ii. 42).[163] We can dispose for good of Owen's complaint about the final Book ruining the poem's pattern. Spenser's promise of a flashback certainly appears to presuppose narrative. In actual fact it inflates an illusion to bursting-point. The elusiveness of glory in Time dictates the mere implicitness of Gloriana's feast in the poem. It also has to muzzle the Letter, if it is to be a valid complement. Hence the Historiographer does not say in so many words that the adventures are festive pageants. True, their origins, which he describes at some length, are explicitly part of the feast. But then, as complaints (L 93, 111, 117) they overcloud its glory. Even so, of course, they testify openly to its hidden presence. That is why they are told in a mere postscript in 1590, withdrawn in 1596. The Letter's glory shines and vanishes like the evening star.

Only once in his historiographical account does Spenser slip out of his assumed role, to gloss the armour Una gives to Red Cross as 'the armour of a Christian man specified by Saint Paul v. Ephes.' (L 102–3).[164] This is enough to prove his fiction metaphorical and to clinch the definition of its tenor, in case 'glory' and 'magnificence' should still seem indeterminate. For Paul did not distribute weaponry among his congregations: he told them, figuratively, to 'be strong in the Lord'; that is, to resist the devil in the knowledge that in Christ he has already been defeated. The biblical reference could not be a short cut to avoid a full inventory. Who shall say whether Red Cross is equipped with all the items in Paul's list? While the prominence of shields in his encounters with the Sans brothers does invite examination in light of the 'shield of faith', one would be hard put to it to decide whether his feet are 'shod with the preparation of the Gospel of peace'. Instead the reference makes Red Cross, and 'by implication' the other knights, symbols of moral perfection. And it makes him a symbol of holiness in particular, in two ways. Firstly, the passage in Ephesians itself presents Man as consecrated earth, as it were, set apart from and to be defended against spiritual evil.[165] Spenser can cite it to suggest holiness as virtue because it emphasizes the active aspect. (Compare and contrast the synonymous but passive metaphors of warfare in Luther's best-known hymn, prompted by Psalm 46: 'Ein feste burg ist unser Gott / ein gute wehr und waffen . . . Mit unser macht ist nichts gethan / wir sind gar bald verloren / Es streit fur unns der rechte man / den Gott hat selbs erkoren.'[166]) Secondly, the Letter's pseudo-prelude to the quest of Red Cross symbolizes holiness in that Spenser gives away his biblical tenor there rather than anywhere else. For holiness, as a '*whole* armour' (πανοπλία), provided by *Una*, focuses virtue as complete identification of God and Man: this aspect of magnificence equals glory *transparently*. The poem similarly localizes the revelation of its theme. Of all the knights it is Red Cross who knows from experience of *Pan*thea, the Faery Queen's bright, if brittle, tower of strength, and who glimpses the New Jerusalem. It is in the Legend of Holiness that Arthur alludes unmistakably to Gloriana's embraces. And it is the fiction of Book I that can 'already—not yet' be taken whole, as narrative.

In his *Wonderful Prophecies from the Beginning of the Monarchy of this Land* (1626) Robert Salter, a soi-disant friend of Spenser's, claims that his dissertation on the 'fourfold state of the man in Christ' has been anticipated in the poet's first Legend.[167] Nelson dismisses this as the earliest attempt to read the Book as a *Bildungsroman*, depicting four successive phases of development;[168] understandably, considering Salter's use of 'period'. Yet the sheer inapplicability of the sequence should have checked him. And so should logic: how could a 'fourfold *state*' develop temporally? In fact, the fourth state, 'the glory of the man's consummation . . . although he do yet walk in the flesh' explicitly involves the first, 'the state of nature, originally derived unto him from his parents'. In Time, Man could not be educated out of nature. Nor could he mature out of the second 'state of his adoption and childhood in Christ through Grace' into the third, 'his full growth and strength of manhood in Christ'—in spite of what the conjunction of metaphors suggests. Moreover, Salter does not even try to quadrisect Red Cross's quest. He seizes upon its apparent introduction in the Letter, elaborating its details with obvious relish, but then falls into generalities. We might infer that here we have an author indulging in a fond aside and winding up hurriedly. Still, it would not follow that what he denies us are narrative divisions. Perhaps he means that each and every episode symbolizes the fourfold state. If so, he bids fair to be right. Thus in the Error episode we see the first state in the Wandering

Wood, one aspect of *silva*, ὕλη, matter,[169] the 'corruption' in which 'the bodie is sowen';[170] the second and third in the knight's quasi-literal progress from faith to work, so that he succeeds 'first passively' and 'after actively'; and the fourth in Una, not yet named but here representing the meaning of her name, inseparability from Christ, as the companion through whose counsel they are 'more than conquerors . . . [like] Daniel *amidst* the lions'.[171] Or take a 'mere detail' such as the badge of the patron of holiness, his red cross. *Qua* 'deare remembrance of his dying Lord' it signifies mortality. It adorns both his shield, of passive faith, and his breast(plate), of active righteousness—or 'innocencie & godlie life', as the Geneva gloss says (I. i. 2). Finally, in the iconograpical tradition it marks the banner of the risen Christ.[172] (That it is also the attribute of England's patron saint does not make for a fifth meaning. 'Saint George' is, etymologically, 'consecration of earth' (compare I. x. 61, 66); or, in one word, holiness. The name forms part of the vehicle.) The Letter's section on Red Cross embodies the same quadruple meaning. Salter brings out the first state, nature. That the armour is Una's gift conveys the second, passive grace. Spenser's biblical reference introduces the third, active virtue, as we have seen. And the setting, Gloriana's feast, implies the fourth, glory. We may or may not wish to give Salter the benefit of the doubt as to his own ability to read *The Faerie Queene*. Perhaps he is stupidly repeating a few general remarks the poet had once tossed off in his presence. How humbling to think that a critical nobody could have set us straight.

Proceeding now to Guyon's adventure, we salute Lewis as he points out the Letter's misrepresentation of its origin (L 110–16): 'But in your poem Guyon and the Palmer are well started on their mission against Acrasia before they come across the babe with the bloody hands.'[173] We are not impressed, though. Just as the Letter generally serves to intimate 'the whole intention of the conceit' (L 131), so its account of Book II purports to convey 'the whole subject thereof' (L 116). Combine this with its apparent falsity and you will conclude that it is a piece of pseudo-narrative blasting itself out of its hinges. Lewis's retort, in denouncing one inaccuracy, introduces another. True enough, in the poem Guyon and his companion are already travelling together before they find the babe. And they have no doubt come from Faery Court (see II. i. 31). But their journey has not been a mission against Acrasia all along. On the contrary, after Red Cross has wished him good speed,

> Guyon forward gan his voyage make,
> With his blacke Palmer, that him guided still.
> Still he him guided over dale and hill,
> And with his steedie staffe did point his way:
> His race with reason, and with words his will,
> From foule intemperance he oft did stay,
> And suffred not in wrath his hastie steps to stray.
>
> In this faire wize they traveild long yfere,
> Through many hard assayes, which did betide;
> Of which he honour still away did beare,
> And spred his glorie through all countries wide.
>
> (34–5.)

Worse than Red Cross, whose strange lack of purpose after the Error episode we noted in Section IV, Guyon, so emphatically guided, has a purpose altogether different from the one Lewis assigns to him. He comes upon Ruddymane 'at last'. The scene and Amavia's story move him so profoundly that he makes a 'sacred vow' there and then to wreak vengeance on Acrasia (60–1). One cannot but infer that his determination to seek her out dates from this moment. If the experience merely rekindles indignation already aroused previously, Spenser would have said so. How incredible it is, too, that Guyon should run into a situation calculated to motivate him anew purely by accident, 'as chaunst them by a forest side / To passe' (35).

Lewis is wrong in yet another way. The poem contains, less overtly, an account of Guyon and Ruddymane that does agree with the Letter. His false correction might be an unconscious acknowledgement of this other version. Guyon, reminiscing about Faery Court before Medina, tells how

There this old Palmer shewed himselfe that day,
And to that mighty Princesse did complaine
Of grievous mischiefes, which a wicked Fay
Had wrought, and many whelmd in deadly paine,
Whereof he crav'd redresse.

(ii. 43.)

The Palmer can hardly have been so vague to Gloriana. Nobody would hesitate to equate the unnamed 'wicked Fay' with Acrasia. Should our knowledge of Canto i prevent us from equating the unspecified 'grievous mischiefes' with the fate of Ruddymane's parents, in accordance with the Letter? If Una and Irena have particular causes to plead, so, presumably, does the Palmer. And then, to Medina it must seem that he carried Ruddymane into Gloriana's presence, again as in the Letter; for Guyon shows Medina the babe without referring to any distinctly subsequent Mordant episode:

Now hath faire Phœbe with her silver face
Thrise seene the shadowes of the neather world,
Sith last I left that honorable place,
In which her royall presence is introld;
Ne ever shall I rest in house nor hold,
Till I that false Acrasia have wonne;
Of whose fowle deedes, too hideous to be told,
I witnesse am, and this their wretched sonne,
Whose wofull parents she hath wickedly fordonne.

(44.)

To be sure, Guyon enlarges on 'that dolefull tale'. But Spenser cuts short his verbatim report, stating only that he

told the storie of the mortall payne,
Which Mordant and Amavia did rew;
As with lamenting eyes him selfe did lately vew.

(45.)

The last line does not necessarily qualify 'told' as well as 'rew'. In all probability Medina gets the version of Guyon's story that the reader gets in the Letter. And so, surely, does Arthur (ix. 9). The Letter's apparent discrepancy draws attention to a contradiction within Book II, to prove its story illusory. All too obviously Guyon does not fulfil his promise to be in hot pursuit of Acrasia to the letter. Nor need he.

Spenser's equivocation in the scene just examined hints that the apparent origin of Guyon's adventure in the Mordant episode *is* its origin at Faery Court. If so, there are no grounds for locating the rest of his adventure away from Faery Court. More positively, there are good grounds for locating his whole adventure at Faery Court. For one thing, Red Cross openly calls it a pageant (i. 33). For another, Guyon's failure to return at the end of the Book could mean that he has never been away. Besides, his assertion that three months have elapsed 'sith last I left that honorable place' (ii. 44) expresses its ostensible meaning so tautologically (of course you measure a period of absence from your most recent departure) that the alternative reading seems preferable: he has not left the place ever since. Book II anticipates the 'revelation' in Book XII that all the quests are pageants; indeed Guyon, uniquely, refers to the annual feast (ii. 42). It does not anticipate its glory, though. The setting does not light up the adventure: the adventure extinguishes the setting. How perfectly this symbolizes the Legend's theme, temperance: God's grace in so far as it temporizes[174] His curse but by the same token shuts out His eternal radiance. Book I, by implication also pageantry, does anticipate the feast's glory in that it conjures up not its perennial duration but, on the contrary, its conclusion, Gloriana and Arthur in each other's arms. As glory 'already—not yet' Guyon and Red Cross are polar opposites within equivalence, the former being as opaque as the latter is transparent.

The opening of Guyon's speech to Medina, 'this thy demaund, O Lady, doth revive / Fresh memory in me of that great Queene' (40), cannot but prompt certain queries. If this memory is 'fresh' (as well it might be even if he should have been away from Faery Court for three months), it is strange that it should be capable and in need of 'reviving'. It is scarcely less strange that he delays the required explanation of his quest by extolling Gloriana at all. The incongruity of this becomes particularly apparent in light of the classical analogue evoked by Spenser's situation and wording, Aeneas' great speech to Dido:

> infandum, regina, iubes renovare dolorem,
> Troianas ut opes et lamentabile regnum
> eruerint Danai.[175]

The allusion to Aeneas conditioned by Troy's ruin, from which he had narrowly escaped, leads one to expect that Guyon is about to reassert his identification with Ruddymane, who survives his parents' death stained with their blood, unable to wash his hands of fallen Nature. That the knight does so ultimately saves a striking parallel. But why does he not do so at once? Even here one would almost agree with Nelson that 'what [Spenser] borrows he makes his own, without the slightest respect for the integrity or the intention of the original'.[176] Yet such irreverence towards venerated sources seems inherently unlikely. Let us suppose that the poet's departure from Virgil is as vacuous as that of Guyon from Faery Court; in other words, that we are silently being instructed to undo the delay by superimposing Ruddymane on Gloriana. After all, her radiant illumination of the poem's rationale from the next stanza, discussed in Section III, ill becomes the Legend of Temperance. This virtue, *qua* reminder of original sin,[177] screens off the perspective of glory which it implies *qua* aspect of magnificence. That is why Guyon screens off Gloriana's presence by utterly immediate forgetfulness. Spenser's procedure testifies incidentally to his temperance in the pursuit of poetic glory. While eager to 'overgo' Ariosto,[178] he allows Virgil to overgo him. (It also testifies to his secret extravagance: *The Faerie Queene* must be bright indeed if the *Aeneid* is dark in comparison.)

Does the Letter's account of Guyon qualify as a complementary allegory, introducing the theme of Book II? It certainly imposes Ruddymane on Gloriana; a fact that stands out precisely because it contradicts the more obvious of the poem's two accounts of the child. Moreover, Ruddymane is brought in by a Palmer; that is, a pilgrim to the Holy Land,[179] the natural, temporal Hell into which God descended. So as a symbol this Palmer focuses redemption as co-mortification with Christ. And then, whereas in the section on Red Cross the Letter had given away the poem's tenor but otherwise 'spared' its narrative, in the section on Guyon it exposes the illusoriness of its quasi-autonomous vehicle as mercilessly as the knight razes the Bower of Bliss.

VII Faeryland

Only one section of the Letter remains to be considered: its account of Book III. But this is better dealt with in a new Chapter, where we can amply acknowledge the enormity of the Middle Books' challenge to the validity of the Letter's programme. Here, as a final preparation of the ground, we may append a note on Spenser's distinction between Faeries and Britons. Although it has been widely discussed in the literature, no truly compelling interpretation has been found so far. Centuries ago John Hughes saw the root of the problem: while there are Faeries and non-Faeries, 'the fairies in this poem are not distinguished from other persons'.[180] Nothing suggests that they have distinctive interests and ambitions peculiar to themselves or that they have mysterious habits and powers that are exclusively theirs. Both Faeries and non-Faeries resort to Gloriana's court. Both are engaged in the same kind of undertakings. All of the poem's action, to the extent that it is described directly, takes place in Faeryland. There are flashbacks to Britain. But Spenser envisages the two realms neither as states with clear boundaries nor even as vaguely delimited spheres of influence. Worse, apart from Arthur the characters that are definitely not Faeries are nevertheless so called. Red Cross is 'the valiant Elfe' (I. i. 17), 'that Faery knight' (v. 1), 'th'Elfe' (vii. 7); while Artegall is addressed by the Giant with the Scales as 'thou foolish Elfe' (V. ii. 37) and referred to by Radigund as 'yond Fayry Knight' (v. 32). Only because the reverse does not apply can we speak of them as 'definitely not Faeries'. And to do seems pointless if the negation is purely nominal. Hence few share the view of Hankins that Faeries and non-Faeries are beings with a different ontological status.[181] Critics tend to concentrate on the one passage that suggests a clue, the scene at Alma's castle, where Guyon and Arthur read the chronicles of Faeryland and Britain:

the smoothness and serenity of Elfin history contrast markedly with the haphazard and disastrous course of British history (II. x). They infer that Faeryland sets idealized models against the reality of Britain and conclude that the poem explores the tension between real and ideal or promotes their coalescence.[182] But Spenser's stubbornly similar Faeries and Britons resist the imposition of any such distinction. Since his characters are personifications, attempts to distinguish between Faeries and non-Faeries as different kinds of creatures or as more and less stylized versions of human beings must be doomed. (The very sameness of Faeries and non-Faeries might well have produced the insight that they cannot be persons.)

Why does Spenser call his knights Faeries at all? They are certainly not 'fairies'. The narrative concerns the worlds of heroic romance and courtly pageantry, not that of 'fayerye'. Literally the knights belie their species as Arthur does his name. One gathers that they have a symbolic anchorage in fairy lore. The poet identifies some points of correspondence for us. Most notably, he uses the fairies' practice of thieving human infants.[183] Red Cross and Artegall are both reported to have been stolen by Faeries when still babies (see I. x. 65–6 and III. iii. 26); while the new-born Arthur was positively handed over to a Faery as 'unfit' (I. ix. 3). Also, Contemplation remarks that the New Jerusalem 'never yet was seene of Faeries sonne' (I. x. 52). Since Red Cross has been so referred to less than twenty stanzas earlier (33), this seems to mean that he is the first Faery to be granted this vision. Aware of his true race, however, we recognize the Hermit's saying as an allusion to another traditional motif. Tuve speaks of a 'privilege which is given to the hero because he is *not* of supernatural birth, but an ordinary mortal . . . entrance into the heavenly kingdom where there are mansions prepared for men but cold shrift for Merlin, Puck, Lucifer, Grendel and the Tuatha da Danann'.[184] If non-Faeries are destined for Eternity, Faeryland must be Time. Which makes sense: Time is 'fairyland', a fantasy world, in so far as it passes itself off as the ultimate condition of life, since in Christ it has 'already—not yet' been transcended. *All* the virtues are Faeries, God's glory unfolded and variously adapted to Time. Eternity has no Time for them. Those which are definitely non-Faeries *as well* constitute temporal variants of eternal qualities. The New Jerusalem is God's *holy* city, whose advent proves Him *just.* So holiness and justice are, as it were, Time's theft. Magnificence is Time's variant of the New Jerusalem's *glory*.[185] Arthur has been delivered into Faeryland rather than stolen because he sums up Man of 'the same minde . . . that was even in Christ Jesus, / Who being in the forme of God, *thoght it no robbery* to be equal with God: / But he made him self *of no reputation*'.[186] Hence also Arthur's exclusion from Cleopolis, 'fame city'. He dedicates himself whole-heartedly to Gloriana as elusive Faery Queen, secure in the knowledge that he is no Faery but 'sonne and heire unto a king, / As time in her just terme the truth to light should bring' (I. ix. 5).[187] Time's termination will reveal his glory. Meanwhile he has all the Time in the world.

That Arthur is a Briton would follow from his personal identity, if he had any. Spenser subtly botches up his Britain, historically and geographically, to prove it a metaphor. Thus tradition associates Rauran hill and the river Dee (I. ix. 4) with Vortigern's Merlin, not with Arthur's. Again, according to Malory king Ryence rules North Wales, not South Wales (III. ii. 18); while the river flowing 'emongst the woodie hilles of Dynevowre' and by Maridunum is the Towy, not the Barry (iii. 7–8).[188] Nor does Spenser's Britain exist over against or alongside Faeryland; we see no traffic between the two. They are contrary aspects of the same thing, Eternity in Time, like their capitals Troynovant and Cleopolis, whose relation we discovered in Section V. The poem does not so much leave Britain to immerse itself in Faeryland. Rather, it orients itself towards phantom Time, taking for granted solid Eternity. When it comes to deal with temperance, it cannot manifest its essential solidity. That is why Book II contains a traumatic chronicle of 'Briton moniments', which breaks off just when at last God (Uther Pendragon) breaks in, 'untimely' (x. 68); thus emphasizing the length and ingloriousness of Time. Guyon's 'Antiquitie of Faerie lond' reinforces this emphasis in its own way. By implication it is equally traumatic. For it skips the reigns of no fewer than 'seven hundred Princes' as 'too long . . . to record, ne much materiall' (74); thus intimating the repetitiousness and futility of Time. Moreover, if even Guyon, to judge from Gloriana's picture on his shield (i. 28, viii. 43, ix. 4) her champion *par excellence*, who performs at her court, has access to Elfin glory only through a book of history, perused in the ruined chamber of Eumnestes, its present splendour must be totally obscured. To be sure, Alma calls him for 'supper' with Arthur; but not until 'the time was fled' (77)—so that this banquet, too, remains undescribed. Guyon is reading 'all this while . . . Ne yet has ended' (70). The whimsicality of the Legend's Proem, which promises enlightenment about Faeryland and then denies it, will now be appreciated as meaningful.

Another relevant motif, which Spenser identifies negatively by interpreting 'Elf' as 'alive' ('quick'—II. x. 71) is the association of fairies with death. 'They are fairies; he that speaks to them shall die', says Falstaff.[189] Bennett notes that 'the medieval queen of fairies was identified with Proserpina, queen of the realms of the dead'. But she opines that, since Gloriana is a complimentary type of Elizabeth, Spenser cannot be taken to atrribute this role to his Faery Queen.[190] He does, though; symbolically. As we have seen, she represents 'perfection in mortalitie' (II. ii. 41), true life in death. Therefore to Guyon, who cannot see Faery Court in its glory while there, it is, in one of its aspects, the 'Gardin of Proserpina' (vii. 53). Not that the motif fails to suggest the perspective of Eternity. Arthur's legendary namesake, after receiving his fatal wound, was transported by the Ladies of the Lake to Avalon, 'the one spot in the British Isles which is a part of Fairyland', as Hankins says, there to await the time for his destined return. And here we may refine the idea of this critic that Panthea means Glastonbury as the seed from which the British Church was to spring.[191] The fiction never *means* history. However, adorning Gloriana's city, Cleopolis, with Panthea, the manifestation of its divinity, it does hint that Arthur's counterpart, Troynovant, will have a similar ornament; which will, presumably, have 'got lost' in Faeryland, like Arthur himself. This must be Glastonbury, not only (because of its association with Avalon) the place where

Arthur died but also the place where the Church (from κυριακός, 'of the Lord' and so 'wholly God's', like Panthea) emerged, only to vanish. The poet does not disappoint our expectations. 'Briton moniments' mentions the Grail city precisely as a dying seed; or rather, it contains an obliterating allusion to it, as befits an allegory of temperance (II. x. 53).

Spenser's story of Arthur, his dream of the Faery Queen and his search for her in Faeryland, imitates Chaucer's 'Tale of Thopas', as Bennett has demonstrated. Yet to her it is self-evident that 'we cannot suppose that he borrowed Chaucer's burlesque *Sir Thopas* as the basis of a grand heroic poem symbolizing the search of Virtue for Glory. He came to that in the end, but we need not suppose that he began there.'[192] Or so one's sense of decorum suggests. But then, 'whether or not the story of Arthur's falling in love and vowing his great quest is part of the debris of an earlier version of *The Faerie Queene*, the poet did include it in the work which he presented so proudly to Queen Elizabeth. If narrative of this kind is what Gabriel Harvey objected to when he described that draft of the poem that Spenser sent him in 1580 as "*Hobgoblin* runne away with the Garland from *Apollo*" the criticism still holds for the work as we have it.' Nelson's point is unanswerable; all the more so because Bennett's evolutionary theory does not hold water. Although his emphasis on the poem's comic elements distorts its overall impact, one must agree that Spenser is 'jesting . . . at his own fiction' and finds 'nothing incompatible in the association of an absurd tale and a deeply moral significance'.[193] But why should this be so? Fowler writes that 'in spite of a possible allusion to the *Tale of Sir Thopas*, it is quite unnecessary and inappropriate to suppose any comic intention. Spenser was well able to take an unfinished thread from Chaucer . . . and work it in entirely to his own purpose. . . . The use of literary material in this way is really a kind of manneristic alienation effect, emphasizing the literary status of the fiction.'[194] This shows tact and insight, but also a certain faint-heartedness. After all, Arthur's story is not simply one among many but a metaphor epitomizing the entire poem. The incongruity of the borrowing lies at the very core of the work.

The 'Tale of Thopas' is not a straightforward parody of

a deplorable romance type but Chaucer's joke at his own expense. The author of *The Canterbury Tales* casts himself in the role of one of his imaginary pilgrims, whose narrative contribution, so far from constituting the gem of the collection, as might be expected of one from a renowned court poet, is rudely interrupted by the Host as 'nat worth a toord'. One suspects, though, that the joke could be at the expense of the Host as well, who, despite his vociferous self-assertion, is hardly one's final arbiter in literary criticism. He may be a connoisseur of 'chaff', but he has no taste for 'fruit'. To him, the imaginary originator of the tales project, it seems a tremendous game. So it is to Chaucer, its real originator; but with a difference: for him its entertainment value enhances it as an exploration of the human condition, the great pilgrimage from which the Host is so eager to be distracted. The apparent ridiculousness of the 'Tale of Thopas' is ironic self-deprecation on the part of Chaucer the narrator, who can do better—witness the *Tales* as a whole. But it is also an implicit indictment by Chaucer the pilgrim, whose mind is elsewhere—

He semeth elvyssh by his contenaunce,
For unto no wight dooth he daliaunce

—of readers who will not see that the work really caters only for 'pilgrims'.[195] The barely disguised didacticism of his 'Tale of Melibee' brings the point home. In basing the epitome of his *Faerie Queene*, the 'unfinished' story of Arthur and Gloriana, on Chaucer's abortive romance, Spenser intimates that *qua* narrative his poem is nothing but a hotchpotch of loose ends. He also intimates why: his mind, too, is elsewhere. We must not take him to be less appropriately preoccupied than Chaucer the pilgrim, in spite of his less than grudging concession to 'the use of these dayes': the failure of most of his contemporaries (or, perhaps, of people generally, conditioned as they are by day-to-day life, temporality) to esteem anything but fictions 'delightfull and pleasing to commune sence' (L 35–7). Indeed, we must not; for this concession, itself 'elvyssh' throughout, is the most magnificent literary expression since *The Canterbury Tales* of Time as a pilgrimage to Eternity.

Two

SCUDAMOUR AND AMORET

I What is Wrong with the Middle Books?

In Books III and IV *The Faerie Queene* seems to lose its bearings: they lack the pattern common to the Outer Books, which, to judge from the Letter, represents a norm. One expects that each Book will be dominated by a single male hero, identified in its title, whose adventures in carrying out a mission undertaken at Faery Court come full circle within its confines. Book III has a woman, Britomart, for its titular hero. Book IV has two titular heroes, Cambel and Telamond (the second of whom appears in the Book itself as the trio Priamond–Diamond–Triamond). No mention is made of Faery Court as the starting-point of the titular heroes' adventures. Cambel and 'Telamond' are not questing at all. Britomart is, but for private purposes, to find Artegall, her destined lover; not to redress a public wrong. Besides, she not only dominates Book III but figures prominently in Book IV as well, where she finds Artegall. Even in Book V she plays a conspicuous part, rescuing Artegall from Radigund. By contrast, the titular heroes of Book IV are no more prominent than its other major characters. And they appear only in four consecutive Cantos (ii–v), thus failing to make the Book distinctly theirs.

The Letter's specific account of Book III (L 116–28) makes an apparently spurious assertion of its conformity. It treats the male Scudamour as the Book's main character and the overthrow of Busirane as its main adventure, analogous to the overthrow of the Dragon and Acrasia in Books I and II. But that does not make Scudamour a titular hero. Nor does it alter his lack of prominence, which differentiates him so markedly from the Outer Books' knights. He figures only in Cantos xi and xii; and even there he is virtually eclipsed by Britomart. Although the poet admits that 'many other adventures are intermedled' with Scudamour's story

(L 125), this strikes one as a disingenuous attempt to maintain his primacy rather than as an honest acknowledgement of the true state of affairs. It would seem that Book III itself does not allow us to determine whether or not he is engaged on a genuine mission, authorized by Gloriana. But her mandate would be unnecessary, even inappropriate, for the overthrow of Busirane, more obviously an obstacle to his private happiness than a public evil to be opposed with disinterested zeal, like the Dragon and Acrasia. Pursuing Amoret, he resembles Britomart in search of Artegall more than he does the Outer Books' quest heroes. And then, it is Britomart, not Scudamour, who overcomes the enchanter. Finally, though in the 1590 edition Scudamour's story, brief as it is, looks complete, he reappears all the same in Book IV, just like Britomart. (Hence, presumably, the different ending to Book III in the 1596 edition.) In short, Book III fails to conform, in spite of the Letter.

One way of solving the problem would be to say that there is none. Simply decide that the Outer Books are apparently not normative, and you will welcome the Middle Books as refreshingly different. This would be to rule the Letter out of court. But then, its implication that the narrative is unreal will go only a little way towards making the Middle Books fall into place. It does not remove or explain the discrepancies. Thus, if Scudamour should be a personification, his subsidiary role in Book III does not disqualify him as its quest hero any more than the subsidiary role of Arthur in *The Faerie Queene* as a whole disqualifies him as the poem's leading character. But why is he so inconspicuous compared with Red Cross and Guyon, his alleged counterparts? Similarly, if Scudamour's story in Book III should be a metaphor, it could mean the same thing as the Letter's account of it. But why does he not depart from and return to Faery Court; or else, like Guyon, perform at Faery Court? Again, if the narrative should be illusory, Books III and IV are conceivable as distinct units like the Outer Books, in spite of having most of their major characters in common. Perhaps, indeed, Spenser's choice of Cambel and Telamond, who figure in Book IV only, as its titular heroes serves to bring home the Middle Books' separateness. Their minor status would be as immaterial as Scudamour's. But it would be equally puzzling. And which of the characters in Book IV performs a mission? Where is its counterpart to the other Books' evil powers, the Dragon, Acrasia, Busirane, Grantorto, and the Blattant Beast? No sequel to the Letter could have offered plausible answers. Moreover, the assumed unreality of progressive narrative across the Books' common frontier does not explain why they share so many characters. Anyway, this unreality seems less compelling than ever. Arthur's story may explode at the slightest touch. And those of the Outer Books' knights may yield when pressed. But in the Middle Books the chief characters do not appear to have bound themselves to perform a single task. Hence the inconsequentiality of their adventures does not make them clearly non-sequential; even though, with the typical mould, its quasi-regimenting effect is also lacking. Like Arthur these characters seek sexual fulfilment: Britomart in Artegall, Scudamour in Amoret, Timias in Belphœbe, Florimell in Marinell. But unlike Arthur they are not manifestly recurrent symbols. Their relationships with their partners undergo overt transformations as Arthur's relationship with Gloriana does not. As a result there is a powerful suggestion of real, developing narrative.

Chapters Two and Three will scrutinize a fair sample of the episodes that appear to make for a Scudamour story and a Britomart story, to establish their disconnection. We shall be flogging a horse that is only logically dead. In this Section we must presume success and sketch the conceptual rationale for the Middle Books' idiosyncrasies, so that, once on our explosive mission, we can promptly reuse the narrative rubble to build the allegorical edifice. To recapitulate, Spenser's theme is the moral, and therefore temporal, manifestation of Man's redemption in Christ. As all-round virtue this is unspecified glory 'already—not yet'. As any individual virtue it is a particular aspect of this. Thus holiness is transparent: glory wholly 'already' even while 'not yet'; whereas temperance is opaque: glory wholly 'not yet' even while 'already'. The several specific virtues are distinct permutations of 'already—not yet'. Hence the Letter's programme of variously uniform quests. However, only those virtues which are temporal variants of eternal qualities are inherently glorious.

Ultimately glory has fewer aspects than there are virtues. Consequently certain virtues have to share one or other of these aspects. Such is the case with chastity, friendship, and justice. As we shall see, they all reflect, in different ways, Eternity's transcendence of separateness; as against, say, its timelessness, reflected in constancy, or its holiness, reflected in the virtue named similarly to signal its transparency. Spenser may be intent on 'the more variety of the history' (L 64). Yet disregard for Book boundaries, displayed more or less extensively by so many characters in the Middle Books, does not betoken a departure from the Outer Books' norm for its own sake. It may be compared with Arthur's inclusive disregard for them. These characters bracket some virtues as relating to glory *qua* oneness just as Arthur brackets all the virtues as relating to glory generally.

To comprehend the triad of virtues it will be best to take the middle term, friendship, first. Spenser means New Testament *ἀγάπη*: Telamond, a titular hero of Book IV, is the son of Agape (ii. 41). St. Paul calls it 'the bond of perfectnes'. Note that he does not say 'the perfect bond'. He means that *ἀγάπη* is Man's perfection in Christ considered as a bond; not only of separate individuals but also of distinct virtues.[1] For it is, in the alternative biblical phrase, 'the fulfilling of the Law': 'the end (*τέλος*) of the commandement is love'.[2] The virtues come to a head in *ἀγάπη*, the love with which Christians are to love their neighbour *as themselves*, because it identifies them with each other as aspects of the Body whose Head is Christ, making them 'perfect in one'.[3] The relevance of so understanding the mother's name is confirmed by that of the son. 'Telamond', as *τέλος mundus*, means 'end world', while, as *τελαμών*, it means 'band'.[4] So the Legend of Friendship concerns the integration of mankind in virtue. However, for the Time being this integration cannot manifest itself beyond togetherness. Already the faithful 'mete together . . . unto a perfite man' (*εἰς ἄνδρα τέλειον*). But this is as yet a body with many members, receiving 'increase . . . unto the edifying of it self *in love* . . . according to the effectual power, which is *in the measure of everie parte*'.[5] Correspondingly, the virtue to end all virtues is still a separate virtue, with a Book to itself. As Paul says in his famous chapter on ἀγάπη, 'when that which is perfite (τὸ τέλειον), is come, then that which is in parte (τὸ ἐκ μέρους), *shalbe* abolished'.[6] Happily the name 'Telamond' conveys a 'perfection in mortality': De Quincey has a reference to 'τελαμῶνες or linen swathing bandages . . . to bind up corpses'.[7]

Since this discussion of ἀγάπη might evoke Nygren's disjunction of ἀγάπη (gift love) and ἔρως (need love), adopted by some Spenser scholars,[8] we should make a point of noting that it is unbiblical, formally and, indeed, substantially. Man fallen 'to pieces' is bankrupt and has nothing to give but his needy, worthless self. He cannot put himself together again. The partial Old Adam lives in debt to the whole New Adam.[9] Ἀγάπη is God's payment of this debt in Christ. The word ἔρως does not occur in the New Testament. Nor does its philosophical meaning, under another name. 'Ohne Zweifel ist es das bleibende Verdienst Nygrens, daß er es als einer der ersten Theologen versucht hat, zu den hinter den äußeren Formulierungen stehenden Motiven als den "wirklichen Triebkräften der betreffenden Anschauungen vorzudringen". . . . Indessen möchten wir meinen, daß er—abgesehen von seinen uns fragwürdig erscheinenden philosophischen Voraussetzungen—der von ihm selbst namhaft gemachten Gefahr, dem geschichtlichen "Material ein fremdes Gedankenschema aufzuzwingen" . . . nicht völlig entgangen ist.'[10]

Friendship approximates humanity's ultimate oneness by associating its constituents. Chastity does so by making each constituent separately whole. This proposition is more obviously true of celibate chastity, which, as Elizabeth's bard, Spenser was in duty bound to honour, than it is of married chastity, which, as a Protestant poet, he must have been eager to champion. For marriage is a particular form of friendship, of being together. Under its sexual aspect it is something else, though. It joins husband and wife into a single entity, 'one flesh', which embodies separately the whole Church of Christ. This is indeed not obvious but, as the apostle says, 'a great secret'.[11] Friendship and chastity, of either kind, are contrary virtues, like holiness and temperance but with a difference. Friendship opens up the self to give access to others. Chastity closes off the (usually dual) self to exclude others. While both are partial reflections of 'God . . . all in all',[12] friendship is almost transparent whereas chastity is almost opaque. However, since their contrariness is nothing but Eternity's oneness divided against itself through Time as togetherness versus wholeness, they are also one virtue, in separation.

Friendship and chastity, each in its own way, heal the wound of separateness partly. Justice heals it completely but secretly. For this virtue addresses itself not to the wrong of Man's fragmentation but to the wrongs of the fragments. Preventing or correcting abuses to which separate existence lends itself, it appears to perpetuate the condition which it adjusts. It is as opaque as temperance. But temperance, Time made into a virtue, is intrinsically inglorious. Justice, by contrast, is opaque in spite of itself. It effects a full at-one-ment, whose glory is merely hidden by separateness. In justice people are united as the specific virtues are in moral perfection: totally though obscurely. As an aspect of magnificence, therefore, justice highlights through darkness the perfect identity of specific and unspecified virtue. While manifestly distinct, it is not a permutation of 'already—not yet' but that paradox itself. To remember that the Bible has one word for magnificence generally and justice in particular, namely 'righteousness', is to see that Spenser's terminological distinction significantly overclouds sameness. Justice heralds darkly its self-revelation on the Day of Judgement, when 'righteousnes and peace shal kisse one another'.[13] For the Time being it is 'the peace of God which passeth all understanding':[14] peace in God's inscrutable will that the consummation of Man and morality must as yet assert itself militantly, as virtue; a peace which will *prove* peace at the last.

This conceptual outline shows that chastity, friendship, and justice demand synoptic treatment. Accordingly Spenser brackets Books III–V, through Britomart and Artegall. These Books stand out from those surrounding them as one massive block of Britomart-Artegall fiction: she dominates Book III, he dominates Book V, and together they figure as prominently in Book IV as does any other pair. That the Middle Books do not have heroes of circular quests in their titles signals that they do not stand on their own, like the Outer

Books. We are encouraged to unite them with Book V. Yet the fact that they do not have the same titular hero as Book V frustrates this merger; as, by implication, does the fact that Book V itself does have a quest hero in its title. Thus the Middle Books are left hanging as 'one in part', in token of their themes. Book III focuses this union in separateness as wholeness in that its titular heroine, Britomart, is Artegall's better half. Book IV focuses it as togetherness in that it has two titular heroes, neither of whom belongs with either Britomart or Artegall. Book V conveys its theme in a similar manner. Its manifest conjunction with the Middle Books hides its self-sufficiency, implied by the coincidence of quest hero and titular hero; whose name, Artegall, testifies to the special identity of his virtue, justice, with magnificence, represented in Arthur. And one begins to appreciate the order of the three Legends. The 'bond' of Friendship joins Chastity with Justice, which comes last as the virtue altogether content to wait for the revelation of what it is already, the end of the world. This argument does not, of course, account for their position in the scheme of twelve virtues. But with that larger question we need concern ourselves only to the extent of stamping out the notion that, following on as they do from Holiness and Temperance, they broaden out from private through social to political virtue—a notion largely due to mistaking the historical allusions in Book V for tenor. *The Faerie Queene* deals exclusively with 'private morall vertues' (L 27–8).

Our conceptual outline also shows a particularly intimate connection between chastity and friendship: they are one and the same virtue as well as two distinct virtues. Accordingly Spenser brackets off the Middle Books through Scudamour, the quest hero of Book III, as the Letter says; and so of Book IV too, as his reappearance there implies. And indeed, among the manifold stories in this Book the only one at all suggestive of a quest is Scudamour's adventure at the Temple of Venus, in Canto x. True, this is only part of its Scudamour fiction, which does not as a whole read like a quest. But then, 'quest' does not really specify narrative. Instead it symbolically defines virtue as glory 'not yet'. The extent to which the label applies literally is itself allegorically significant. That only a single section of the quest hero's fiction bears out his status makes him glory 'already' for the most part: friendship. Conversely, of the considerably lesser amount of Scudamour fiction contained in Book III, everything except the passing reference to him in vi. 53 reads like a quest; which makes him glory 'not yet' for the most part: chastity. Even considered in isolation, though, the Temple of Venus episode remains defective as a narrative quest, in that it lacks a counterpart to the Outer Books' evil powers. And the Busirane episode remains likewise defective, in that it lacks action on Scudamour's part. However, this defectiveness of the episodes separately is precisely such as to make them jointly a single quest analogous to those in the Outer Books. The Busirane episode takes over where the Temple of Venus episode leaves off, the latter providing the action and the former the evil power. The sequence of Canto numbers, IV. *x* to III. *xi–xii*, supports this reading; especially since there is no Scudamour fiction in III. i–x and IV. xi–xii: Book IV wants to lie on top of Book III. Apparent chronology clinches the matter. Scudamour's confrontation with Busirane seems to follow on, via his marriage to Amoret (IV. i. 1–4), from his adventure at the Temple. Just as singly his chastity fiction and his friendship fiction are markedly, though variously, inconclusive, to signify that these two virtues merely approximate glory, so collapsed they are a fiction continuing into itself, which highlights the circularity common to all the quests for the same thematic purpose. Either way they are 'endless work'. To restore the balance Spenser brackets them in with justice, 'end work'.

Scudamour's composite quest still appears to deviate from the norm in several respects, though. There is, to begin with, his preoccupation with Amoret. To see that this is less of an anomaly than it seems, we need to remind ourselves of the Red Cross Knight's love for Una. His adventure is none the less a public quest for having a private dimension. The same goes for Scudamour, albeit not so evidently: unlike Una, Amoret is herself the victim of the evil power opposed by her knight and so his cause as well as his prize. Yet this distinction proves vacuous as soon as it has been made. Una, so far from being just a formal reward, is her knight's other self quite as much as Amoret. The heroes' relations to their ladies are allegories of the virtues they patronize. That Red Cross does not have to deliver Una but enjoys her veiled company all along (except when, by way of synonymous metaphor, they suffer an 'Archimaginary' alienation) signifies the completeness with which holiness equals elusive glory. That Scudamour does have to win or free Amoret and never possesses her securely signifies the approximateness of friendship and chastity. Dedication to knighthood looks like an end in itself in the case of Red Cross whereas it does not in the case of Scudamour, certainly; because this impression is thematically appropriate. It does not follow from Scudamour's deficiency as a knight that we should regard him as a lover instead. For his love life complements his military career, as an allegorical variation; whence its lack of fulfilment. Nor should we exaggerate his deficiency. It is true that, uniquely, he fails to overthrow his ultimate antagonist, as even the Letter roundly admits (L 121–2). But this further deviation from the norm, too, is more apparent than real; or rather, significantly, real in part only. Although Scudamour cannot wrest Amoret from Busirane at his House in Book III, Busirane cannot wrest her from Scudamour on the island of Venus in Book IV. The validity of this mere inference emerges from a comparison of the Middle Books, run together, with the Outer Books: their evil powers control their victims from the start.

Scudamour deviates from the other quest heroes also in that he does not depart from and return to Faery Court. But in this respect Book II has already taught us to be prepared for meaningful complications. After describing the Garden of Adonis and Amoret's training there, Spenser adds:

> To Faery court she came, where many one
> Admyrd her goodly haveour, and found
> His feeble hart wide launched with loves cruell wound.
>
> But she to none of them her love did cast,
> Save to the noble knight Sir Scudamore,
> To whom her loving hart she linked fast
> In faithfull love, t'abide for evermore,
> And for his dearest sake endured sore,

> Sore trouble of an hainous enimy;
> Who her would forced have to have forlore
> Her former love, and stedfast loialty,
> As ye may elsewhere read that ruefull history.
>
> (III. vi. 52–3.)

This clearly alludes to Amoret's sufferings at Busirane's castle. We are not told, though, how he abducts her from Faery Court; nor, indeed, *that* he does. Considering that he distinguishes himself from the other evil powers by an obvious taste for what may loosely be called pageantry, we may take these lines to imply that Amoret's 'hainous enimy' torments her at Faery Court and therefore that Scudamour's efforts against him (as also his exploits at the Temple, which lead up to them) take place at Faery Court, like Guyon's quest. And although, unlike Guyon's quest, Scudamour's is not openly referred to as a pageant, there are hints to its status as such, almost explicit in Book IV, barely implicit in Book III. In Book IV only his adventure at the Temple reads like a quest, so that his other adventures in that Book must be pageantry. That they do not quite read like that conveys that friendship is not quite glory. Moreover, the Temple of Venus episode heavily qualifies its own status of quest; in general through providing a fixed rather than a shifting background for Scudamour's enterprise, and in particular through mentioning that he undertook it 'what time the fame of this renowmed prise / Flew first abroad' (4). Spenser's collocation of 'time' and 'fame' conjures up Cleopolis. And since the knight hears of Amoret 'abroad' as a 'prise' rather than at Faery Court as the theme of a complaint, we infer with ease that he moves in to perform at home. That he does not quite take his reward for granted—in other words, that the pageantry retains an element of quest—again conveys that friendship is not quite glory. The ambiguity of his decision to 'purchase . . . some place *among the best*' makes the same point: the phrase in italics, which manifestly goes with both 'purchase' and 'place', can just about be taken to go with 'place' alone. In Book III the poet puts Scudamour's adventure in a position where, considering its brevity and frustration, it does not seem to belong. Yet the last line of the passage quoted above suggests that this placement is deliberate. With difficulty we infer that this adventure constitutes an emphatic variant of the anticlimactic returns to Faery Court in the Outer Books. (Spenser *returns* to it, having alluded to it before.) Now a quest which *is* a return both does and does not have a de-part-ure (thus signifying wholeness in part). In so far as it does not, it is a pageant. Characteristically, Book IV eases the difficulty. The Temple of Venus episode, which precedes this return, itself obviously *returns* to Faery Court, being Scudamour's flashback to his performance there, as well as the final Scudamour fiction. The placement of this tale of success makes it an unemphatic variant of the other quest heroes' returns, anticlimactic merely by implication: the knight is *remembering* his glory.

We may now admire the unobtrusive skill with which the Letter's quasi-narrative account of Book III defines chastity allegorically. At first sight it seems to misrepresent it, slightly, as altogether opaque, stressing as it does Scudamour's failure. However, it is just possible to grasp that the complaining 'Groome' (L 116) is none other than Scudamour himself, Amoret's bridegroom. Thus the knight's dual appellation hides for the most part but not completely both his single identity and his union with a woman, his glory. Also, the equation implies that Scudamour succeeds in his failure. Because he as it were recycles himself, we cannot regard his powerlessness, to which his complaint already testifies, as the whole truth about him. (Since Book IV reveals Scudamour as bridegroom, its appearance necessitated the withdrawal of the Letter, in that it made it too easy, for the purposes of chastity, to guess the equation.) Furthermore, in summarizing Book III the Letter does not force us to smash the narrative, as it does in summarizing Book II. It does not contradict the poem outright. Instead it presents a part, Scudamour's quest, as though it were the whole by correlating it with the quests of Red Cross and Guyon. In this way, too, it symbolizes chastity as wholeness *ἐκ μέρους*. Besides, it surveys the rest of the Book's fiction as a series of manifestly separate adventures, with the warning that these 'are intermedled . . . rather as Accidents, then intendments'

(L 125-6). That is to say, it breaks up the story into self-contained fragments yet pledges their entire synonymity, just as chastity divides yet contains glory, 'the *whole intention* of the conceit' (L 131).

II The Busirane Episode

(i) *A Separate Whole*

The preceding sketch argues mostly by deduction, rather like GROUNDWORK. Its explanatory power shows the limitations of empiricism as a heuristic method in Spenser. Needless to say, deduction does not supersede close reading as, among other things, validation. The 'actual text' could, actually, have elicited greater understanding than it has. Given its manifest inconsequentiality, it positively invites examination of junctures, for instance. But the common approach has been impressionistic. The Scudamour–Amoret fiction seems to consist at once of autonomous episodes and of continuing narrative. Instead of worrying over the contradiction critics 'respect' it. Thus Roche offers separate accounts of Amoret with Busirane, in the Garden of Adonis, and at the Temple of Venus. He even treats the 1590 ending of Book III independently. Yet he deals with the last three of his units in a section entitled 'Amoret's Education', which opens with an overview of her appearances readjusted in their 'proper', chronological, order. This must be a narrative summary; especially because Amoret's wedding is regarded as taking place after her capture by Scudamour in the Temple and as providing the occasion for her capture by Busirane. Indeed, Roche bases his reading of the Busirane episode on its supposed occasion. While he sees that Spenser's characters are anchored in concepts, he finds them not consistently representative because 'subject to the tugs and pulls of storytelling'.[15] Similarly, for C. S. Lewis 'it goes without saying that Amoret's childhood in the Garden and her womanhood in the Temple of Venus are not really two successive stages in a biography. We should think of them, rather, as two co-temporal aspects of the way of life she symbolizes.' Yet this does not prevent him from ascribing the 1596 ending of Book III to 'the exigencies of the plot' and claiming that 'no doubt in the complete *Faerie Queene* the original passage would have been used somewhere else'; that is, one gathers, at a suitable stage in the narrative.[16]

Such complacency exasperates those of us not attuned to romance. Too bad, you might say. However, the sympathetic understanding of the *cognoscenti* becomes dubious when they turn out to be at cross purposes. For Roche it does *not* go without saying that the Garden episode and the Temple episode are non-sequential. He imagines, in his summary, that Amoret 'is brought to the Garden . . . as an infant but at some point goes to the Temple'. Let the poem arbitrate. It never describes, suggests, or even implies any such move. As we have seen, it says that 'to Faery court she came' (III. vi. 52). Nor does it permit the conclusion that her residence at the Temple must have occurred in between her departure from the Garden and her arrival at Faery Court, or else after her stay there. For the three stages of Amoret's career in Book III, Garden, Court, and House of Busirane, are run tightly together. Moreover, it is at Faery Court that Amoret meets Scudamour; it is there that he becomes one of her many admirers; it is there that she freely bestows her love upon him. So he cannot win her either previously or subsequently, and that against her will (IV. x. 57). To save the narrative one might postulate that the Temple episode, which is, after all, Scudamour's tale, has a personal slant. But 'point of view' cannot create a non-event; unless Scudamour should be fantasying, or lying. Such desperate scepticism with regard to his tale seems unwarranted, though. Spenser himself vouches for its authenticity, explicitly near the beginning of Book IV (i. 2) and implicitly a little later, when he traces Blandamour's hostility to Scudamour to the fact that 'his love he wonne by right' (i. 39). Alternatively, one might suppose that Scudamour's tale presents truly but *allegorice* his relation with Amoret *at* Faery Court. This will not do either. The tale is an allegory to the reader but not to the audience in the poem; exactly like Arthur's account of his dream. Within the fictional world it tells 'in order dew / All that adventure, which [he] did assay / For that faire Ladies love' (ix. 40). Its lack of the chronological moorings it would demand as part of a sequence of literal narrative proves it to be pure allegory. To specify its tenor temporally when even its vehicle is timeless would be perverse. Anyway, we already know that Faery Court itself is not a place but an allegory. So it could not be the setting for any genuine story, with a development to be inferred from the correct order of its episodes suitably de-allegorized. Minute as it is, the Faery Court 'episode', the first to connect Amoret and Scudamour, rules out sequence.

It must be conceded that this mini-episode advertises neither its importance nor its function. Coming as it does where the core Canto of Book III peters out, all it seems to say is 'to be continued'. Considering the central position and the engrossing subject matter of the Garden episode proper, critics should not, perhaps, be blamed for thrusting into the middest, even where it most concerneth them. Unpardonable, however, is their interpretation of Amoret's plight at the House of Busirane as an allegory of the condition in which she finds herself on her wedding day. For Spenser's reference to her marriage comes in Book IV, which did not appear until six years after the Busirane episode was first given to the public. The poem of 1590 never alludes to any such occasion. Only the Letter does, obliquely, by introducing the 'Groome', whose identity they have not guessed and could not have guessed, assuming real narrative. Now how can they base their reading on information which the poet does not provide, when nothing suggests that it is being withheld? The 1590 ending hardly encourages one to expect more Scudamour-Amoret fiction: rapturously final, it leaves one momentarily persuaded that *The Faerie Queene* could be complete in three Books. Maybe they take it that the publication history reflects external factors, which cannot be allowed to condition interpretation. Could it not be that Spenser was averse to having his work published and refused to monitor the process? Many poets in his time sought appreciation among a limited circle of patrons and fellow *literati*, shunning public acclaim or even despising the vulgar. But surely Spenser cannot have been among them. The scale of his undertaking and its theme, the redemption of Time, militate against the idea of authorial contentment with ephemeral praise. One who so feelingly bemoans the effects of 'cursed Eld the cankerworme of writs' (IV. ii. 33) will naturally have sought to avail himself of the means to guard his own production against the (imagined?) fate of Chaucer's; which, indeed, it purports to reverse (34). If he gives even a private, occasional poem such as *Epithalamion* to the world to be 'for short time an endlesse moniment' (line 433), he must have been eager to bring out his epic; for, according to the 1596 Dedication to Queen Elizabeth, he meant 'these his labours to live with the eternity of her fame'.

Was he, perhaps, so eager to give an earnest of his heroic poem in the making that in 1590 he took advantage of Ralegh's interest and rushed into print with what happened to be in finished form? Or, supposing he had Book IV ready by that time, may his publisher not have declined to commit himself to more than three Books, initially? One can do little more than speculate about the poet's rate of composition. *Amoretti* LXXX implies that six Books were completed when he married Elizabeth Boyle, in June 1594, on the assumption that he wrote the sonnet sequence during his courtship: it came out in 1595. Since the Six-Book *Faerie Queene* appeared only in 1596, it is possible that in 1590 Spenser was similarly 'ahead of schedule'. Marlowe's imitation of a stanza from Book I in *II Tamburlaine*, first performed in 1587–8,[17] and Abraham Fraunce's quotation of one from Book II in his *Arcadian Rhetoricke*, of 1588,[18] do not enable us to infer when they received the text of the episodes in which these stanzas occur,[19] let alone when these episodes were written; conceivably much earlier: one thinks, again, of E. K.'s allusion to II. iii. 25 in his commentary on 'June'. Although, as self-contained allegories, they may well have been composed in advance of their destined context, like the Mutabilitie Cantos, it is very possible indeed that by 1590 Book IV was finished. But we have no positive evidence. All we know is that Spenser planned an *Epithalamion Thamesis* as early as 1580; as an independent poem, to be sure, of greater scope than the Canto describing the marriage of Thames and Medway (IV. xi).[20] However, no matter why only three Books were printed in 1590, the poet could easily have referred to the wedding of Scudamour and Amoret in Book III, even if it had been matter for a full-blown episode in Book IV. In fact it takes up less than two stanzas of apparent linking narrative right at the beginning of Book IV, so that one wonders why he did not transpose it, provisionally at least, to Book III. Was he in such a hurry that he forgot? This seems most unlikely. For he did find time to write a 'gratuitous' climactic ending specially for the first instalment. One must conclude that correct interpretation of the Busirane episode does not presuppose knowledge of the wedding. Juxtaposed on opposite sides of a Book boundary accentuated as a publication chasm, they cry out to be left apart.

Nor will they join. According to Book IV 'that mask of love which late was showen' (i. 3), namely III. xii. 1–28, occurs at the wedding. But in Book III Spenser implies that it occurs every day (28). What we witness with Britomart would be a repeat seven months later (xi. 10; compare IV. i. 4). We do not see Amoret on her wedding day. Of course, all agree that the Mask is a symbol; Spenser's symbol, that is: nobody takes Amoret to be, allegorico-dramatically, reliving her wedding day again and again, *à la* Miss Havisham in *Great Expectations*. Now Busirane could not possibly have brought in Spenser's symbol. Even magicians cannot transcend logic. Roche says that 'the initial impact of the mask in canto 12 is one of horror and evil, ill-suited for a wedding feast, but we should remember that it *was* presented at the wedding'. Not so. Its inappropriateness virtually precludes the situational reading. He sees an analogy with the wedding mask in Beaumont and Fletcher's *A Wife for a Moneth* (1624). But it breaks down at the crucial point: Evanthe, the bride at whose marriage it takes place, is not the kind of ghastly figure at the centre of Spenser's Mask (19–21). She does not even participate. Renaissance wedding masks, he says, generally reflect the male sense of conquest and were often performed in a context of 'bold bawdry' with little consideration for the feelings of the bride about to be bedded.[21] Perhaps. His civilized concern betrays another male prejudice, though; that of woman weak, sweet, and clean. Pre-Victorian females may have been roused rather than disgusted by such an atmosphere. They were certainly not required as a matter of course to enact a dreadful symbolic travesty of their supposed victimization. Nor does Spenser constrain us to believe that such, nevertheless, is the fate of his Amoret. For what he explicitly presents as a mask is also manifestly not a mask. Not only do its participants not go masked but it supervenes unexpectedly, disrupting the wedding celebration and preventing the consummation of the marriage. Now masks cannot do that without ceasing to be what they essentially are, organized ritual. Surprise introduction and audience participation may be among their features, but these too will be programmed. Indeed, it seems to have been customary for them to involve the abduction of the bride; but only 'by way of sport'.[22] Spenser actually uses these words to specify Amoret's abduction in Book IV. Yet they cannot cancel out the impression in Book III that she is captured in earnest. So we have here two incompatible conceptions of what happens to her. And both are at odds with her being among the maskers all along. Or does she have a double, like Una and Florimell? Intriguingly, the magician's prisoner in III. xii receives no name until after her liberation. But if she is Amoret then, she must be Amoret before. In any case, he 'conveyed quite away' the original (IV. i. 3). Again, the organization of a wedding entertainment would hardly have been entrusted to 'that same vile Enchauntour Busyran'. Yet it is he who brings it in. Nor can this be taken to mean that he is its leading actor rather than the master of the revels: in III. xii he is very much the man behind the scenes. Let us wind up. If the Mask of Cupid both is and is not a mask, it cannot be an event. Therefore Amoret's wedding, at which it is performed, cannot be an event either. Consequently there is no such thing as Amoret's plight on the day of her marriage for the Busirane Cantos to symbolize.

But would a troubled wedding not follow on naturally from Amoret's unwillingness to go with Scudamour towards the end of IV. x? Roche takes such continuity for granted without stressing it. Indeed, given his assumption of sequence he makes unjustifiably little of it, saying that 'the extreme reluctance of Amoret to leave the temple is *overcome* by the picture of Cupid on Scudamour's shield'. This is hardly the drift of Spenser's text—

> when Cupid with his killing bow
> And cruell shafts emblazond she beheld,
> At sight thereof *she was with terror queld,*
> *And said no more*
>
> (55)

—even though 'she' refers, strictly, to Womanhood, not to Amoret. Nevertheless, Roche remains a valid target, because his interpretation of the Busirane Cantos tallies with the correct reading of the lines quoted. He regards the House of Busirane as 'the objectification of Amoret's fears of marriage', which 'are based on moral and physical grounds. Scudamour can dispel neither' because 'unwillingly he is the cause of these fears'. So they cannot have arisen all of a sudden at the introduction of the Mask. Roche admits that it 'crystallizes' them. How, then, can he say that Amoret 'turns from a joyful acceptance to a cold rejection of the claims of the physical'? This is his definition of Amoret's plight: 'The dreary assortment of ills that follow Cupid corresponds precisely with the Christian interpretation of adulterous love. These are the effects of love outside Christian marriage, but presumably the marriage of Amoret and Scudamour is a Christian marriage. Amoret makes no distinction between them.' Hence Busirane is 'an abuse of marriage because the mind he possesses cannot distinguish between the act of marriage and adulterous love'.[23] Does this make sense? How can Amoret possibly fail to distinguish when Scudamour is in the very process of marrying her 'as did him behove' (IV. i. 2)? One could think of three explanations, none of them at all convincing. Christian marriage might in some ways be treacherously similar to adulterous love. But Roche makes no attempt to argue that this possibility is less absurd than it sounds. Alternatively, Amoret may have been impervious to the prolonged education she has been receiving in the Garden and at the Temple. But it is hard to see the one product of these eminent training centres with which the poem acquaints us as a failure. Spenser has Amoret 'lessoned / In all the lore of love, and goodly womanhead' (III. vi. 51), without qualifying her docility. In view of the unmistakably sexual character of her schooling Fowler's suggestion that Amoret's fears 'focus on the action of physical sex' strikes one as curiously inept. He wisely hastens to admit that 'sexual penetration appears less unambiguously in Busyrane's masque' than in Colonna's *Hypnerotomachia*, the alleged analogue that prompted the idea.[24] Personally I have not been able to spot it at all. A third possibility is that Amoret's fears are nothing but a momentary delusion. But if so, why on earth should Spenser have made such heavy weather of it? As Hankins says, 'Busyrane seems too sinister a figure to represent merely a bride's nervous qualms before her first sexual experience'.[25]

It might seem that Kent Hieatt's corrective to Roche's position avoids all these difficulties. Giving due weight to the fact that 'Amoret is swept away protesting' from the Temple and noting Scudamour's repeated boldness, highlighted in Womanhood's 'sharpe rebuke, for being over bold' (IV. x. 54), he argues that 'it is not a shortcoming of Amoret . . . that she must view her relation to Scudamour in terms of the abusive Masque of Cupid, and that she must confuse her marriage with "adulterous" or "courtly" love. It is Scudamour who forces her into this position by his own practice of an aggressive mastery in the Chaucerian sense.'[26] But 'maistrye' is Chaucer's term for repressive domination *within* marriage. Since the marriage of Scudamour and Amoret never gets under way, he is not in a position to practise it upon her. More important, Womanhood objects not to Scudamour's manner but to his having designs on Amoret at all,

> Saying it was to Knight unseemly shame,
> Upon a recluse Virgin to lay hold,
> That unto Venus services was sold.

And clearly Hieatt does not agree that Scudamour should leave Amoret alone. Now for one thing Scudamour's retort is beyond reproach:

> Nay but it fitteth best,
> For Çupid's man with Venus mayd to hold,
> For ill your goddesse services are drest
> By virgins, and her sacrifices let to rest.

The knight's supposed 'amorous passion' does not prevent

him from speaking the language of sweet reasonableness. For another thing, though he does behave somewhat forcibly towards Amoret, he does not do so with a will. On the contrary, he shows a lack of determination, having to '[shake] off all doubt and shamefast feare' (53). Even when he proceeds to the conquest, he looks anxiously 'upon the Goddesse face . . . for feare of her offence'. It is because she smiles reassuringly that he feels 'em*bold*ned with more confidence' (56). Venus, for Hieatt a symbol of harmony and concord, would not have countenanced Scudamour's flouting of her values. These criticisms of the corrective are surely more conclusive than Roche's own rejoinder:

Hieatt's suggestion that Scudamour is to blame because of his aggressive mastery of Amoret is not an answer to my position, nor is it the most fruitful way of viewing Scudamour's action at the Temple of Venus. . . . He is a universal that the occasion of Amoret's and Scudamour's wedding allows Spenser to bring into his poem *before we learn about the occasion*. Spenser devotes no time to an explanation of why Amoret is in this situation and never alludes to the culpability of either Amoret and Scudamour.[27]

Roche is more perceptive than Hieatt. But his insights are uncompelling for want of an intelligible rationale. Hence they do not make his account of Amoret's plight immune to 'adjustment'. As this example shows, the recognition that Spenser's symbolism is bound to affect his fiction's coherence as narrative tends to result in premature resignation to an uncertain grasp shading off into the implicit conviction that there is nothing to grasp: Hieatt is taken to task for being unfruitful, as though we were beyond right and wrong. Thus we get fundamental carelessness with regard to the stories as such (often enough hidden within a condescending taste for primitive quaintness or an abject lust for archetypal titillation), instead of the rigorous close reading which alone can expose their literal shame responsibly, to their allegorical glory.

(ii) *Personifications*

'There is no such thing as Amoret's plight on the day of her marriage for the Busirane Cantos to symbolize.' More generally, there is no tenor Amoret for the vehicle Amoret to symbolize. This formulation should bring out the absurdity of critical assumptions to the contrary. Amoret could not be variously real and symbolic as the fancy takes us. She does not differ in status from the maskers, Ease, Fancy, and so on. Consider 'her trembling hart . . . drawne forth, and in silver basin layd, / Quite through transfixed with a deadly dart' (III. xii. 21). No person would survive in this state even for a moment, let alone show at the same time 'a seemely grace, / And . . . move a comely pace' (19). Or are we to postulate that Amoret displays an artificial duplicate? This would ruin the impact of the scene, which derives from its 'reality', impossible as it is. Insistence on literal sense reduces her to an actress. (*Qua* participant in the Mask she is only metaphorically an actress, 'mask' being a metaphor, like 'pageant' and 'quest'.) Nor would the idea that she enacts her state of mind compensate for the loss. Such exteriorization would seem pointless, tasteless hyperbole. We must have no truck with 'meanings' that diminish the fiction.

If the episode should be about Scudamour and Amoret as (representative) individuals, why does Spenser do so little to register their presence? Both are lacking in narrative prominence and personal consciousness alike. Scudamour's role is confined largely to the first half of Canto xi. There he voices, unsolicited, a highly rhetorical lament (9–11), which, passionate though it is, defines his anguish on account of Amoret philosophically rather than existentially, in terms of abstract right and wrong rather than of personalities in a mutual relationship. The reader feels indignation at an intolerable injustice but cannot share sympathetically the experiences of the frustrated lovers, since these are not specified and, indeed, hardly ever referred to. For Spenser does not reveal either how Amoret, herself not introduced until the second half of Canto xii, feels about Scudamour during her sufferings. Nothing indicates any awareness of his existence, whether as the cause of her plight, culpable or otherwise, or as her potential rescuer. It is Britomart who, in order to stem the tide of Amoret's effusive gratitude at her release, first mentions him, almost as an afterthought. And the response she elicits, warm enough in itself, strikes one, in its context, as too laconic to warrant the inference that Amoret must have had him in mind all along:

> Henceforth faire Lady comfort to you take,
> And put away remembrance of late teene;
> *In stead thereof* know, that your loving Make,
> Hath no lesse griefe endured for your gentle sake.
>
> She much was cheard to heare him mentiond,
> Whom of all living wights she loved best.
>
> (40–1.)

The 'huge affection' and 'sweete ravishment' she manifests, in 1590, on finding Scudamour come rather as a surprise (45). Her disappointment, in 1596, on finding him absent seems almost casual:

> But most faire Amoret, whose gentle spright
> Now gan to feede on hope, which she before
> Conceived had, to see her owne deare knight,
> Being thereof beguyld was fild with *new* affright.
>
> (44.)

These lines do not suggest that her acute torments inside the Castle are the effect of separation or alienation from Scudamour.

Furthermore, most of the episode 'digresses' to provide circumstantial descriptions of the tapestries and the Mask, which halt the action without explaining it *qua* action. For example, how does exhaustive scrutiny of the loves of the gods prepare Britomart for her task? It does not. C. S. Lewis more than implies this when he says: 'To the characters participating in an allegory, nothing is allegorical. They live in a world compact of wonders, beauties, and terrors, which are mostly quite unintelligible to them. . . . Our own experience . . . is divided between sharing the experiences of the characters in the story and looking at their life from somewhere outside it, seeing all the time meanings that are opaque from within.' So he acknowledges, obliquely, the inconsequentiality of the narrative. However, Spenser's characters do not have points of view of their own. It is just not true that 'we see all this erotic imagery through Britomart's eyes'.[28] The poet describes it directly, dropping Britomart altogether. He does not punctuate his account with 'she sees', 'next she turns to'. And he proceeds too systematically to suggest the naturally haphazard wandering of a visitor's gaze. Much the same applies to the Mask. Spenser presents it objectively, without hinting at Britomart's reactions to the various maskers, without conveying mounting tension as the show continues or horror at the appearance of Amoret. Nor, for that matter, does Amoret allow empathy: she seems totally anaesthetized. There is only one point of view, the reader's. Lewis underestimates more than mildly the difficulties of interpretation. Readers must not hope to 'receive the allegory so easily that they forget they have done so, as a man in health is unaware of breathing'.[29] The poem addresses us as sick unto death, caught in original sin. Yet for all his (imagined) affinity with Spenser it is Lewis who impedes a unifying response, by childishly relishing the marvels of romance for their own sake and thus playing off the fiction against the meaning.

The Busirane episode itself powerfully undercuts the illusion that it is about Scudamour, Amoret, and Britomart. To insist that it is all the same, allegorically, would be to confuse the status of the discourse and to attribute to Spenser a counter-productive method: novelistic fiction would have served his purpose far more adequately. Of course, the novel did not yet exist. But there are no signs of Spenser straining to invent it. His characters are personifications, complementary metaphors for what the long stretches in which they do not figure also symbolize. We face a consistently allegorical canvas, whose components are interpretatively equidistant from the reader, with convergent meanings. Semantically centripetal and lacking in temporal dynamics, it slows us down to a leisurely pace. Instead of requiring us to will a story, it prompts us to let go, so that we may linger over every stanza and absorb it in its concreteness until it becomes diaphanous, a 'shining one'. Having recognized this, we may safely admit that the roles of the main characters, extremely fragmentary though they are, do look as though they could be elaborated so as to result in a story. This impression does not sanction such suppletion, however: it is an allegory of oneness barely perceptible, chastity.

Let us now purge the episode of the entirely hypothetical constructions with which the narrative approach contaminates it. We may revert to Roche:

> Amoret's fears are based on moral and physical grounds. Scudamour can dispel neither. Unwillingly he is the cause of these fears, and any attempt on his part to dispel them would be self-defeating since it would mean her eventual surrender, the basis of her fears. Britomart, on the other hand, can attack these fears on both the moral and physical grounds. As a woman she understands Amoret's attitude towards the physical side of love, and as the exemplar of chastity she is able to make the moral distinction between marriage and adulterous love. Her entry through the wall of flame gives her an intimate knowledge of the House of Busyrane, and her understanding finally allows her to release Amoret from her fears.[30]

How extraordinarily remote this is from the text and what it can reasonably be taken to imply. For a start, the argument is all about Amoret's *fears.* Yet in the poem she actually undergoes excruciating torture. She does not merely anticipate it. To be sure, this torture is an enchantment, which is dispelled. And physical wounds cannot just be dispelled, whereas false imaginings can. Still, the text presents a sudden physical recovery, not a mental readjustment (38). We cannot dismiss Busirane as a mere illusionist, as we must, without realizing all the more the horrifying extent of his power. No other great antagonist in *The Faerie Queene*, whether the Dragon, Acrasia, Grantorto, or the Blattant Beast, communicates its wickedness as disturbingly as does Busirane. Then why reduce the magician from an enemy to morality that Everyman has to confront to untypical, or even pathological, anxiety? But perhaps modern critics, keyed to psychology rather than ethics, sense no reduction.

Scudamour's efforts are self-defeating, says Roche, because unwillingly he causes Amoret's fears; not 'unwittingly'. And indeed, only utter insensitivity could have kept the knight unaware *that* Amoret's sudden panic results from his sexual demands, even if he cannot understand *why*. Now for Scudamour to see this *is* to perceive that from Amoret's point of view any solution meant to ensure that he will have his way must be a threat. In other words, he knows that it is futile to try. So his efforts lay him open to the charge of sadism. But there is not a shred of evidence in the text that Scudamour sees why he fails, or feels guilty about wanting to succeed, or knowingly adopts a policy of 'gently does it'. On the contrary, his lament shows him to be completely bewildered. He has been trying desperately and reviles himself for *not* succeeding. His efforts are simply in vain. Nor does the text show any difference of approach between Scudamour and Britomart. She never scolds him for going about things selfishly or tactlessly. She does not seek to dissuade him from trying at all. Together they draw near to the flaming porch, which terrifies her no less than him. Yet she steels herself and passes through safe and sound. Keen to emulate her, he follows her lead, only to fail, *for no apparent reason.* Spenser does say that 'Mulciber would not obay / His threatfull pride' (xi. 26). But this cannot be taken as censure, because Britomart is, if anything, more proudly self-confident than Scudamour. Also, Britomart's attempt to dispel Amoret's fears would be meant to ensure her surrender to Scudamour, exactly like his own.

Nor, *pace* Roche, is Britomart better qualified to do the dispelling, 'as a woman' and 'as the exemplar of chastity'. For one thing, as a woman Britomart is less experienced than Amoret. She has not been educated in the Garden and at the Temple. And she has not yet met her own lover in the flesh. What could she possibly have to offer? Surely not her 'intimate knowledge' or 'understanding' of Busirane's House (an accomplishment which Spenser, incidentally, denies her, in xi. 50 and 54). For it can hardly be as profound, after three days, as Amoret's seven months' experience of the place. Anyway, Britomart does not reveal her sex to Amoret until IV. i. 13. For another thing, what could justify the assumption that Britomart is more of an exemplar of chastity than Scudamour, one of Gloriana's paladins, and Amoret, the foster-child of a Venus reconciled with Diana (III. vi. 25)? What really ails the couple, on Roche's view, is not that they are less than chaste but that Amoret has a distorted notion of chastity and that Scudamour is not sufficiently imaginative to meet her on her own ground. They would need pastoral counselling, not an exemplar of chastity. But even supposing their shortcomings could be construed as flaws in their chastity, how could Britomart's moral superiority be the remedy? Just look at the text. Do we see Britomart lecturing on the definition of chastity and sympathetically exposing fateful misconceptions? No. Do we see her behaving with exemplary chastity? No. Are there any signs that Scudamour and Amoret come to see each other in a different light? No again. Britomart forces an evil magician to undo his work. This action is an allegory; that is, it constitutes the vehicle of a metaphor for a given tenor, chastity. We must not think up a tenor *story* that 'really goes on' in and, more often, behind the ascertainable vehicle story and that is therefore doomed to remain a wildly speculative construct, cluttering up the surface narrative. Spenser's vehicle pure and simple, without any admixture of 'interpretation', makes far better sense *qua* story, as far as it goes. Busirane has imprisoned Amoret, lusts after her, and tortures her 'all for she Scudamore will not denay' (xi. 11). Meanwhile Scudamour does all he can to release her, in the spirit of true knighthood, but without success. Then Britomart comes along and proves more efficient. The lovers are united (1590) or, alternatively, remain as yet separated because Scudamour has left, convinced of Britomart's failure after all (1596). This may be a largely meaningless pattern from the common stock of romance. But it has enough content to rule out the ludicrous notion that Scudamour causes Amoret's plight and so to forestall the fanciful explanations this notion inevitably entails. The apparent narrative falls readily into place as Scudamour's quest against Busirane. The knight is not of the magician's party, whether consciously or otherwise.

If Amoret and Scudamour are personifications, how do they personify chastity, wholeness in part? Amoret, to judge from her name, stands for small-scale love. She is one of the twin daughters of Chrysogonee (III. vi. 4–10). Her mother's name means 'golden generation' (from χρυσός and γονεία). This is a paradox, for gold represents glory,[31] while generation, which produces separateness, deprives of glory. Accordingly, Chrysogonee is 'yborne of high degree', generated from Eternity; the real child, not the foster-child, of a Faery who cannot be just a Faery, as her name confirms: Amphisa, 'both equally' (4). In token of her correspondence to her mother and grandmother we find Amoret begotten miraculously 'through influence of th'*heavens* fruitfull ray' (6). (Being an 'idol', not a human infant, she does not illustrate Spenser's considered opinion on how conception works—a point obscured by Fowler's solemn astro-genetic exegesis of stanzas 8–9.[32]) Here Amoret symbolizes chastity, glory almost opaque, in particular, in view of Chrysogonee's sense of 'shame and foule disgrace' despite her 'guiltlesse conscience' (10): a fine contradiction in terms.

Amoret is adopted by Venus 'in her little loves stead, which was strayd' (vi. 28). Cupid had fled from 'her blisfull bowre of joy above' (11). To find him Venus

left her heavenly hous,
The house of goodly formes and faire aspects,
Whence all the world derives the glorious
Features of beautie, and all shapes select,
With which high God his workmanship hath deckt.

(12.)

Possibly this alludes to the astrological house of the planet Venus. The goddess chasing Cupid on earth could 'be' Hesperus in the same sense as Gloriana. The identification does not entail that the 'goodly formes' that beautify 'all the world' are confined to a particular section of the sky. If those 'formes' are Neoplatonic Ideas, their house would be the Divine Mind. However, its characterization as a 'blisfull bowre' suggests rather that Spenser simply means heaven, the true Bower of Bliss.[33] Venus in her heavenly house stands for love in Eternity. But Eternity is not yet. Hence we do not see Venus in heaven. Her loss of Cupid is not a contingent misfortune in the celestial world, the excuse for a playful literary arabesque, but a symbol of love, eternal union, fragmented beyond recognition, 'disguiz'd in thousand shapes', in Time (11). Her search signifies commitment to Time, virtue. Appropriately, Venus never finds Cupid. She does adopt Amoret, who therefore, as a substitute Cupid, properly belongs in heaven. However, 'she brought her to her joyous Paradize, / Where most she wonnes, *when she on earth does dwel*' (29), the Garden of Adonis. 'Great enimy . . . to all . . . That in the Gardin of Adonis springs, / Is *wicked Time*'

(39). Amoret's introduction into an enclosure which contains multiplicity, 'a thousand thousand naked babes', only partially in that it lets them out into separateness as well as back in (32) and on which Time casts a dark shadow makes her, again, symbolic of chastity.

Spenser criticism has mostly gone awry in its eagerness to hail the Garden episode as 'that great philosophic poem in praise of life and generation',[34] almost as though it were a counterblast against Belphœbe. We must blame C. S. Lewis. In contrasting the natural sex of the Garden with what he sees as its artificial perversion in the Bower, he equates it with chastity by sleight of hand. Sex does become chaste through marriage. However, marriage is not a natural relationship but a divine institution. Spenser recognizes the chain of generation as evidence of Man's oneness and celebrates it as such. Obviously, though, generation unfolds rather than infolds the whole Man. It is a natural process which needs a moral dimension, chastity, to control or even check it. Spenser calls the Garden 'so faire a place, as Nature can devize' (29). 'Mr Lewis takes it to mean that the garden is a place so fair as nature alone can devise; whereas it is equally possible that Spenser meant it was the best that Nature could do.' Brooke's early remonstrance hits the nail on the head.[35] The episode does not urge us to live according to nature and, by means of generation, make ourselves 'eterne in mutabilitie' (47) to boot. So understood the oxymoron would be a mere manner of speaking, offering no real consolation for personal mortality. We cannot but live according to nature, for the Time being. The episode symbolizes chastity, through which Man is as a matter of fact 'eterne in mutabilitie', whole even while caught up in generation.

Amoret comes 'to Faery court . . . where many one . . . found / His feeble hart wide launched with loves cruell wound' because of her (52). 'Many one', the multifarious unity of love, glorious with Gloriana, orients itself to virtue, which, as chastity, approximates eternal life so distantly as to seem a mortal injury. Since the quotation describes Amoret, too, as we see her in the Busirane Cantos, we have all the more reason for not taking it literally, to mean that a certain lady Amoret becomes the flame of many a knight.

True, Amoret 'to none of them her love did cast, / Save to the noble knight Sir Scudamore' (53). Apparently she discriminates. Does this not imply that the 'noble knight' contrasts favourably with the others? Surely not. All we know about them is that they are love-stricken. We cannot disapprove of them without disapproving of Scudamour himself: 'none of them . . . save' is inclusive, so that it is impossible to differentiate his love from theirs. Scudamour is not a person, the only one among a crowd to be worthy of Amoret's affection, but the sum of them all in isolation, thus proving Amoret's equal as a personification of chastity. Hence their commitment to each other. She suffers 'for his dearest sake' (53) because they are synonymous. Conversely, as Britomart says to Amoret, he 'hath no lesse griefe endured for your gentle sake' (xii. 40). To literal readers this is, of course, preposterous, since he does not share Amoret's physical plight. But they might say that she is telling a white lie, to stimulate Amoret's love. Does Scudamour not accuse himself precisely of being culpably exempt from torture: 'Yet thou vile man, vile Scudamore art sound' (xi. 11)? Not at all. He symbolizes love, which *is* soundness, agonizingly unable to manifest itself as such—a paradox built into his very name: Scud-amour, 'shield love', love as shield, protecting by bearing the brunt; or, love as (mere) faith. The episode does not tell of two lovers, one in pain, the other going scot-free. It unfolds love, highlighting it as suffering in Amoret and as protection in Scudamour, the quest hero. Intense suffering and ineffectual protection are complementary metaphors for the darker side of love in Time, chastity, in being just perceptibly qualified by insensitivity and soundness. With telling effect, Spenser at once defines the knight in frustrated dissociation from his identifying attribute:

> A little off, his shield was rudely throwne,
> On which the winged boy in colours cleare
> Depeincted was, full easie to be knowne,
> And he thereby.
>
> (7.)

This brings us to the 'winged boy', Cupid, whose brightly attractive appearance here as nothing less than the principle to which the noble Scudamour has sworn allegiance would be most uncharacteristic if we were to follow C. S. Lewis in associating him with 'courtly love' or 'the whole tradition of polite adultery'.[36] But we will not. The frame of reference for his seminal discussion of the Middle Books is far-fetched, and perhaps imaginary. Scholars no longer agree about the nature, or even the existence, of courtly love. Anyway, married love, the alleged theme of these Books, cannot plausibly be treated as courtly love dialectically *aufgehoben*. Lewis admits that Spenser does not so treat it but confidently ascribes this to the poet's poor historical perspective. We may confidently ascribe to Lewis's rich imagination (half-creative, as becomes that of an arch-romantic) his tendency to hypostatize a 'false Cupid', which falsifies the poem. Allusions to a good Cupid are certainly quasi-incidental and inconspicuous, and hence easily overshadowed by the altar image of the cruel Cupid (xi. 47–9) and the tyrant Cupid in the Mask (xii. 22–3). Nevertheless, their very existence rules out the idea that to Spenser 'false Cupid' was virtually tautologous. Cupid is false as presented by Busirane; or rather, as misrepresented by Busirane, an enchanter, whose business it is to distort. The god is (true) love in a false perspective, not a false variety of love exposed in all its horror. Outside the House of Busirane Cupid is nothing worse than painfully ambivalent. The god who 'hath with spoiles and cruelty / Ransackt the world, and in the wofull harts / Of many wretches set his triumphes hye' is definitely, if almost unrecognizably, the selfsame god who 'laying his sad darts / Aside, with faire Adonis playes his wanton parts' (vi. 49). And consider the opening of Scudamour's lament, which definitely apostrophizes Cupid; though not openly, by name:

> O soveraigne Lord that sit'st *on hye*,
> And raignst in blis emongst thy blessed Saintes,
> How suffrest thou such shameful cruelty,
> *So long* unwreaked of thine enimy?
>
> (xi. 9.)

Apparently an accusation of divine indifference, this really conveys the god's 'soundness'. It sets up the same paradox as Scudamour's self-accusation two stanzas later. How is it that love, the glory of eternal union, suffers—undergoes as much as tolerates—the shame of temporal separateness? Cupid, biding his Time, giving and receiving wounds that largely obscure his divinity, is yet another personification of chastity.

Busirane resides at Faery Court, as we concluded in Section I. He is its evil genius. Of course, the realm of Gloriana, Eternity descended into Time, is in no way evil *per se*. However, Time tends to pass itself off as an ultimate, because as yet Man can see himself only in its mirror. The power of this spell corresponds to the degree to which any virtue hides glory. It is most powerful under the rubric of temperance. But there it is harmless, since that virtue has no transcendent aspirations anyway. Its evil potential becomes manifest under the rubric of chastity, a virtue which partakes scarcely of glory. Hence Busirane, the enchanter, in Book III. Seizing on the gloomy aspect of love, he tries to absolutize it. His tapestries reiterate as though endlessly the humiliating metamorphoses of the gods, multifarious Eternity, through Cupid's power, in order to conceal that it unites them even so. They culminate in the revelation that Cupid does not

> spare (so cruell was the Elfe)
> His owne deare mother, (ah why should he so?)
> Nor did he spare sometime to pricke himselfe,
> That he might taste the sweet consuming woe,
> Which he had wrought to many others moe.
>
> (45.)

Such overwhelming evidence seemingly warrants a logical impossibility, the casual identification of the god as an Elf. More than that, it appears to turn the worship of eternal love as refracted by Time, 'an Image *all alone* [i.e. 'many as one'], / Of *massy gold*' with wings like the peacock's tail or the rainbow (47), into an idolatrous cult of 'the Victor of the Gods', trampling what is surely (though not, perhaps, exclusively) a self-devouring serpent (emblem of Eternity) *manqué* (48–9; compare IV. x. 40). Indeed, nothing apparently prevents Busirane from clinching his point through the Mask of Cupid, in which 'that Elfe' (xii. 22) looks manifestly self-destructive, exulting over his captive counterpart Amoret.

Formally a 'triumph', it is a ghastly travesty of the real Cupid, who will 'set his triumphes *hye*' (vi. 49), even as he inflicts pain. Yet only if we have our eyes skinned for practically hidden details, such as Amoret's going unnamed, can we see through the magician. His name associates him with Busiris, the mythical Egyptian king. 'Busiris . . . was told that the shedding of a stranger's blood would restore Egypt's lost fertility. Busiris sacrifices the very seer who came to impart this intelligence.'[37] The concern of Busiris for fertility intimates Time's demand for generation. Amoret, love as chastity, meets the needs of Time as it really is, finite. But she lives subject to, even as she resists, the illusion of Time's perpetuity, which blots out her *raison d'être*, so that love appears to make the whole Man fritter himself away in generation.

Commenting on the Mask of Cupid, Fowler once wrote that 'the most outstanding feature in the arrangement is, of course, the contrast between the orderly grouping of the characters (phases of emotional experience) that precede the triumphant god and the hurried confusion of the rout that follows. This is clearly meant to convey the difference between earlier and later stages of a sexual relationship.' In a subsequent, more detailed, study he finds himself in a quandary, though:

> The first part of the procession includes such traditional obstacles to love as Doubt and Danger, while the last is a 'confused rout' of 'maladies'. We are tempted to speculate that Busyrane's procession may also resemble Ovid's in following the sequence *opposition to love / submission to love / love's consequences.* Here we meet a difficulty, however. The triumph of Ovid's Cupid has a definite sense: namely, the yielding of the lover to passion. . . . But Amoret never returns Busyrane's love, so that the masque cannot celebrate her submission to him. On the other hand, her love for Scudamour is socially too acceptable . . . to have such evil consequences.[38]

This leaves one wondering uneasily whether the triumph of Spenser's Cupid has an indefinite sense, or even no sense at all. For Fowler's 'focused' synthesis of Roche and Hieatt, Scudamour's penis, goes limp for want of textual life-blood. But then, the personifications preceding and following Cupid cannot be bracketed as 'opposition to love' as against 'love's consequences'. 'The first part of the procession *includes* . . . obstacles.' This implies, correctly, that it does not consist entirely of them: Ease, Fancy, Desire, Hope, for instance, do not qualify. Even Doubt and Danger themselves are not certainly obstacles, for, unlike Ovid's 'Mens Bona . . . et Pudor, et castris quidquid Amoris obest', they are not bound, 'manibus post terga retortis'. Actually, the Latin analogue does not have the suggested sequence in the first place. For one thing, it does not specify where the personifications representing opposition to love come in the procession. For another, the personifications that follow Ovid's Cupid, 'adsidue partes turba *secuta* tuas', are described as love's instruments rather than as love's consequences: 'his tu militibus superas hominesque deosque.' Those specified, 'blanditiae . . . Errorque Furorque', have counterparts, if at all, among the personifications *preceding* Spenser's Cupid, Fury and, arguably, Dissemblance (17, 14). Conversely, Shame, the only one of Spenser's personifications with a definite counterpart among Ovid's obstacles to love (Pudor), follows Cupid (24).

Spenser's maskers do not objectify Amoret's experience. Being a personification, she does not have a psyche. Instead they unfold love as distorted by Busirane (Cupid as Elf, Amoret as anonymous 'dolefull Lady'). Love is at ease in Time because whole even while broken. But in Busirane's perspective Ease, who introduces the Mask, with his name 'in *golden* letters cyphered' and with his laurel branch, emblem of eternal victory, appears in 'garments, fit for tragicke Stage' and conveys, in a dumb show, 'some argument of matter passioned'; which is strangely at odds with what he stands for. Hence he identifies himself as Ease only as he 'backe retyred soft away' (3–4), to intimate that the Mask will present (love as) departure of ease. And so it does. The maskers preceding Cupid personify so many aspects of separate existence *qua* threat to wholeness. Spenser sums them up in the gripping picture of 'Amoret' with her heart, her very selfhood, torn out. Inevitably love in Time involves Fancy, Desire, Doubt, Danger, Fear, Hope, and the rest. Busirane's power is not creative but parasitic upon reality. He cannot prevent that 'thus marched these sixe couples forth *in faire degree*' (18): though disruptive, they are even so harnessed by chastity. However, as in the tapestries and the image, he loads the dice. In dismissing Ease he virtually ensures an uneasy response to the personifications preceding Amoret, whose supposed malignity surfaces briefly in the 'confused rout' of those following her. Without Eternity chastity is meaningless. And without chastity generative love is 'Shame . . . Lewd Losse of Time . . . Death with infamie' (24–5), the very opposite of Time's redemption into glory. Only if we resist Busirane are Cupid's followers no more than 'phantasies / In wavering wemens wit'. If we do not, they are 'punishments in hell' (26). Spenser does not trace the emotional experiences, as they develop, of an (un)representative lady: as always, he defines a virtue in relation to its medium.

(iii) *Variant Endings*

The existence of two different endings to Book III appears to undermine our contention that the Busirane episode has a single meaning. If its constituent scenes are complementary metaphors, the same could, in principle, be true of its alternative conclusions. But the diametric contrast between them seems, in fact, to rule out equivalence. The 1596 ending also appears to establish a narrative link with Book IV. The 1590 ending had made the Busirane episode a self-contained Scudamour story. However, this ending was discarded. We must not deny appearances but assess whether they are real or illusory.

But first let us ponder this question: supposing Scudamour does have a real story running across the Book boundary, why should Spenser have written a provisional ending at all, and a misleadingly conclusive one at that? Climax and fulfilment, it might be said, are aesthetically satisfying at the end of an instalment. Since *The Faerie Queene* was serialized at very long intervals, keeping the reader in suspense would have served no purpose. But then, the ending of the second instalment, with Book VI, forestalls suspense without in the least resembling a grand finale. Spenser could have done something similar in 1590. This would certainly have been more in line with his treatment of the other major narratives in Book III, which he abandons unresolved. In the case of Britomart, the Book's titular and most conspicuous hero, he even promises a continuation, more or less. Indeed, he does so in the provisional ending and thus mars its characteristic finality:

> Britomart halfe envying their blesse,
> Was much empassiond in her gentle sprite,
> And to her selfe oft wisht like happinesse,
> In vaine she wisht, that fate n'ould let her yet possesse.
>
> (46.)

Or are we barking up the wrong tree? Could it be that in 1590 Spenser simply did not yet envisage a sequel to Scudamour's story? Hardly. If he planned the reappearance of Britomart, that of Scudamour and Amoret cannot have been an afterthought, for their story in Book IV is inseparably intertwined with that of Britomart, whom we invariably see in the company of either. Anyway, what could be the 'continuity' of a story that has not been conceived as a whole and whose parts have not even been welded together? Spenser does not bother to motivate Scudamour's change of behaviour. In 1590, 'halfe desperate . . . of the hardie Britomarts successe' (43), the knight stays put. In 1596, where he, likewise, 'his expectation to despaire did turne', he decides 'thence to depart for further aide t'enquire' (45). Both reactions are too natural to require explicit motivation independently; but on seeing them juxtaposed one demands some modification in circumstances to account for the change; in vain. How awkward, also, that Scudamour's sudden burst of initiative should be occasioned by Britomart's supposed failure rather than by the prolonged sufferings of his own Amoret. Our present understanding of *The Faerie Queene* makes it unlikely that Spenser decided on quest heroes as he went along. And, for all we know, Book IV may have been written by 1590. The 'conclusive' ending serves to underline what is implied by the 'perverse' decision to allow publication to sever the Middle Books, namely that Book III, so obviously partial in comparison with Books I and II, is even so whole, and thus about chastity.

Now for the evidence that the appearance of narrative continuity is illusory. To begin with, contrary to what the 1596 ending of Book III leads one to expect, the opening of Book IV does not present Britomart and Amoret searching for Scudamour. Britomart, still to all intents and purposes a man, treats Amoret as 'his' own 'pray' (4), abusing her ignorance (7). The text does not specify this behaviour as light-hearted jesting. It is, in fact, gratuitously cruel, and the very opposite of what you would expect from an exemplar of chastity. Nor does she reassure Amoret at once, spontaneously: only the custom of the castle and the complications it causes (9 ff.) precipitate the revelation of her sex. Amoret, for her part, so far from reminding Britomart of her duty towards Scudamour and of her own commitment to him, for the consummation of which she has supposedly been rescued, is entirely preoccupied by her sense of obligation to her liberator; and with full authorial backing:

> For well she wist, *as true it was indeed*,
> That her lives Lord and patrone of her health
> Right well deserved as his duefull meed,
> Her love, her service, and her utmost wealth.
> All is his justly, that all freely dealth.
>
> (6.)

To be sure, 'nathlesse her honor dearer then her life, / She sought to save'. But this cannot mean that she wants to preserve her virginity for Scudamour instead: she is 'profest a *virgine wife*'. Even when Busirane's magic has been dispelled, Amoret persists in her 'aberration'; which she shares with the Faery Queen. After the revelation of Britomart's sex they do go in search of Scudamour (16). However, this search, like that of Arthur for Gloriana, remains undescribed. Spenser says only that '*long* wandred they, yet *never* met with *none*, / That to their willes could them direct aright'. Their next adventure, Blandamour's attack and defeat (33–6), does not exemplify seeking. The poet refers to Amoret's desire to find Scudamour twice later on, only to drop her story at once (v. 30; ix. 19).

At IV. i. 38 Scudamour and Glauce enter the fiction together just as they had left the House of Busirane together at the end of Book III. Spenser does not remind us of their starting-point, though; nor, for that matter, of their purpose:

we do not see them enquiring for further aid. He makes Scudamour the object of Paridell's attack, launched at the instigation of Blandamour, who hates Scudamour 'because his love he wonne by right' (39)—obviously an allusion to his conquest of Amoret at the Temple of Venus. The energetic confidence with which Scudamour meets the challenge suggests that, if the scene follows on from any other scene at all, it must be from the Temple episode, not from the Busirane episode. His effortless victory does not tally with knightly powers sapped by seven months of hopeless frustration. Indeed, in view of Amoret's seemingly irremediable captivity, it would hardly be logical for him to vindicate his possession of her. Paridell does not tell Scudamour why he attacks him. Does Scudamour, perhaps, fight in mere self-defence, unaware of the issue? Certainly not, for to Blandamour and Paridell it seems that he initiates the clash:

> ere long they chaunced to espie
> Two other knights, that towards them did ply
> With speedie course, *as bent to charge them new.*
>
> (38.)

Moreover, Scudamour does not betray any surprise at Duessa's admonition to Blandamour, 'why do ye strive for Ladies love so sore' (46), as he should if it reveals to him what the fight was all about. Nor does he inform his antagonists that he has long since lost Amoret. In short, the scene makes little sense if Scudamour assumes his lady's captivity; as he must if it is continuous with Book III.

But then, Scudamour readily infers that the 'stranger knight' in favour of whom Ate gleefully insists that Amoret has abandoned him (not without apparent justification, as we have seen) is none other than Britomart (50, 52–3). Yet Ate's specification is none too specific:

> a stranger knight, whose name
> I wote not well, but in his shield he beares
> (That well I wote) the heads of many broken speares.
>
> (48.)

Surely only Scudamour's knowledge that he left Amoret in Britomart's care previously could explain his inference?

As a suspicion, yes. But it does not explain his complete lack of hesitation, for which Ate's indefiniteness allows ample scope. Why does it not occur to him that Amoret may have been seduced by somebody other than Britomart? Is it really altogether natural for him suddenly to lose all faith in one whose 'huge heroicke magnanimity' and 'bounteous brest' had recently inspired eloquent and unquestioning trust (III. xi. 19)? Or if it is, why does it not occur to Glauce, at least, to suggest alternatives? All we learn is that she 'his flaming furie sought to have assuaged / With sober words, that *sufferance* desired' (IV. i. 54). Later in Book IV Scudamour can still think of only one possible culprit (v. 30 ff. and vi. 7 ff.). One wonders how Glauce could know Ate for a liar 'by assay' (50), since she has been with Scudamour, not with Britomart. One would have thought that she knows it on principle, knowing Britomart's sex. Yet she never thinks of using this knowledge to refute Ate and extricate herself from a situation where Scudamour's anger puts her life at risk. How absurd, as story. In fact, Scudamour's denunciation of Britomart does not specifically evoke the Busirane episode:

Discourteous, disloyall Britomart,
  Untrue to God, and unto man unjust,
  What vengeance due can equall thy desart,
  That hast with shamefull spot of sinfull lust
  Defil'd the pledge committed to thy trust?

(53.)

If we nevertheless take this as an allusion, we must find it odd that the implication of Ate's words, that Britomart must have released Amoret from her captivity first, does not, as far as we can tell, force him to adjust his assumptions. After all, he had left the castle 'misdeeming *sure* that her those flames did burne' (III. xii. 45-1596). Moreover, after his grand encounter with Britomart, Scudamour himself speaks to her of her victory over Busirane as a matter of course, requesting 'tydings of my love, / My Amoret, sith you her freed fro thence, / Where she captived long, great woes did prove' (IV. vi. 34). Nobody has told him about it; nor has he seen his lady with his own eyes. Once he knows

Ate's story to be a lie, he 'ought to' think that Amoret is still with the magician. Yet he speaks as though he had witnessed her delivery himself. He has; but only in the 1590 ending, allegedly discarded to ensure narrative continuity.

With no real Scudamour–Amoret story crossing the Book boundary, the 1596 ending cannot be a narrative *trait d'union* reflecting 'the exigencies of the plot', as Lewis would have it. The Busirane episode remains self-contained. But how are its variant endings equivalent? We cannot answer that question unless we see first how what they have in common, Amoret's liberation, equals her captivity. Does Spenser not employ precisely the contrast, emphatic captivity versus marginal liberation, in order to symbolize chastity? He does. And his irresistible invitation to regard them jointly as a symbol already precludes sequence. To appreciate the equivalence we need to remind ourselves that Scudamour and Amoret oppose Busirane throughout, however indecisively. The narrative approach misses the significance of this. It cannot but interpret their stance as the inadequate means to a literal end. It assumes tacitly that, but for Britomart, Scudamour and Amoret would in the long run have had to yield to Busirane. Freedom from Time's spell *consists in* refusing to acknowledge its finality. One can do no more; for it will not go away, just yet. Accordingly Spenser qualifies Amoret's liberation, in 1596, by Scudamour's disappearance. Their separation means, far less dramatically, of course, what exposure to Busirane's magic also means. Again the narrative approach misses the significance. It cannot but interpret the separation as a contingent misfortune, a delay due to Scudamour's laudable but, as it happens, premature decision to seek assistance. Within the fiction the lovers will not be united, ever, any more than Arthur and Gloriana.

The 1590 ending may seem to disprove this categorical assertion. It does not really, though. For in their Hermaphroditic embrace (46) Scudamour and Amoret are still only one in part, unlike the androgynous Venus behind the veil (IV. x. 40–1).[39] Spenser merely plays down their separation. He can afford this positive note, proper to friendship, because it sounds too briefly to balance the horrors of the

Busirane episode. The 1596 ending pre-echoes, faintly, this same note. The 'further aide' Scudamour sets out to seek is not literal assistance, as we have seen, but his reappearance as the vehicle of friendship. The impression, derived from the fiction as narrative, of a largely vacuous separation from Amoret has a complementary significance. Realizing the equivalence of the two endings, we can make the most of their difference. In 1590 the poet does shift forward the emphasis belonging to Scudamour's second quest as he does not in 1596. That is to say, the Middle Books, collapsible in 1596, are collapsed in 1590. Thus the first instalment enacts structurally the wholeness of the single broken virtue chastity-friendship, the second instalment its togetherness. The later view complements rather than supersedes the earlier one. In serializing his poem Spenser shows how he can redeem the Time of publication precisely through placing himself at its mercy. He orients himself towards poetic virtue, as against poetic glory.

III The Temple of Venus Episode

(i) *Preliminaries*

The Scudamour–Amoret fiction in Book III, the Garden of Adonis episode and the Busirane episode, ceases to be conceivable as story once we try to relate it chronologically to the Temple of Venus episode. It is whole only in part, within the confines of the Legend of Chastity, to symbolize that virtue. Yet the illusion that there must be such a chronological relation remains extremely powerful. Spenser provides almost unbroken story, to symbolize friendship. The same situation should obtain *a fortiori* within the confines of the Legend of Friendship. One would expect that its several Scudamour–Amoret episodes are emphatically together in merely implicit separateness. If in the following pages we stress their separateness, it is because that needs demonstration. We will respect the powerful illusion for its significance but we will not mistake it for reality. Take the Amoret fiction. Apparently nothing prevents us from reading it as a sequence. In addition to her adventures in Canto i, she performs at the beauty contest after Satyrane's tournament

(v. 13–30) and finds herself captured by and released from Lust (vii. 1–36). From viii. 19 onwards she enjoys the protection of Arthur, in whose company she is during his stay at Slander's cottage (viii. 23–36), his vindication of Amyas (viii. 38–ix. 16), and his settling of the dispute between Druon, Claribell, Blandamour, and Paridell, on the one hand, and Britomart and Scudamour, on the other (ix. 32–41). We could say that she goes through all these experiences one after another. That would be an empty statement, though, since not only do her several episodes have nothing to do with each other objectively but she does not even connect them subjectively, being herself an object rather than a subject throughout.

Scudamour is more of a 'presence'. Accordingly his adventures form a more palpable sequence. Even the Temple of Venus episode contributes to this impression. For we naturally take its marked self-sufficiency, its complete, unified, wellnigh Aristotelian plot with beginning, middle, and end, as a purely formal property imposed by Scudamour the narrator. We have already noted that Blandamour's hostility to Scudamour, in Canto i, seems to presuppose his conquest of Amoret at the Temple as a previous event. We may add that Scudamour's restless night at the House of Care, in Canto v, seems to relate to Amoret's alleged seduction as effect to previous cause. So, also, does his urge to take revenge on Britomart (given his rash identification of the culprit), which he satisfies in Canto vi. His reconciliation with Britomart seems to follow on from his recognition of her innocence. The constructive redirection of his energies into a search for Amoret similarly stands to reason, in view of Britomart's explanation that 'she wandred was, or gone astray' (36). And although neither their joint resistance to 'sterne Druon, and lewd Claribell, / Love-lavish Blandamour, and lustfull Paridell' (ix. 20) nor Scudamour's own narration of his conquest is an instance of seeking Amoret, each does seem to advertise itself as part of a developing story: the foursome attack remembering 'the fowle upbraide, / The which the Britonesse had to them donne, / In that late Turney for the snowy maide' (28), while Scudamour tells his tale at their request—a natural expression, surely, of their changed disposition, meeting with the natural response, to seal their newly found concord.

However, if the Scudamour fiction is more intelligible as sequence than the Amoret fiction, it is also more calculated to explode its narrative appearance. To begin with, we cannot connect Canto x and Canto i except via the fateful wedding of Scudamour and Amoret, because of Spenser's (unique) reference to it at the start of Book IV. Now Busirane's capture of the lady so unmans the knight that the connection between the Cantos becomes incredible, as we have seen. True, the magician intervenes 'by way of sport': thus the poet instructs us to make light of his intervention, for the purposes of Book IV. But if we read literally, we cannot carry out this instruction, in view of the spouses' separation. Busirane does not end his sport, as far as we can tell. The lovers' unconsummated marriage symbolizes Eternity interrupted, broken, by Time. Under the aspect of chastity Busirane's Mask virtually obliterates the fact that there is really a wedding in progress. Inherently glorious *qua* mask, Faery Court pageantry, it masks glory almost beyond recognition. Under the aspect of friendship, by contrast, Busirane's Mask is obviously no more than the mad prank of Gloriana's court jester, as it were. That virtue approximates heaven so closely that Time cannot take itself very seriously. Nevertheless, it will have a go while it lasts. Being a symbol rather than an event, the wedding of Scudamour and Amoret cannot be a narrative link between Cantos x and i any more than between Books IV and III. It marries segments of fiction only to keep them separate, as it does the lovers themselves.

On the supposed continuity between Ate's insinuations in Canto i and Scudamour's stay with Care in Canto v, let us hear Thomas Warton first:

> The occult meaning of his bringing Scudamore to the house of Care . . . clashes with what he had before told us. By this allegory of Scudamore's coming to Care's house, it should be *understood*, that 'Scudamore, from a happy, passed into a miserable state'. For we may reasonably suppose that before he came to Care's house he was unacquainted with Care; whereas the poet had before represented him as involved in extreme misery.[40]

Quite so. But then, contrary to Warton's assumption, shared

by critics generally, the episode allegorizes not the care of any one Scudamour but Care as an aspect of what Scudamour stands for. To be sure, Scudamour suffers literally from care. Grief, in the Mask of Cupid, unmistakably a personification, similarly suffers from grief (III. xii. 16). It also causes grief; a fact which prompted Coleridge's acute, but unjustifiably adverse, comment that 'this confusion of agent and patient occurs so frequently in his allegorical personages that Spenser seems to have deemed it within the laws and among the legitimate principles of allegory'.[41] The *symbol* Grief can neither act nor suffer; metaphorically it can do either, or both. It is not as though in the Care episode Spenser laudably avoids the confusion of Coleridge's 'two incompatibles'. He simply unfolds the active and passive aspects of Care, whereas he leaves those of Grief infolded. Not that Care inflicts *care* on Scudamour: it harasses him with unbearable noise, raps on the head, and scaldings in the side (IV. v. 41, 42, 44), which *mean* care. Scudamour's literal care remains strangely unspecified. Only once in the entire episode does Spenser hint at any preoccupation with Britomart and Amoret:

> Yet in his soundest sleepe, his dayly feare
> His ydle braine gan busily molest,
> And made him dreame those two disloyall were:
> The things that day most minds, at night do most appeare.
>
> (43.)

These lines distinguish between the dream, in which 'these two' are actually 'disloyall', and waking experience, when the active brain merely fears what in sleep, idle, it experiences as certainty. Yet some few stanzas earlier Scudamour had stormed into the Canto 'bent to revenge on blamelesse Britomart / The crime, which cursed Ate kindled earst' (31), utterly convinced of her guilt as in Canto i. The incongruity becomes even more striking when we see Scudamour, on his arrival at Care's cottage, intrigued, aloof, apparently as unacquainted with Care as Warton would have him:

> Sir Scudamour there entring, much *admired*
> The manner of their worke and wearie paine;

And having long beheld, at last *enquired*
The cause and end thereof: but all in vaine.
(38.)

We must read allegorically. *Qua* friendship, love is Care without end, since it stays approximate all the Time, but also without cause, since it approximates glory for all to see. It wonders what its Care is all about. Alternatively, it is Care unmasking itself as a mere nightmare, whose real impact looks unaccountable:

With that, the wicked carle the maister Smith
A paire of redwhot yron tongs did take
Out of the burning cinders, and therewith
Under his side him nipt, that forst to wake,
He felt his hart for very paine to quake,
And started up avenged for to be
On him, the which his quiet slomber brake:
Yet looking round about him none could see;
Yet did the smart remaine, though he himselfe did flee.
(44.)

Coleridge, with his characteristic crazed perceptiveness, got at least part of the point:

At night, and in sleep, cares are not only doubly burdensome, but some matters, that then seem to us sources of great anxiety, are not so in fact; and when we are thoroughly awake, and in possession of all our faculties, they really seem nothing, and we wonder at the influence they have had over us.[42]

However, his excited psychologizing blinds him not only to Scudamour's remaining physical smart but also to his 'soundest sleepe' and 'quiet slomber'. Ordinary readers, whom the higher Spenser criticism has not yet rendered obtuse, will be taken aback by the poet's apparent mindlessness, as a result of which Scudamour's experience seems too self-contradictory to qualify as an event. They should congratulate themselves, rather, on discovering the poet's point.

In accordance with the italicized lines in stanza 44, Care's disturbance of Scudamour's sleep leaves him with uncertain and unverifiable 'gealous dread' (45). It does not derive from and force him back upon any waking obsession with Ate's revelation. So his continuation of 'his former voiage' (46), in the certainty of Britomart's guilt, does not follow on from Canto v. But neither does it follow on from Canto i, supposing we could just ignore the Care episode in order to save the story. For in Canto i he does not set off in pursuit of Britomart but challenges Glauce instead. We do not hear of any designs against Britomart until his re-emergence in Canto v. It 'explains' the new course of his vengeance by presenting as counter-productive Glauce's attempts to make him see reason, which, in Canto i, are said to prove ultimately effective and thus earn her the lofty comparison with Orpheus, David, and Menenius Agrippa in the opening stanzas of Canto ii: a fine contradiction. Nor does Spenser describe Scudamour's search for Britomart. His grand encounter with her in Canto vi, while apparently its intended culmination, is entirely accidental. It results from his chance meeting with Artegall, who happens to bear a grudge against Britomart himself. Actually, 'results' is saying too much; for Artegall, so far from seeking out Britomart, waits in the woods so that he may attack this 'stranger knight . . . When ever he this way shall passe by day or night' (5). That she comes his way at all, and that at once, is purely fortuitous. And then, how can Artegall's reference to her 'Hebene speare' identify her for Scudamour? As far as we can tell, he has never seen her wield it or, indeed, a spear of any description. And the epithet 'Hebene' is peculiar to IV. v (8, 20): elsewhere the spear is, if anything, 'enchaunted'.

Let us see if the grand encounter itself will survive scrutiny as narrative. It is awkward that Scudamour attacks Britomart without stating his grievance, so that she has no opportunity to undeceive him by voluntarily revealing her sex. But perhaps this could be accounted for 'naturalistically' by postulating blind fury, due to (intermittent) certainty of her crime. What passes credibility, however, is that he should address her as 'Sir' (34) *after* the revelation of her sex; a revelation which affects him so powerfully (24, 28) that it could not possibly have slipped from his mind. Nor is the address simply a slip of the pen on Spenser's part: Britomart herself clearly reassumes the role of Amoret's male lover, here—

Ne ever was there wight to me more deare
Then she, ne unto whom I more true love did beare

(35)

—and in Canto ix, where, again in Scudamour's presence, she speaks of her painful search for 'my former love . . . that gentle maide' after having been addressed by Arthur as 'sir Knight' (38, 37). Scudamour now tolerates and accepts as his search companion one who openly professes to be a rival lover. How could he, even if he should no longer believe Ate? Are we to insist, with supreme indifference to the actual text, that really he must know Britomart's true sex? If so, can we accept the corollary, that Spenser has written an *exemplum* of agonizing jealousy due, trivially and most untypically, to mistaken sexual identity? How could we be morally enlightened by the knowledge that Scudamour's anxiety happens to be much ado about nothing? Only if we interpret symbolically. Friendship almost realizes the glory of love. Amoret's fearfulness and Britomart's dubious behaviour (i. 5, 7), Blandamour's taunts to Scudamour—'so hast thou to thy selfe false honour often wonne' (44), 'thy vaine boast, and spoile of love misgotten' (51)—and Scudamour's vulnerability to Ate, 'delusion', are so many reminders that, for the Time being, love cannot manifest its glorious essence. That is why Glauce 'sufferance desired, / Till *time* the tryall of her truth *expyred*' (54). Yet we are never in doubt that Amoret's fears are unfounded, that Britomart means well, that Blandamour does not deserve credit. And Scudamour proves more than a match for Paridell. Canto vi conveys the same emphasis. Although Britomart cannot register as woman (glory), Scudamour takes 'him' on trust as Amoret's lover; not as a person joining forces with a rival, which would be absurd, but as one personification signalling its equivalence to another. He allows her to identify herself with him, as he does in the Busirane episode. But there they are at once parted by the flaming porch, so that each becomes separately the other's whole counterpart, in token of chastity. Here they remain united to represent each other separately together, in token of friendship.

Developments during their joint search for Amoret leave

something to be desired as narrative. Granted, it makes sequential sense for the quarrelsome quartet to remember Britomart as having 'shamefully fordonne' them at Satyrane's tournament—or at least for Blandamour: Druon and Claribell are not mentioned by name in Canto iv, and who shall say whether even Paridell, who earlier on in the Book wisely shuns an encounter with Britomart (i. 34–5), was among the 'full many others . . . likewise dismounted' (iv. 46)? But had Britomart 'eke the famous prize of beauty from them wonne' (ix. 28)? Theoretically, yes (v. 20). But she had refused the snowy Florimell, whom the cestus would not fit and who preferred Braggadochio anyway. Why should the kinghts delay their pursuit of false Florimell (v. 28; ix. 24) even more than they are doing already, by attacking Britomart as well as each other? After all, she is not responsible for her disappearance. Indeed, she could be said to have ingratiated herself with them by renouncing her rightful claims (v. 21). To match this incongruity we have Britomart's statement to Arthur that she has lost Amoret as a result of the tournament and the beauty contest (ix. 38). This is untrue: in v. 29 she rides off with Amoret for companion. She does not indicate any such causal connection in vi. 35–6; nor does Spenser, in vii. 3–4.

As for Scudamour's tale, it does not suit its occasion quite well enough to allow literal reading. One expects that, having told the climactic story of how he once conquered Amoret, he will revert ruefully to his present forlorn condition. But he does not. Nor is this story calculated to stabilize good relations. It rubs in the notion of his glorious achievement, the very cause of Blandamour's hatred. Of course, Scudamour does not force it upon his audience: it is they who ask for it. And they specifically want to hear 'all that adventure which [he] did assay / For that faire Ladies love' (ix. 40). Its pervasive note of triumph might simply reflect the scope of their request. Moreover, Claribell realizes that they are imposing 'so sad a taske'. 'Nessun maggior dolore / che ricordarsi del tempo felice / nella miseria.'[43] But then, why do they make the request at all? If they are intent on sealing the reconciliation, they should not prod Scudamour's wound. Presumably it implies that they, including Blandamour, are ready to accept the tale's truth. Spenser does not say so, though, and refrains from giving their reactions. Indeed, he refrains from continuing the Scudamour-Amoret fiction altogether; for good, as far as we can see, thus leaving it oddly suspended. Scudamour confirms our growing suspicion that the scene is not in the nature of an event by saying:

> For from the first that I her love profest,
> Unto this houre, this present lucklesse howre,
> I *never* joyed happinesse nor rest.
>
> (39.)

If this is true, he cannot go on to tell about any past 'safe' conquest of Amoret. Yet he does precisely that. And note the crowning absurdity. When Britomart and Scudamour voice their complaints about having lost Amoret, she is, with Arthur, in their very presence (20). If, as Lewis thinks, Spenser intended to reuse the original ending of Book III, with its rapturous union of Scudamour and Amoret, this would have been the place to do so. Upton feels that we should make good the poet's omission.[44] He ought to have wondered why the poet did not forestall us. Spenser both generates and thwarts a compulsion to supply the happy ending so that we may infer both that love is not yet finished yet also that the manœuvre would be superfluous: Amoret's obvious proximity to Scudamour is synonymous with their Hermaphroditic embrace. The difference in intensity between the two scenes corresponds to the relative position of the Middle Books' quests, unfolded in 1596, infolded in 1590.

(ii) *At the Temple*

Critics regard Scudamour's story in Canto x as an allegory of a courtship, even though it can almost be read literally as a quest while the knight refers to it as such: 'this same brave emprize' (4), 'that hard adventure' (5). One can see how the mistake has arisen. The story occupies only one out of twelve Cantos. It features no single power of evil. It apparently leads up to the wedding in IV. i. 2. And, what has perhaps been most decisive, it seems to be an exponent of a familiar genre whose mainspring is the thirteenth-century French *Roman de la Rose*; a poem which, according to C. S. Lewis's influential reading, presents, by means of personifications, the love story of two people, the dreamer and the lady. But this reading will not do. Lewis is rightly struck by the contrast between the 'presence' of the personifications and the virtual 'absence' of dreamer and lady. However, his explanation issues not so much from the *Roman* itself as from his comparison of it with 'a curious little dialogue [by] Mr. Aldous Huxley', which he declares to be 'the best preparation for a study of Guillaume de Lorris' (astonishingly, in view of his more-than-one-hundred-page endeavour to get 'courtly love' and 'allegory' into a proper historical perspective). 'In the first place [the poet] practically abolishes the hero, as one of his dramatis personae, by reducing him to the colourless teller of the tale. The whole poem is in the first person and we look through the lover's eyes, not at him. In the second place he removes the heroine entirely. Her character is distributed among personifications.' Where, pray, do we see Guillaume doing any such thing? How do we know that what is not there has been abolished or removed? And why should we undo Guillaume's labours of annihilation? We had better stick with the rose and the insubstantial hero—whom, incidentally, there is little point in calling 'dreamer' or 'narrator', since the narrated dream is coextensive with the poem: there are no waking experiences or other people. Now 'rose' and 'I' are not persons emptied out but personifications (of 'cunnus' and 'will'). If, as Lewis correctly observes, 'you cannot really have the lady, and, say, the lady's Pride, walking about on the same stage as though they were entities on the same plane', that stage will not support a lover either, no matter how residual. Anyway, the *Roman* is too exhaustive and too schematic an account of courting to qualify as the story of individual lovers. One would be hard put to it to extract a single, intelligibly motivated development. Speech and action of the personifications supposedly representing the lovers' progress suggest self-definition rather than interaction. Their liveliness and occasional verisimilitude cannot make them ersatz persons. Moreover, Lewis sees perfectly well that not all the personifications qualify as moods of lover and lady. He ought to have questioned his conception of Guillaume's mode, instead of rushing to the conclusion that the poet's execution is flawed.[45]

In so far as Spenser's Temple of Venus episode belongs generically with the *Roman*, it resists the Lewis approach even more than does the *Roman* itself, on precisely the same grounds. Let us take them in reverse order. The 'bevie of fayre damzels', Womanhood, Shamefastnesse, Cherefulnesse, Modestie, Curtesie, Silence, Obedience, can hardly represent a succession of attitudes that Amoret adopts towards Scudamour, since the poet crowds them together in a small space and places Amoret 'in the midst of them' (48–52). They cannot even be regarded as an analysis of a single, complex attitude; for Amoret is not in fact cheerful, nor unhesitatingly obedient, nor silent, when Scudamour leads her away (55–7). Similarly, Love and Hate are too patently contrasting abstractions to symbolize stages in Amoret's feelings or the paradoxical 'odi et amo' of Catullus (32–6). Lewis's decision that Daunger, while signifying 'danger' in III. xii. 11, stands for 'refusal, or difficult granting, of love' in IV. x. 17 begs the question.[46] How could such an attitude involve 'hatred, murther, treason, and despight . . . in ambushment . . . awayting to entrap the warelesse wight' (20)? These unfold 'danger', rather. Furthermore, Scudamour's adventure, so far from being a series of quick, on-the-spot reactions to a lady's whims or at least a strategy being put to the test, has all the orderliness and serenity of a prefabricated ritual. It is virtually mapped out for him, and he could almost be said to tick off its various stages as a matter of routine. On its own small scale it is, if anything, even more exhaustive and schematic than the *Roman.* And then, since persons and personifications cannot possibly interact, Spenser's hero and heroine must be personifications, just like the other characters. For example, we do not see Scudamour coming to grips with his own doubt or dispelling somebody else's: we see him forcing the porter Doubt to give way by the display of his shield. So he cannot be a person; unless 'Doubt' should be a nickname for somebody whose real name, Tom, Dick, or Harry, remains undisclosed (12–14). But with his 'double face' the porter classifies himself so evidently with what Joseph Spence calls 'ridiculous imaginations'[47] that he has no serious claims to personhood. Now if Scudamour and Amoret are personifications, it would be gratuitous indeed to assert that they are personifications of themselves.

Spenser's couple is perhaps less apt to create the impression of being abolished than are the *Roman*'s alleged protagonists. Yet, as in the Busirane episode, they are not really 'there'. Amoret figures only in the last few stanzas. And these do not explain her reluctance to leave the Temple in terms of any negative response to her captor. As for Scudamour, his prominence is almost vacuous, in that the sheer objectivity of his tale nearly extinguishes him as a 'consciousness'. Instead of thinking all the time of the prize to be won, he seems to savour the several stages of his adventure for their own sakes. His dealings with his antagonists are effortless and leisurely, without any gradual building up of tension as, approaching his goal, he finds yet more obstacles or distractions. Even the sight of Amoret herself occasions not a lover's awestruck or enraptured awareness of 'the other' but a fleeting, impersonal uneasiness about the adventure's propriety:

> Whom soone as I beheld, my hart gan throb,
> And wade in doubt, what best were to be donne:
> For sacrilege me seem'd the Church to rob,
> And folly seem'd to leave the thing undonne,
> Which with so strong attempt I had begonne.
>
> (53.)

Nor, of course, does he respond at all to Amoret's entreaties: he carries her off as though she were an inanimate object (just as in the 1590 ending of Book III they embrace 'like two senceles stocks'—45). One would have to sympathize with those who find him culpably masterful, were it not that his obliviousness of Amoret is all-pervasive. Yet the 'negative presence' of the pair constitutes no very powerful temptation, as it does in the *Roman*, to treat them as people exteriorized in the personifications. For not only do these not qualify as moods or attitudes, as we have already observed: they are also notably perfunctory, lacking the vividness and *enargeia* that mark so many of the *Roman*'s characters.

So even *qua* mini-*Roman* Canto x is not the prelude to a marriage. The generic similarity implies that Scudamour cannot really be a narrator any more than Guillaume's 'I'.

Literally he does adopt that role at the end of Canto ix. But supposing he should be a person there, he could not conceivably start reminiscing about previous exploits as a personification. Also, in his *exordium* Scudamour says: 'Of my love at length I rest *assured*, / That to disloyalty she will not be allured' (x. 2). Now it is not given to people to know the future with certainty. Could it not be, though, that he simply expresses his personal conviction? No; for we have conclusive evidence, earlier on in Book IV, that he lacks such conviction. Or is it, perhaps, that he speaks of a recently acquired conviction? Does 'at length . . . assured' not mean 'persuaded at long last'? After all, Amoret is, when he tells his tale, 'she whom I behold' (4). Might his faith not be inspired by her visible presence? No again; for he has had her more than just visibly present before, as his tale testifies, only to lose her. More important, he does not merely 'count as naught, and tread downe under feet' (2) any anxieties *now*: repeating the burden of his complaint in ix. 39, namely that he '*never* joyed howre, but *still* with care was moved' (x. 1), to bring out the endless prolongation of his trouble, he aligns himself with those to whom 'all the cares and evill which they meet, / May nought at all their *setled mindes* remove' (2). Despite his permanent 'martyrdome' he is permanently assured, certain, thanks to 'grace . . . given . . . from above', of his love's consummation 'at length', in Eternity, thus symbolizing friendship, *almost* transparent glory.

Scudamour's tale itself may seem to lack the qualification altogether. Or are we to supply the fateful wedding? By no means. The appearance is deceptive. We cannot, as in real stories, detach the action from the setting and summarize it as 'Scudamour tries to get Amoret and succeeds'. To begin with, not only are they not individual lovers but, unlike 'I' and 'rose' in the *Roman*, their relation, even as personifications, is not one of purposive drive as against object of that drive. They are equivalent personifications, whom this Canto polarizes as purpose and goal in the same sense in which Canto v polarizes Care and Scudamour as agent and patient. Moreover—and this is another crucial difference from the *Roman*—the fiction does not symbolize anything remotely like 'plucking the rose'. Scudamour and Amoret are defined, independently but similarly, through the setting. They almost infold into the androgynous Venus behind the veil. The goddess, too, almost manifests her true self. The veil is 'slender'. Her twin legs are joined by the self-devouring serpent of Eternity (40). She stands upon an altar of 'costly', if still 'brickle', material, 'likest glasse', 'yet glasse was not' (39), closely approximating the fabric of *Pan*thea (I. x. 58) while still sacrificial.

And all about her necke and shoulders flew
  A flocke of little loves, and sports, and joyes,
  With nimble wings of gold and purple hew;
  Whose shapes seem'd not like to terrestriall boyes,
  But like to Angels playing heavenly toyes;
  The whilest their eldest brother was away,
  Cupid their eldest brother; he enjoyes
  The wide kingdome of love with Lordly sway,
And to his law compels all creatures to obay.

(42.)

Heaven shines through. Cupid reigns, with a cruelty alluded to only implicitly. True, he is still 'away', 'the whilest', hiding his oneness for the Time being. But Venus, who in Book III had 'left her heavenly hous' (vi. 12) to pursue him on earth and adopted as a substitute an Amoret of highly vulnerable wholeness, here stays in her Temple, also a heavenly house, adopting as a substitute a multiplicity of 'little loves', Amoretti, with mere streaks of purple in their wings (in contrast with Prays-desire's completely purple pall—II. ix. 37) and so undifferentiated in their togetherness as almost to obliterate their separation. Moreover, she has with her the one true Amoret as well, whom she does indeed let go, to convey commitment to virtue, but without any misgivings. Amoret herself is specified by a 'bevie of fayre damzels' gathered so closely together as to keep her almost infolded. And are Womanhood, Shamefastnesse, Cherefulnesse, Modestie, Curtesie, Silence, and Obedience not all qualities that take the sting out of separateness? Now Spenser symbolizes exactly the same meaning through Scudamour and Amoret together, united by consent of Venus in her innermost sanctuary but in a union as yet to be lived out beyond its precincts, safely in the midst of danger (58). We must not regard Amoret's reluctance to follow Scudamour, with Hieatt, as an implicit indictment of his character. Roche rightly insists that 'Scudamour's *keckheit* is not culpable but absolutely requisite for his task'. However, it is blandly wrong to assert that 'from this initial discord of the lovers will grow their love'.[48] There is no discord between them. Amoret's reluctance to leave the Temple equals Scudamour's reluctance 'the Church to rob' (53). Instead there is discord between Eternity and Time, which remains an enemy to love even as friendship.

Only consistently allegorical reading bears out the adequacy of the Legend's thematic rubric. Half measures make nonsense of it; and of themselves. Thus, in an effort to do justice both to the supposed story of Scudamour and Amoret and to the unmistakable theme of concord Roche, who calls the Canto 'an emblematic exemplum of the theme of *discordia concors* in a courtship', finds himself claiming that sex is 'subordinated to the non-physical aspects of love, to love as it appears in society' in that Spenser names the pairs of friends but not the pairs of lovers (25–7).[49] Let us for a moment suppose that, as Lewis also says, the episode concerns 'love as a conventional social form', 'Nature and Art in happy symbiosis'.[50] How could sex, the constitutive factor of that love, be subordinated? How are the non-physical aspects of love not sexual? How is love as it appears in society non-physical? Be that as it may, the subordination could not without incongruity be proclaimed by Scudamour, allegedly in the very process of seeking to make Amoret his bedfellow. Nor could this proclamation take the form of extolling male friendship. For this is not a socialization of sexual love. In fact Scudamour quietly identifies himself with the lover who, in a great Lucretian passage, addresses Venus as the genius not only of natural harmony but of generation (43–8). If there is to be subordination at all, one would have to side with Lewis, who says that 'friends are found to be merely "another sort of lovers" ' (26).[51] But then, 'merely' is not in Spenser's text, not even by implication. Since sexual lovers are mentioned before male friends, Scudamour's indefinite envy of '*their* endlesse happinesse', mentioned subsequently, cannot apply specifically to the former. Anyway, Lewis's statement is illogical. Unlike Spenser he uses 'love' to mean 'married sexual love'. The love of male friends, presented emphatically as non-sexual in the very stanza he quotes from, could not possibly be a subcategory of that.

These tangles can be avoided. Scudamour does not *exemplify* erotic love, apparently to the exclusion of male friendship: he *personifies* ἀγάπη, companionship irrespective of sex. St. Paul uses ἀγαπάω not just generally for the love of the brethren but also specifically in injunctions to husbands to love their wives.[52] He does not mean that marriage is a social convention in conforming to which they will sublimate their sexual passion, presumed rampant. He means, rather, that marriage, apart from being one of the two states in which to attain sexual wholeness, constitutes, as a lasting mutual commitment, the most revealing form of non-sexual togetherness; *non-sexual*, because this togetherness virtually equals the oneness that makes the distinction between male and female inoperative.[53] (Of course, the distinction remains in fact. And spouses should make the most of it. The point is that sex is strictly for wholeness. If mistaken, as it easily can be, for a means of togetherness, it is really lust. Hence Lust appears not in the Legend of Chastity but in the Legend of Friendship, as pseudo-ἀγάπη, philandering.) All this is not to deny the sexiness of the episode. Scudamour and Amoret are, after all, lover and lady as well as knight and prize. It is to specify it as a property of the fiction *qua* vehicle, as we did the far headier sexiness of the Bower of Bliss, in Section IV of Chapter One. It might be objected that in our Canto sex invades the heart of the tenor: its pivot is a Venus *genetrix* who must be goddess of procreation conceptually, since nothing suggests that Scudamour and Amoret, who are defined in relation to her, literally want a baby. Fair enough. But does this imply that for Spenser friendship does not come into its own without a stiff dose of sex? Surely not. Venus does not stand for generation here any more than she does in the Garden of Adonis Canto. Instead she symbolizes love, transcendent union, as affected by generation, the cause of separateness. Committing her divine glory to Time, like Gloriana, she happily embraces generation: in Book III, as chastity, to contain the process; in Book IV, as friendship, to join its results.

Let us now go through the Canto to make sure that the (significantly) strong appearance of internal sequence is indeed illusory. The 'background' of the story readily segments it. The greater part, from the twenty-first up to but not including the last stanza, is set 'within the compasse of that Islands space', with 'right in the midst the Goddesse selfe'.[54] The ten stanzas preceding this segment and the one following it are set on the bridge connecting the island with the mainland. Scudamour's first action, his defeat of the twenty knights and his winning of the shield, take place on the mainland itself (7–10). One might think that both these knights and Doubt, Delay, and Daunger, who man the bridge, are simply obstacles trying to prevent access or, failing that, to hamper progress. Not so. As for the knights, their 'office was, against all manner wights / By all meanes to maintaine that castels ancient rights'. Only shoddy reading translates this as 'no entry'. The castle 'warded all which in or out did wend' (7). This suggests regular traffic across the bridge. The reference might be to, say, routine food supplies. Nothing warrants this specification, though. What the 'ancient rights' are is not said explicitly; but one infers that they include a positive invitation to enter for those who can win the shield:

> Blessed be the man that well can use his bliss:
> Whose ever be the shield, faire Amoret be his.
>
> (8.)

This, the pillar's inscription, could be regarded as a trap, since we learn that the shield was 'of many sought in vaine'. On this view Scudamour would be an unforeseen exception, putting a stop to an evil practice. The truth is less perverse. '*Many* sought in vaine.' But friendship, which is nearly 'one', succeeds by definition, almost. And are we not made to take Scudamour's success just about for granted? After all, we have known him practically from the first as the possessor of the shield (from III. xi. 7; vi. 53 does not mention it). Indeed, he derives his name from it. Now, as the inscription implies, the winning of the shield guarantees the conquest of

Amoret. Therefore it cannot really be the first in a genuine sequence of entry tests, as though Scudamour could still fail later on. He hardly needs the shield as a means. It is primarily a prize. Only he cannot yet have it as a trophy 'hangd *on high* with *golden* ribbands laced', just as he cannot remain with Amoret in the Temple.

As for Doubt, Delay, and Daunger, who certainly try to impede Scudamour's progress, they contradict the function of the bridge, a passage way (6). On the incorrect assumption that they represent the attitude of an individual Amoret, this would be a forbidding attitude. Hence, whether real or pretended, it could not possibly *be* the bridge to her heart. Scudamour overcomes the three without changing their dispositions; naturally, since they are personifications anchored in their meanings. On the psychological approach this would suggest that he rapes Amoret's (apparent) feelings: not exactly an exploit to be recounted proudly in public. However, it is strange, on any approach, that further obstructions should be put in the way of someone who has just qualified for entrance; especially since they would not really be *further* obstructions: the battle with the twenty knights has already put in doubt, delayed, and endangered Scudamour's access. Sequential reading does not make sense. Conceptual reading does. Friendship is already manifestly Time's bridge to Eternity—a bridge, not quite Eternity itself, owing to the persistence of separateness, which, however, causes no more than negligible Doubt, Delay, and Daunger to oneness.

Since the bridge is a metaphor, Scudamour does not enter heaven after crossing it. This warning may be in order, for the island is notably paradisiacal. Indeed, Scudamour 'thought there was none other heaven then this' (28). This phrasing puts us on our guard, though. Red Cross, too, 'weened well, / That great Cleopolis . . . The fairest Citie was, that might be seene' (I. x. 58). And Spenser himself says of the Garden of Adonis: 'Well I wote by tryall, that this same / All other pleasant places doth excell' (III. vi. 29). Red Cross recognizes his mistake. And Spenser expects us to realize that he did not, of course, 'try' heaven. It would seem that Scudamour does not retract his interpretation. Probably, though, few have followed him in his error. On the contrary, most readers, assuming that his words are loosely hyperbolic, will not sense any error at all. They take it that the scene is the poet's idealized, but strictly non-figurative, picture of friendship in a harmonious setting, meant to prompt their enthusiasm as it does Scudamour's. It certainly evokes the life of Horatian *otium* to which some Renaissance minds aspired. But the evocation serves precisely to suggest the scene's absurdity. Could the poet really be urging us to dedicate ourselves to a perpetual stroll through an actualized *locus amoenus*? Is friendship only for those with estates and no work on their hands? And how about the climate at British latitudes? Anyway, what is so attractive about a place where 'thousand payres of lovers walkt . . . Ne ever ought but of their true loves talkt' (25)? Let us not credit Spenser with such imbecile dreams and pretend that they charm and morally rejuvenate us. The scene multiplies couples of lovers and friends in order to symbolize friendship as separate multiplicity for the most part ingathered. Its very closeness to a literal *exemplum* constitutes an allegorical expression of that virtue's near approximation to glory. In this complex metaphor Scudamour's rapturous misinterpretation is the component that brings out its apparent heavenliness. By contrast, the setting, while supporting this emphasis, highlights the qualification, 'almost'. In ἀγάπη nature is transformed beyond recognition: 'All which by nature made did nature selfe amaze' (24). But nature has not yet vanished. Nor has it been restored to pre-lapsarian splendour: 'Art playing second natures part' supplies 'all that nature did omit' (21). The Island Paradise is an aspect of the Bower of Bliss.

Scudamour *does* retract his interpretation: implicitly he razes the Paradise as Guyon does the Bower. His entry belies its message, for without Amoret he is the odd one out. To be sure, it leads to his union with Amoret. But then, on his return with her he does not, as one would expect, join the happy couples. He does not even mention the Paradise again. Has it mysteriously disappeared? If so, why does he not register surprise and disappointment? Because he dispels it himself (and the story with it). The sacrifice remains implicit because, while harrowing to temperance, it is almost painless to friendship. This idea of a sacrifice could indeed be dismissed as an interpreter's fantasy, were it not that Scudamour is more clearly disruptive inside the Temple, actively and passively. In the face of logic, it is when 'past all perill' (21), with Daunger left behind on the bridge, that he has to seek Amoret 'through paines and perlous jeopardie' (28). In the Temple porch he is 'halfe dismayed' (36)—strangely, for a knight who has dauntlessly unseated twenty adversaries and mastered the bridge without any misgivings, especially because Love and Concord restrain Hate for him: he does not have to lift a finger in his own defence. Once inside he associates himself with 'great sorts of lovers piteously complayning' (43). His shield, 'on which the winged boy in colours cleare / Depeincted was' (III. xi. 7), has undergone a frightening transformation, to reveal 'Cupid with his killing bow / And cruell shafts' (IV. x. 55). And, of course, he 'robs the church' of Amoret, leading her into Daunger. In survey Scudamour's role looks so *ominously* approximate that one hastens to plunge it back into its context. His envy of the couples in their Paradise, his fear of Hate, the plight of his fellow lovers, and his heartfelt amen to their spokesman's complaint get a stanza or less each only; while the complaint is in fact a hymn apart from the last line: 'O graunt that of my love *at last* I may not misse' (47). Even the fateful abduction of Amoret takes place under the benign auspices of a laughing Venus. The meaning of the episode agrees almost with its impact *qua* narrative: Scudamour triumphant. That the triumph is, as yet, ἐκ μέρους goes almost unnoticed, like the non-Aristotelian rationale of the fiction.

Three

BRITOMART AND ARTEGALL

I The Flashback

(i) *Canto ii*

If the Scudamour–Amoret fiction is only apparent narrative, the Britomart fiction, with which it intersects at so many points, cannot be real narrative. However, her 'story' contains theirs as a mere strand. And her changing relationship with Artegall, from search in Book III through discovery in Book IV to rescue in Book V, strongly suggests genuine sequence. So a logical short cut will not carry conviction. To explode the Britomart narrative this Chapter examines her two great Artegall episodes, in Books IV and V. And since the former is also one of her two great Scudamour episodes, we shall reconsider the other, in Book III, from her angle. But first we must attend to the flashback (III. ii. 17–iii. 62), which contributes most to the illusion that she has a developing love story, just as the illusion of Arthur's purposeful advance through the several Books derives largely from the recollection of his erotic dream (I. ix. 8–15). The flashback consists of three sections, the mirror scene, the consultation of Merlin, and the departure for Faeryland. These do not even constitute a continuous mini-story. Instead they introduce in small compass the three temporal aspects of eternal oneness, which the Legends of Chastity, Friendship, and Justice embody on a large scale.

Long ago Merritt Y. Hughes called the mirror scene a 'prelude of sentiment and idealism' to Britomart's love story, 'indispensable for Spenser'.[1] Modern interpreters, mindful of the teachings of the New Critics, are careful not to profess any such insight into the poet's psychological make-up, or at least to disguise it respectably by submerging his mind into the collective unconscious. Yet their response to the passage has not changed as much as critical sophistication and a volte-face in literary theory suggest. Even the two critics who positively insist on the inadequacy of novelistic reading treat the scene very much as though it were indeed the prelude to a real love story. C. S. Lewis concedes that 'occasionally, of course, [the poet] makes a very brief approach to the kind of fiction now valued in the novel: the conversation between the lovesick Britomart and her nurse, for example'. According to him Spenser regards Britomart's looking in the mirror to see her future husband as 'the ordinary action of a normal woman'.[2] Alpers would have us adopt towards Britomart the attitude of experienced middle age, smiling in sympathy with a girl profoundly discomfited by the pangs of first love, patting her reassuringly on the back in the knowledge that 'her feelings are perfectly natural' and that 'she will finally meet her lover'.[3] Perhaps the episode does invite the kind of distanced empathy commonly required of novel readers. However, we must respect Spenser's presentation of his heroine's plight. We are not entitled to normalize and domesticate it as these critics do. It is by no means natural for Britomart to see her future lover in a mirror: '*By straunge occasion* she did him behold, / And *much more strangely* gan to love his sight' (18). True, she seems to believe as a matter of course that the mirror will reveal 'whom fortune for her husband would allot' (21). But Spenser's emphatic reiteration implies that magic cannot be taken for granted. We might regard her action as the courtly counterpart of a regular Celtic folk custom, as described, for instance, in Mary O'Holleran's reminiscences of girlhood scenes with Nora Barnacle in Galway:

> we would steal a head of cabbage out of a garden we never stood in before on a moonlight night on Hallow eve and have a mirror we would go into a field and stand on a dunghill and eat the head of cabbage and looking through the mirror to see if we could see the face of our future husband . . .[4]

Not surprisingly, we do not learn that Nora actually saw the portrait of the artist she was to marry. Again, it is by no means natural for Britomart, supposing she has simply fallen in love, to be adamant that her plight is unique and irremediable:

> neither God of love, nor God of sky
> Can doe (said she) that, which cannot be done,
>
> For no no usuall fire, no usuall rage
> It is, O Nurse, which on my life doth feed.
>
> (36, 37.)

These are hardly the words of your typical teenage lass. Nor is it natural for Glauce to attempt to exorcize the passion through magical rites; and, ineffectual though they are, the seriousness of the situation forbids us to take them as a grotesque comedy of superstition. Lewis and Alpers have perpetrated a critical crime: they distort the scene's tonal and atmospheric impact, neutralizing its mystery and fatefulness out of existence.

This ironying out, so to speak, of local texture clearly results from the conviction that there is a real, continuing Britomart-Artegall love story, presided over by an ultimately benign Providence offering the cue for the reader's stance. Prompted by the 'impossibility' of the magical event, critics treat it as a symbol only to make it mean incipient love as part of a story. Thus Nelson:

> despite its magical trappings, the process Spenser describes is real enough. Love begins, he is saying, not at first sight, but with an envisagement of what the beloved should be. This envisagement depends, in turn, upon the nature of the lover himself. . . . The ideal having been imagined, the lover must then find its fleshly counterpart.[5]

Alternatively, MacCaffrey:

> love's consummation ensues upon the recognition of the beloved as he is, not as a projection of desire. When [Britomart] falls in love with Artegall, he exists for her only in the 'world of glass' that is Merlin's mirror. Loving this 'shade', she lives in the world of imagination, and that . . . is . . . a kind of death. . . . Britomart must pull herself away from the self-regarding world of glass and enter the world of actual men and women.[6]

Both quotations, contradictory as they are in their valuation of the mirror, illustrate to perfection the pernicious inbreeding of vehicle and tenor that has been the bane of Spenser studies. Britomart does not 'envisage' or 'project' Artegall before she meets him in the flesh. How could she conjure up an identifying image (IV. vi. 26) of a person she does not know? She literally sees him in a mirror. This mirror might conceivably symbolize *the* imagination. It could not possibly symbolize *Britomart's* imagination, though. People *use* their faculties; they do not consult symbols of them. (Nor, for that matter, of anything else. Thus to say that 'the *looking glasse* . . . is not a mirror . . . but a "glassie globe" . . . which signifies fragile marital harmony in Renaissance iconography (Panofsky, 1962, 162)' is a useless, if learned, assertion, as well as a false denial.[7]) Since its impossible properties make the mirror a symbol, Britomart must be a symbol too. And as such she cannot have a love life, except metaphorically.

The nature of Britomart's distress is unintelligible to a literal reader. It is not the miraculousness of Artegall's appearance in the mirror that bowls her over (see 26). Neither does the experience of love *per se* disturb her, to judge from her rejection of Glauce's diagnosis, 'aye me, how much I feare, least love it bee' (33). Nor does she seem to be apprehensive about the character and inclinations of Artegall, whom, after all, she does not know, or dismayed at the prospect of having to search for him. Instead she despairs because 'th'only shade and semblant of a knight . . . Hath me subjected to loves cruell law' (38). This is extraordinary. Mirrors, even magical mirrors, produce images, not substances, or they would not be mirrors. She cannot logically expect anything else. Is she, perhaps, suddenly overcome by doubts about the existence of the image's corresponding reality, in view of Glauce's consoling admonition that 'no shadow, but a bodie hath in powre' (45)? She never says so. And her self-deprecation, 'I fonder, then Cephisus foolish child . . . I fonder love a shade, the bodie farre exild' (44), makes sense only if she assumes that the substance does exist. The girl's implicit faith in the mirror's magical control of the future when she might have been entirely sceptical can only have been strengthened by its performance. And since it presents a picture of what promises to be an admirable knight, who does not fail to take her fancy, her anguished response seems not just premature but utterly gratuitous. We have here a stark incongruity that eludes sympathetic understanding and offers no scope even for paternal drooling.

Britomart's own explanation for her profound distress leaves one blank with incomprehension. However, alert scrutiny of the actual text enables us, just about, to supply a cause that might save the story. Merlin made the mirror such that 'what ever foe had wrought, or frend had faynd, / Therein discovered was' (19). And he gave it not to Britomart, so that she might know her amorous destiny, but to her father, king Ryence,

> for his gard,
> That never foes his kingdome might invade,
> But he it knew at home before he hard
> Tydings thereof, and so them still debar'd.
> (21.)

As a matter of fact, Britomart does not make for the mirror with the set purpose of finding out whom she will marry. She comes upon it accidentally ('it fortuned'), looks in it casually ('her selfe a while therein she vewd in vaine'), and then, reminding herself of its powers, watches more carefully in order to discover nothing more specific than what 'mote to her selfe pertaine' (22). If, in the next stanza, her curiosity becomes specifically marital, it is not because sex asserts itself but because marriage traditionally determines a girl's whole future, stamping it with the character, status, and occupation of her husband:

> Not that she lusted after any one;
> For she was pure from blame of sinfull blot,
> Yet wist her life at last must lincke in that same knot.

Now if the mirror was fabricated for the express purpose of revealing hostile projects, Artegall might be not simply Britomart's destined bridegroom but an enemy to Ryence's kingdom. Spenser's congratulation of Ryence on possessing Merlin's present, 'happie this Realme, had it remained ever since' (21), must be ironic, since the disappearance of Deheubarth implies the inefficacy of the mirror. So does the illogicality of its protective power: it does not help the king to *debar* foes, showing, as it does, their *invasion* (in process, not merely planned, for secret schemes hardly produce 'tydings'[8]). If Artegall should be invading the realm, Britomart's distress stands to reason.

Although this explanation is purely inferential, it derives implicit support from the poet's sources. It is a commonplace of Spenser criticism that Britomart and Artegall are broadly modelled on Ariosto's Bradamante and Ruggiero. These characters are not simply lovers: they are champions of different nations engaged in a religious war. Their commitment to each other is acutely at odds with their commitment to their respective leaders, Charlemagne and Agramante. Spenser's borrowing from his Italian predecessor could be meant to signal a similar complication in the love of Britomart and Artegall. And there is another, even more telling analogue. As Hughes points out, the story of Glauce and Britomart in Canto ii is 'Spenser's greatest single debt to Virgil. . . . His source was the *Ciris*.'[9] He contents himself with listing similarities in wording and characterization. It never occurs to him to wonder *why* Spenser should have echoed so distinctly a passage from this (pseudo-)Virgilian poem. *Ciris* tells of Scylla's fateful love for Minos, the Cretan king besieging Megara, the city of her father Nisus, the safety of which depends on his lock of hair. Carme, Scylla's nurse, tries her magical charms on king Nisus, so that he may give up his opposition to Scylla's desire—in vain. Scylla, driven on by her passion, cuts the lock and Megara is ruined. Surely we are meant to take the whole dramatic situation of the Latin poem as a matrix for Spenser's episode. Artegall is to Britomart and her father's kingdom what Minos is to Scylla and her father's city. Britomart resembles Scylla in helplessly causing the state's doom in her love. After all, she casts her shadow Artegall. The poet encourages us to embrace this large-scale parallelism by contradicting Virgil in his more obvious small-scale borrowing: Glauce, Britomart's nurse, tries her magical charms not on king Ryence but on Britomart herself. Though this contradiction also makes for self-sufficiency, its message cannot be simply 'never mind Virgil', in an episode so unmistakably Virgilian.

Yet, fitting and, indeed, inescapable though the overall parallels are, they will not be accepted without demur. For

Spenser does not recreate 'the whole dramatic situation' in Virgil. *Ciris* presents an emergency, with the unbending wills and drives of its protagonists vividly realized. We detect clearly the logic of fate. Scylla's love is uncontrollable. Nisus refuses to compromise by letting her leave the city, even after Carme's efforts. Hence she is bound, as a last resort, to cut her father's talismanic lock, thus ruining the city to gain access to Minos. *The Faerie Queene* allows us to say no more than that Artegall's appearance in the mirror is ominous by implication. Deheubarth's fall through him remains an inference. We do not see Artegall actively warring on Ryence; nor does the poem elsewhere hint at any hostile designs on his part. Also, Britomart equals Scylla only in reverse, as it were. The latter cannot help ruining the state for the sake of the man she loves; the former cannot help loving the man who (presumably) ruins the state. Hence Britomart's love looks disturbingly misguided but not evil *per se*, like Scylla's. Moreover, though her desperate anxiety favours the view that in consulting the mirror she has done a deed as baleful as Scylla's cutting of the lock, the mirror exists in order to safeguard the kingdom. We cannot blame Britomart for its paradoxical inefficacy, nor even for not leaving the cussed thing alone: how could it serve its purpose without being consulted? And it does, even as it fails to do so, if Spenser's sources are indeed to be regarded as matrices. For Ariosto leads us to expect a happy ending. Whereas Minos overthrows Megara, Ruggiero, while never betraying his loyalty to Agramante, must resign himself to his party's defeat. But he discovers that on the strength of his ancestry he belongs with Charlemagne's party and so adopts Christianity and marries Bradamante without qualms. Although in this episode Spenser does not allude specifically to Ariosto, as he does to Virgil, it would be arbitrary to ignore the Italian's perspective altogether.

The immediate, dark, Virgilian backdrop almost obscures the distant, luminous, Ariostan horizon so that the episode may symbolize the virtual opacity of chastity. It is to enhance this symbolism that Spenser imports *Ciris* whole in part and 'heals' that part into an autonomy appreciable only in light of its manifest de-part-ure from its source. For the same reason Britomart's anguish can be understood literally only in relation to a property of the mirror seemingly irrelevant to the apparent love narrative and so self-contradictory as to preclude literal reading. Merlin's gift to Ryence represents Time, the mirror in which eternal glory sees itself as moral perfection in mortality:

> It *vertue* had, to shew in *perfect* sight,
> What ever thing was in the world contaynd,
> *Betwixt the lowest earth and heavens hight*,
> So that it to the looker appertaynd.
>
> (19.)

All-inclusive in its scope yet excluding heaven itself, 'it round and hollow shaped was', spherical, unlike mirrors as we know them, to signify perfection, 'and seem'd a world of glas', to signify brittleness. More particularly, it represents Time as it reflects heavenly love, because it is first referred to as 'Venus looking glas' (i. 18). For this specification alludes only in part to its capacity, in the narrative, for revealing Artegall as Britomart's future lover. Gavin Douglas's poem *The Palice of Honour*, whose broad thematic kinship with *The Faerie Queene* has been pointed out by Hankins,[10] also features a mirror of Venus; one singularly reminiscent of Ryence's but even less amatory. It surpasses 'the costly subtil quent spectacle of Rome', which 'enabled the Romans to see the lands all round them and whether they intended peace or war', as well as 'the myrrour send up to Canyce', which 'could show coming adversity and a lover's inconstancy'. In it one 'mycht se at a sycht / The dedes and fetes of every erdly wycht, / All thinges gone lyk as they wer present'.[11] Considering its 'present' survey of sacred and profane history *in extenso* it must stand for Time in the perspective of Eternity. The mirror in Spenser mirrors that in Douglas: it stands for Eternity in the perspective of Time. Now Time breaks heavenly love even as the virtues reflecting it, chastity, friendship, and justice, heal separateness: for the Time being they do so *ἐκ μέρους*. Hence the paradoxicality of Merlin's gift. It is in his rhapsody on ἀγάπη, the middle term of Spenser's triad, that St. Paul, as he looks forward the beatific vision 'face to face', observes that '*now* we se *through a glasse* darkely'.[12] 'Venus looking glas' *is* the apostle's mirror.

Britomart's consultation of this looking-glass aligns her with Venus, implicitly: like the goddess she represents eternal union, but 'darkely'. By way of complementary metaphor she looks in the mirror, thus signifying inevitable commitment to Time, while it lasts. For her consultation is not a contingent event any more than Venus' loss of Cupid in Canto vi. Spenser writes 'it fortuned', there (11) as here (ii. 22), to convey that commitment to Time involves immersion in fortuitousness. And he adds that 'her *selfe a while* therein she vewd *in vaine*' to suggest that Time, though a mere pastime for Eternity, overclouds its essence. How thoroughly it does appears when we see her image, Artegall: literally another person and allegorically the patron of justice, a virtue as opaque as temperance, even though merely in spite of itself, as we saw in Section I of Chapter Two. That Britomart falls irrevocably in love with this image implies its 'likeness'. (As with Arthur-Gloriana and Scudamour-Amoret love means conceptual equivalence.) But if she recognizes herself in it at all, it must be with extreme difficulty. Indeed, she repudiates it emphatically as a mere 'shadow, the bodie farre exild' and accepts only tacitly Glauce's vital qualification, 'no shadow, but a bodie *hath in powre*'; which means not that Artegall exists as a person but that the shadow *is* the body, though *in posse*, not *in esse* (to use the Schoolmen's terminology). In short, Britomart's 'experience' with the mirror symbolizes chastity. She languishes for the same thematic reason as Amoret at the House of Busirane. Her physical and mental premonitions of death (35, 39, 44, 52), so far from being a touching mark of sexual inexperience or, alternatively, the manifestation of self-destructive tendencies inherent in narcissism,[13] bring home how little chastity can apparently do to transcend generation as Time's desperate rearguard battle against mortality. Her condition is an emblem of Man observed from a position where his dual allegiance to Eternity and to Time seems most painfully impossible. 'Neither God of love, nor God of sky / Can doe (said she) that, which cannot be done', stressing the incompatibility of Eternity (love) and Time (the realm of the ever-moving sky) as though they were not both in the care of the One God.

If Artegall personifies justice, he does indeed mirror Britomart, love as, reluctantly, chastity; for justice reverses chastity's horror of separateness. But he cannot be quite her image unless he allows her to catch a glimpse of his secret glory; that is, unless he personifies chastity as well. Otherwise she could not have identified herself with him at all, despite their common heavenly essence. How does Spenser make him symbolic of both virtues? By spelling his name 'Arthegall' (25) he highlights the special connection between justice and magnificence, mentioned in the opening Section of the previous Chapter, to suggest that for his present purposes the knight partakes of Arthur's peculiar status of containing several virtues. The fact that Artegall wears the armour of Achilles strengthens the Arthurian connection. For it is not simply as though 'the near identification with Achilles works to establish Artegall as a supreme warrior and hero, worthy to bear the armour of the greatest of the Greeks, a trophy his survivors had competed for'.[14] Its inscription, 'Achilles armes, which Arthegall did win', makes him not only another Achilles but also another Hector, since Hector actually *won* the (old) armour of Achilles, by killing Patroclos. (The inheritor of his new armour, Ulysses, secured it against the claims of Ajax through rhetoric.[15]) So Artegall equals Arthur *qua* Hector–Achilles (compare Section V of Chapter One). Of course, just as the poet weights Arthur to suit holiness, the rubric under which he appears in this capacity, so he weights Artegall to suit justice. Whereas on Arthur's crest it is the dragon that lies low (I. vii. 31), the animal symbolic of all that keeps Man from God, Artegall's, by contrast, 'was covered with a couchant Hound', surely a greyhound (especially in view of his association with Lord Grey in Book V), Dante's *veltro*, symbolic of the just mon-arch and so, in Spenser, of justice in its ultimate rule as oneness.[16] Again, whereas the poet reveals the solar splendour of Arthur's shield, which the Prince himself 'never wont disclose' (34), we can only guess that the same splendour also characterizes Artegall's, 'enveloped sevenfold' and featuring a 'crowned litle Ermilin' with a 'pouldred skin' which totally belies its traditional function as an emblem of uncorrupted, unblemished purity[17] and hence the crown. Moreover, unlike Arthur Artegall is explicitly aligned with Achilles and only implicitly with Hector. As a result he looks completely anti-Troy. Although he is truly on a par with Arthur *qua* Hector the proleptic victor of Achilles in Patroclos, his armour contrasts markedly with Arthur's, whose blazing like the midday sun (29) intimates transparently Achilles' defeat by Apollo: it is merely 'round about yfretted all with gold', to remind us of Prays-desire's pall, under the rubric of temperance, virtue opaque. Besides, his quasi-exclusive relation to the Greek hero enables us to envisage him as the Achilles who, in the process of being made invulnerable, was left fatally vulnerable in part (in his heel). Nor should we forget that the *Iliad* tells how 'the greatest of the Greeks', instead of leading them to triumph, frustrates their common cause: Homer sings his wrath, which divides his own party against itself. However, one ray of light penetrates, albeit uncertainly, this intense gloom. Artegall 'lookt foorth, as Phoebus face out of the east, / Betwixt two shadie mountaines doth arize' (24). True, even this parallels Achilles' 'sunrise' to slay Hector. But it is a sunrise nevertheless. That this single element has a dual meaning symbolizes justice, unity eclipsing itself. That in its semantic deviation within a cluster of synonymous metaphors it determines, all on its own, their collective meaning symbolizes chastity, wholeness in part.

Let us now consider the little Egyptian allegory in stanza 20. Spenser compares Ryence's mirror to Phao's tower, 'ybuilded all of glasse', like Panthea (I. x. 58). Its maker is Ptolomæe, the ancient astronomer,[18] whose name, up until the sixteenth century, epitomized cosmology. However, not only was his particular model seriously challenged in important details by Copernicus in 1543 but, by Spenser's time, speculation that there might be a plurality of worlds[19] nearly obscured the notion of a single universe obvious in Ptolemy—*nearly*, for that notion, itself logically inescapable, it would seem, was still suggested by the wholeness in miniature of each constituent world. Thus the poet's anachronistic reference, conjuring up as it does the contemporary state of the art, signifies chastity. As a hieroglyph for any *uni*verse of moving heavenly bodies the tower symbolizes oneness immersed in temporality. 'Phao' derives from *φάος* or *φῶς*, 'light'; in the New Testament often a synonym of 'glory'. Thus the injunction of Jesus to his disciples to let their light shine, since they 'are the light of the worlde',[20] corresponds exactly to the injunction of Paul to 'glorifie God in your bodie'. The Letter to Ralegh endeavours to give 'great light' to the reader, namely glory, the meaning of the poem. Panthea, under the rubric of holiness, virtue transparent, 'seemd the brightest thing, that was'. Phao, though, does not let her light shine. On the contrary, she 'long did lurke / From all mens vew, that none might her discoure', as though she were virtue opaque, temperance. But Ptolomæe will not accept that. He must see her glory, if need be at the cost of shattering his universe: 'Yet when his love was false, he with a peaze it brake.' For this does not make literal sense. The tower, 'impregnable', with Phao locked inside, would preclude adultery, supposing it had been designed for that purpose; an unreal supposition, since 'she might all men vew out of her bowre'. (More precisely, literal reading is just possible enough to expose its impossibility. 'Impregnable' could mean 'capable of pregnancy' if only it did not mean 'impregnable'.) Spenser calls Phao 'false' because, totally hidden, she belies herself, 'light'. She shines whole in separateness, the tower in smithereens, in token of chastity. Not that Ptolomæe's action changes the stanza's meaning from temperance to chastity. Whole, the tower is Phao's vessel, *φωσ-φόρος*, and so equals Venus *qua* morning star, love dawning uncertainly, as it does in Artegall's sunrise.

It may be felt that this type of exegesis, with its tense conceptualizing of a few selected stanzas, distorts the mirror scene as much as do the half-literal readings it seeks to supplant. Who could deny that the Canto comes alive dramatically in Britomart's conversation with her nurse Glauce? Spenser may not enable the reader to enter their minds. Yet the two women do seem to be genuine personalities that he can relate to. The confrontation of the innocence of youth, with its blissful self-sufficiency for the first time rudely challenged, and the wisdom of age, as ineffectual in its sympathy as it is heart-warming, has great human appeal.

And the scene is none the less touching for being far more 'strange' than critics tend to allow. But then, to press for allegory is not to suppress emotions. Spenser positively appeals to them, just as novelists do. Only he does to a different purpose, to earth our understanding of concepts rather than to provide scope for vicarious experience. Let the fiction absorb us, by all means; as long as we yield to the actual text, with all its illogicalities. We are meant to enjoy ourselves 'in this delightfull land of Faery'. However, if we persist in chasing phantom stories, we shall soon be complaining, if we are honest, of 'weary steps' and 'tedious travell'. Following the poet we are to be 'nigh ravisht with *rare thoughts* delight' (VI Proem 1). Where he thinks in sense-images more consistently and on an incomparably vaster scale than any of the Metaphysical Poets, we should unite our faculties, instead of perversely cultivating a 'dissociation of sensibility'.

Like Britomart's behaviour, Glauce's is literally incomprehensible. She tells Britomart that she should 'with *reason* yet represse / The growing *evill*' (46) and attempts to exorcize it through magic (49–51). This contradicts fundamentally her previous attitude. She had protested reassuringly that 'though no reason may apply / Salve to your sore, yet love can higher stye, / Then reasons reach' (36). She had insisted that both Britomart's 'mind' and her 'fortune' are good, contrasting them emphatically with the mind of Myrrha, Biblis, and Pasiphaë and with the fortune of Narcissus (40–5). She had sworn solemnly 'by this most sacred head / Of my deare foster child, to ease thy griefe, / And win thy will' (33). Spenser never explains Glauce's second thoughts. But since in Canto iii she reverts to her original attitude as a matter of course, sequential readers feel free to ignore them. They are not. So blatant an incongruity, which baffles even geriatric psychology, ought to prevent them. Glauce could not be said to try magic first, before setting out to find Artegall, to see if she can save herself the trouble. Her prompt, extravagant vow, 'death nor daunger from thy dew reliefe / Shall me debarre' (33), shows that she is not the type to consult her own convenience. Or is this mere consolatory hyperbole? Hardly; for her subsequent performance bears out her total commitment. Glauce and the mirror are complementary metaphors, as stanza 45 suggests, where she states its properties with an authority as though she controlled it herself. She is another 'Glauce' (glassy) world of Time. Her ambivalent response to Britomart parallels Merlin's (un)protective present. In two minds, she safeguards the girl broken, as Ptolomæe's tower does Phao. And just as Britomart decries the mirror even as she trusts it, so she denounces Glauce even as she confides in her. For the nurse's magical rites, though meant to remedy Britomart's condition, are not intended to dispel her love, as we have so far assumed. Her attitude to love corresponds to that of her Virgilian model, Carme:

> non ego te incepto (fieri quod non pote) conor
> flectere, Amor, neque est cum dis contendere nostrum![21]

—as well it might, seeing that Spenser's Amor, unlike Virgil's, is intrinsically good. Instead she directs her magic against herself. True to her self-abnegating vow, she asks her charge to spit upon her face (50). 'That sayd, her round about she from her turnd, / She turned her contrarie to the Sunne.' (51) 'From her', to signal that Time's separateness repels love *qua* chastity; while ensuring its commitment: 'round about' makes the dissociation vacuous. 'Contrarie to the Sunne'; that is, against Artegall and Arthur, who seem to relish separateness. Glauce is to Britomart what Timon is to Arthur, foster-parent Time; but in reverse. The old man warns the young man against love as 'losse of time' (I. ix. 9–10). The old woman warns the young woman against Time as loss of love. The males are glory geared to virtue. The females are glory caught in virtue. Timon, as *τιμῶν*, is Time glorying in its own moral perfection. Glauce, as *γλαυκή*, 'grey', is aged Time suffering from its own effects and missing the hound which Artegall willingly subdues; while, as *γλαῦξ*,[22] she is Time *qua* 'owl', the bird 'that of deth the bode bryngeth'.[23]

(ii) *Canto iii*

It would be nothing new to say that a relation of overt parallelism obtains among many episodes of *The Faerie Queene*, and among certain Britomart episodes in particular.

This line of argument was started more than twenty years ago in an early essay by Fowler.[24] Unfortunately, his carefully articulated comparison between the Malecasta episode and the Malbecco episode was soon to be overshadowed by Northrop Frye's altogether more sweeping approach in 'The Structure of Imagery in *The Faerie Queene*'; perhaps the most influential piece of Spenser criticism to date.[25] It is a dire prophecy, already voluminously fulfilled in Nohrnberg's *Analogy*. The title of Frye's paper intimates what has happened. The poet's fiction has come to be regarded as a free-floating mass of imagery. Its structure consists in the pattern of resemblances among its constituent images. This approach has one advantage: it conveniently disposes of the need to press for a narrative rationale. However, it neither demonstrates that there is none nor accounts for the appearance to the contrary. Also, it refrains from explaining why images should keep recurring. Worse, it seems to be frantically adducing ever more parallels, even the merest skeletons, for the very purpose of stifling this obvious but unwelcome question. Spenser's admirably seaworthy vessel, with its well-briefed captain and its 'jolly Mariners' (I. xii. 42), has been taken over by one-eyed pirates, cut loose from its conceptual moorings, and set adrift, dismantled to an unreliable raft, like another *bateau ivre*. Let us rescue it from its disastrous, if intoxicating, course. The poem's episodes cohere thematically. It is natural that such coherence should be expressed through analogous imagery; but not necessary. Thus the constituent scenes of the flashback fail to resemble each other; so much so that they seem readily intelligible in sequence, as real story. What more natural, on a suspension of disbelief in magicians, than that Glauce, at her wit's end in Canto ii, should decide that the thing to do is to consult Merlin? And what more natural than that, after Merlin's encouraging revelation of the designs of Providence, Britomart should set out in quest of Artegall?

Once again, however, we should not allow our disposition to presume a narrative rationale to blind us to the logic of the actual text. Nor should we impatiently dismiss any incongruities we find as quite acceptable by romance standards (ill defined and ill understood as these are). Glauce decides to go to Merlin in order to learn Artegall's whereabouts (iii. 6). He is certainly a good person to consult, being omniscient (15), as she knows (21). Curiously, though, Spenser motivates Glauce's decision otherwise. He has her turn to Merlin as maker of the mirror (see 6 again). This is odd, because it implies that as such Merlin is responsible not just for the proper functioning of the mirror but for the image that has appeared in it as well, as though it were an imperfect replica of some vision of his own. Imperfect? The mirror 'vertue had, to shew in *perfect* sight, / *What ever* thing . . . So that it to the looker appertaynd . . . *Ne ought* in secret from the same remaynd' (ii. 19). If we take the poet at his word, Glauce's consultation of Merlin is entirely superfluous. Merlin could not have anything to add to what has already been revealed by the mirror. Nor does he. This assertion will seem preposterous, in view of the magician's lengthy prophetic outburst. But then, genealogical prophecy by no means answers Glauce's simple questions, 'what meanes shall she out seeke, or what wayes take? / How shall she know, how shall she find the man?' (iii. 25). The prophecy does contain an answer, the single line 'he wonneth in the land of Fayeree' (26). This is practically useless, though; for subsequently we find Britomart 'searching all lands and each remotest part' (iv. 6). Merlin's speech is mostly beside the point and, to the extent that it is not, totally uninformative.

But does this incongruity not make sense literally? Could we not see Merlin as a sage inhabiting visionary spheres, who, if unconcerned with immediate practicalities, offers something far more significant, namely the assurance of providential election to a crucial historical role? Surely we are to regard Britomart here as rising above the narrowly private reaction to her plight thanks to the mighty vista of 'destined descents' (iii. 2) and thus acquiring the balance and purposiveness of maturity? This objection registers valuably the scene's overall impact, the sense of a liberating breakthrough. Yet this proper atmospheric response does not quite amount to narrative understanding of the fiction. After all, liberating though the prophecy may be as testimony to the divine approval of Britomart's love, as a forecast of events that will happen in fact it is the very opposite, rigorously deterministic. Nor is the predicted course of events a triumphant tale of progress, which might have taken the sting out of the determinism. On the contrary, Merlin presents history as a tremendously costly and wasteful process, continually threatening Britondom with extinction and allowing it only intermittent resurgence. Admittedly, the prophecy culminates in the climactic reference to Elizabeth (49). However, if we should have to think of Britomart as happily embracing her destiny for the sake of the glorious Tudor queen, her 'mature decision' would be too patently the poet's compliment to his dedicatee to qualify as genuine motivation. We would feel tempted to extrapolate the whole prophecy from its apparently spurious context and discard it as one of those regrettably obligatory epic catalogues, perfunctorily inserted in servile flattery. Spenser never specifies why Britomart conceives 'hope of comfort glad' (51). Implicitly, however, he rules out that it is because of Elizabeth, by ending the prophecy in a highly dramatic aposiopesis:

> But yet the end is not. There Merlin stayd,
> As overcomen of the spirites powre,
> Or other ghastly spectacle dismayd,
> That secretly he saw, yet note discoure.
> (50.)

What could this 'ghastly spectacle' be if not the certain collapse, yet again, of British rule with the end of the Tudor succession, at the death of the Virgin Queen? Merlin's prophecy does release Britomart into history. Yet history will constrict her race, as she fully realizes, witness her anxious response (43 and 50). Nor does the magician's recital imply an altogether happy fulfilment of Britomart's passion at least in personal terms: Artegall, though destined to love her and give her a child, is to be 'too rathe cut off by practice criminall / Of secret foes' (28). Literal interpretation does not really account for Britomart's hopefulness. And it does not bear out the poet's assertion that she returns with Glauce 'well instructed . . . *Of all*, that needed them to be inquird' (51).

Like Glauce, Merlin is another mirror. His revelations are

a broken image of Britomart. Spenser unfolds Douglas's mirror, presenting something like its survey of history separately. As a result this is a mirror scene by implication only. The poet minimizes the impact of Time, to signify love as almost glory, friendship. The announcement of Artegall's residence in Faeryland complements his appearance in the mirror, since Faeryland and mirror are alike symbols of Time. But it complements it most unemphatically. With his name spelled 'Arthegall' (26), he still shares Arthur's capacity for more than one virtue. Since 'ne other to himselfe is knowne this day, / But that he by an Elfe was gotten of a Fay', he seems akin to the patron of temperance. However, Merlin asserts that he is 'no Fary borne, ne sib *at all* / To elfes'. Essentially glory, hidden from itself, he stands for justice. He stands for friendship as well in that his lack of eternal self-awareness, which makes him Britomart's antitype, barely qualifies her glorious conception of him. (That he gains his second status, which enables her to recognize him as closely approximating herself, through an external perspective rather than through internal bivalence, as in Canto ii, symbolizes friendship as oneness in togetherness, as against wholeness.) Hence Britomart's cheerful mood; not because she now knows where to find him, as literal readers suppose. Nor does Merlin expect her to join him in Faeryland. The sheer uselessness of his information implies as much. But we can be more precise. The magician calls Artegall 'renowmed . . . From where the day out of the sea doth spring, / Untill the closure of the Evening' (27). One infers that the knight, in the mirror a mere uncertain sunrise, here equals the sun commanding a multitude of midday positions, glorious zeniths, separately together. As virtue ('warlike feates') he is 'renowmed', so that in him God's *fama* must be widespread and almost unquestionably justified. Accordingly his solar role is nearly explicit. Yet, like Glauce, Merlin turns Britomart 'contrarie to the Sunne'; though altogether less dramatically, in accordance with the shift of emphasis from chastity to friendship. For he does not tell her to go and declare herself to Artegall in Faeryland but to get him out 'from thence . . . To this his native soyle', as though his efforts were in the wrong direction. However, *qua* friendship he is already emerging 'from temporality into his eternal essence' as it is. So he forestalls the need for Britomart to journey literally into Faeryland to talk him round. In merely implicit contrariness they are at one together, 'firmely bound with faithfull band': love for the most part apparent while still a matter of faith.

It has been conceded that Merlin's prophecy, unlike his revelation of Artegall's whereabouts, which almost gets drowned in it, comes very close to seeming a stage in a developing Britomart narrative; a fact that classifies it with the Temple of Venus episode, and with the Scudamour-Amoret fiction in Book IV generally, as symbolic of friendship. Whereas the incongruities of the mirror scene proper stare us in the face, those of the consultation scene remain largely hidden. To emphasize them would be to distort a meaningful variation. However, to neglect them would be to forgo understanding. The cheering effect of the prophecy should not deceive us into thinking that Britomart needs encouragement, as though Merlin had to help her make up her mind. Literally her mind is already made up, or she would not have gone to ask him where to find Artegall. Also, Merlin's assertion that although 'the fates are firme . . . Yet ought mens good endevours them confirme' (25) contradicts itself, as Glauce's pointed query suggests. If he foresees the future with certainty, it cannot depend on a moral imperative that Britomart might conceivably ignore. Moreover, if the vicissitudes of her posterity are fixed, they should have been as incapable of arousing her anxiety as those of her ancestry would. But even if we were to pretend that they are not fixed, her sympathy, spanning more than a thousand years, overtaxes literal belief. So does Merlin's dismay at the prospect of the Stuart succession; it would be out of all proportion even on the assumption that it expresses directly that of Spenser, who may be presumed to have remained unprophetically ignorant of what the seventeenth and eighteenth centures were to bring. Anyway, the prophecy, as an extensive, detailed, and unambiguous history forecast—a straight continuation, in the future tense, of the chronicle of 'Briton moniments' Arthur reads at Alma's castle—does not seem credible as an act of prophecy; though one must allow for Merlin's omniscience. But how credible is that?

And then, how strange that the imaginary characters Britomart and Artegall should have historical descendants.[26] Neither Virgil nor Ariosto offers a precedent. Their heroes are legendary or at least pseudo-historical (straight from 'Turpin'). Spenser's, by contrast, are pure invention and unique to him. Nor do they simply fill a blank. They take the place of Arthur, the most famous and most amply 'documented' historical Briton in the chronicle literature. And there are other, less spectacular divergences from the Galfridian tradition. Some of these might be accounted for by citing other chroniclers.[27] But such an explanation would imply that Merlin's prophecy is randomly eclectic and idiosyncratic or else represents Spenser's considered opinion on *wie es eigentlich gewesen.* As for the latter alternative, surely the poet cannot have wanted to publish a rival version of history as part of a poem, where it has to stand unargued, in an age which did argue critically about this matter. As for the former, the impression of randomness is indeed undeniable—and serves a purpose: implying the equal (in)validity of historians disagreeing in retrospect, it usefully subverts literal belief in the authority of the prophet's uniquely determining preview; which mirrors history so as to symbolize friendship. Just as Merlin asserts that Artegall is no Faery, never mind the knight's own conviction to the contrary, so he merges in reverse the various chronicles, acknowledging only tacitly their differences, which, however marginal they seem to us, totally obscure the singleness of the past. Still, this does not prove the impression of randomness true.

Merlin's prophecy also mirrors Britomart. It is 'Arthegall', like Arthur, in its overall similarity to 'Briton moniments', which complements the Prince under the rubric of temperance. Britomart's anxiety represents her contrariness to this Artegall. But it looks negligible in comparison with that in Canto ii. This stands to reason. Merlin *prophesies* 'Arthegall'. Now what could Time prophesy, metaphorically, if not Eternity? While the contents of Merlin's speech correspond to his admission that Artegall thinks himself a Faery, its genre corresponds to his declaration that as a matter of fact he is not. Nor is this the only way in which Spenser conveys the shift of emphasis. 'Arthegall' appears as the history of *Briton*dom even as it goes down under, obtruding that aspect of himself which enables *Brito*mart to identify herself with him. Again, whereas 'Briton moniments' excludes Arthur, the prophecy includes Britomart and indeed merely unfolds her in her posterity. Moreover, the Tudor culmination of the prophecy seems already the consummation of justice; that is, Britomart herself rather than her image:

> Thenceforth *eternall union* shall be made
> Betweene the nations different afore,
> And *sacred Peace* shall *lovingly* perswade
> The warlike minds, to learne her goodly lore.
> (49.)

In this light Merlin's qualification, 'but yet the end is not' (50), on literal reading almost a banality, becomes intelligibly momentous. A biblical echo, it conjures up its original, haunting, context, Christ's great eschatological discourse:

> And ye shal heare of warres, and rumors of warres: se that ye be not troubled: for all these things must come to passe, *but the end is not yet.* For nacion shal arise against nacion, and realme against realme, & there shalbe pestilence, and famine, and earthquakes in divers places. All these are but the beginning of sorowes.[28]

This is the 'ghastly spectacle' that dismays Merlin, negating his vision of peace. But it remains unuttered, in accordance with Christ's admonition, 'se that ye be *not* troubled'. After all, it is nothing 'but the beginning of sorowes', the birth throes of Eternity.[29] The magician regains his 'chearefull looks'. Britomart and her nurse 'unto their home retird' with so much 'lighter hearts' (51) that their dissociation from the prophecy barely registers.

Spenser's substitution of the imaginary Britomart and Artegall for Arthur makes it impossible to read his genealogical list as such. Their joint appearance instead of him reminds us of his oneness (as against his unfolding) only to qualify it as togetherness in separation, just as the appearance of a second hero, Cambel, in the title of Book IV qualifies Telamond's demonstrative perfection in one. Let us pause for some other felicities of detail. Merlin says of Artegall that '*sooth* he is the sonne of Gorlois' (27). This differentiates him from even as it aligns him with Arthur, who, begotten by Uther magically transformed into the likeness of Igerna's husband, is *apparently* the son of Gorlois. Since Arthur's supernatural conception betokens glory, Artegall's natural conception must betoken ingloriousness. Even so his parentage proves him 'no Faery'. Similarly, while Arthur and Artegall alike are to perish through treachery, Arthur will be vindicated supernaturally by his return in glory, whereas Artegall will be vindicated naturally, by his lineal descendants, unnamed son–Vortipore–Malgo–Careticus (28–33), who unfold him, though even so transmit his essence. For this vindication must be metaphorical. One would be hard put to it to apply to a person Merlin's paradoxical description, to Britomart, of Artegall's son as 'his Image *dead*, / That *living* him in all activity / To thee shall represent' (29). The magician's words mean: like father, like son; both stand for eternal glory mirrored almost to the life in mortality. Also, lineal descent flies in the face of Spenser's authority. Geoffrey has Arthur succeeded by his nephew Constantine and Constantine by his nephew Aurelius Conanus, while he does not specify the relationship of the others: 'Vortiporius came after Conanus. . . . Malgo came next. . . . After Malgo came Keredic.'[30] To be sure, the latter part of the succession formally allows of Spenser's specification. Also, in the former part the poet at least approximates history. According to Geoffrey the dying Arthur handed the crown to Constantine, son of Cador. And Conan took it by violence from an unnamed uncle 'who ought to have reigned after Constantine'—a brother of Constantine, one infers. Now Merlin predicts that Artegall's son

from the head
Of his coosin Constantius without dread
Shall take the crowne, that was his fathers right,
And therewith crowne himselfe in th'others stead.

(29.)

This looks like an invitation to identify him as Conan and Constantius as Constantine's presumptive brother; especially because Constantius, his cousin, could well be a son of Cador, Artegall's brother (27). So construed Spenser falsifies history only in making Conan belong to the same generation as Constantine and Constantius. His near accuracy symbolizes Time as virtually Eternity, friendship. So does his deviation from history. Spenser mirrors Geoffrey in that he leaves the robber of the crown unnamed, rather than his victim. By the same token he equates them. They are obviously one, apart. With his crown *constantius* manifests glory 'too steadfastly', too like Eternity, for friendship. Without it he would not manifest it at all (justice), were it not that he continues *constantius*, 'more steadfastly' than that, suggestive of Eternity (friendship). The thief steals the crown in 'his fathers *right*'; that is, to suppress glory, as justice does. Like Artegall he focuses Arthur, Man in Christ thinking it 'no robbery to be equal with God', as Man positively robbing himself of equality with God. Yet he then crowns himself, while, as of the same generation with Constantius, he ascends up the family tree, virtually cancelling out his descendance from Artegall; thus signifying friendship. Nameless, he is undistinguished, without name or *fama* (hence justice), yet even so too unified to require a distinctive name (hence friendship).

Being a compound metaphor Merlin's prophecy cannot form the second stage in a story of incipient love. The illusion that it does derives particularly from the fiction preceding the prophecy proper, which ostensibly links Cantos ii and iii. So let us explode it, with all due respect for the thematic significance of its quasi-narrative strength. We could agree with literal readers that it is natural for the nurse and her foster-child to travel incognito (7): their mission calls for discretion. But why do they not present themselves openly to Merlin? Surely they must realize that their disguise will be pointless if he can see through it and counter-productive if he cannot. Why does Glauce prevaricate in describing Britomart's condition if she is so anxious to have it remedied? How does she expect to learn Artegall's whereabouts if she is 'loth to let her purpose plaine appeare' (17)? No doubt we are meant to identify ourselves with what seems to be Merlin's good-humoured common sense and join him in finding the women's behaviour rather pathetically funny (17, 19). But he needs more than mere common sense, supernatural perceptiveness, to detect Glauce's mismanagement of Britomart's affairs. On literal reading it is by no means a matter of course that her weird strategy has the happy outcome it does have. We too need supernatural perceptiveness, namely allegorical understanding. Glauce's reluctance to reveal Britomart's plight parallels Womanhood's reluctance to let Amoret leave the Temple of Venus: she anxiously asserts love's essence and protests against its inevitable disguise by Time. 'Th'old woman wox half blanck' (17) when Merlin deliberately mistakes her not because she has apparently not made herself clear—a failure of communication easily rectified—but for fear of having been only too outspoken. And she has, in spite of herself; what with her emphasis on the 'sore evill, which this virgin bright / Tormenteth, and doth plunge in dolefull plight' and her anticipation of death (16). She wants Merlin to recognize love's glory. Hence her relief when he makes light of her 'colourable word' (19). Britomart may seem less happy about Merlin's penetration:

> The doubtfull Mayd, seeing her selfe descryde,
> Was all abasht, and her pure yvory
> Into a cleare Carnation suddeine dyde;
> As faire Aurora rising hastily,
> Doth by her blushing tell, that she did lye
> All night in old Tithonus frosen bed,
> Whereof she seemes ashamed inwardly.
>
> (20.)

It looks as though the magician is teasing her about a 'secret' amorous predilection. But on sequential reading she has long since passed that stage. Our interpretation should be informed by the simile, no mere vapid decoration. As Aurora, Britomart ushers in the day of Eternity, like Phao's tower *qua* φωσφόρος but with an intense luminosity poles apart from the morning star's vanishing twinkle. That she blushes her glory shows her commitment in reverse to Artegall, justice, glory in hiding like 'old Tithonus', immortal but lacking eternal youth, nocturnal darkness wedded to yet overshadowing diurnal light. This commitment is a 'secret' symbolically. As Merlin says, she herself, heavenly love, is no 'more hidden . . . then Sunne in cloudy vele' (19), in token of friendship.

The final scene of the flashback seems to follow on from the consultation scene as convincingly as the mirror scene seems to lead up to it: Britomart, having learnt that Artegall 'wonneth in . . . Fayeree', makes ready to depart thither. Indeed, a mere dozen or so stanzas long, it could pass for transitional narrative in its entirety, linking the flashback with the direct narrative. But then, Spenser provides a very peculiar connection:

> Ne rested they, till that to Faery lond
>   They came, as Merlin them directed late:
> Where meeting with this Redcrosse knight, she fond
>   Of diverse things discourses to dilate,
>   But most of Arthegall, and his estate.
>
> (62.)

This ignores her previous clash with Guyon and her journey together with him and Arthur until 'at length' these companions leave her for the fleeing Florimell (i. 4–19). Also, it glosses over how she found Red Cross stymied before Castle Joyous and how they fared inside (i. 20–67). Moreover, the poet had emphasized that Red Cross did not tell Britomart anything about Artegall of which she was not already aware. Although he 'him in every part before her fashioned' (ii. 16), 'yet him in every part before she knew' (17), as the mirror episode goes on to 'explain'—between inverted commas, because the mirror does not literally convey the same information as Red Cross. In short, the flashback, so far from leading into the direct narrative, leads into itself as a manifest breaker of narrative. Or is this too drastic? Surely the flashback does not need to refer to Canto i and genuinely leads into Canto ii in that it is perfectly natural for Britomart in love to enjoy getting the same report of her beloved all over again? True. We can sense the presence of real, unbroken narrative. The fact remains that the link eclipses its unity, as justice does glory *qua* oneness. Take Britomart's statement,

Faire Sir, I let you weete, that from the howre
I taken was from nourses tender pap,
I have been trained up in warlike stowre,
To tossen speare and shield, and to affrap
The warlike ryder to his most mishap.

(ii. 6.)

This is, of course, strictly absurd. We cannot envisage such a daunting toddler. Story readers will say that she is exaggerating, to impress Red Cross, without expecting him to take her quite at her word: she means merely that her military experience dates from long before their meeting. In view of her protracted association with Guyon and Arthur, this meaning would be compatible with Glauce's reference, in the final scene of Canto iii, to Britomart's military inexperience: 'Our weake hands (whom need new strength shall teach) / The dreadfull speare and shield to exercize' (53). Although the girl had already proved a formidable antagonist to Guyon when they first met, this merely goes to show the justness of Glauce's (less than self-evident) claim: 'Ne ought ye want, but skill, which *practize small* / Will bring and *shortly* make you a mayd Martiall.' However, just because the close of Canto iii does not allude to Canto i whereas it positively mentions Britomart's 'discourses', of which the statement quoted forms the beginning, it obscures the continuity of her military development by a stark contrast: inexperience versus experience, the superfluousness versus the importance of extensive training.

The departure scene similarly eclipses its own story. Nothing could persuade us that it does not tell how Britomart prepares to leave Britain in search of Artegall. Yet we do not see it telling anything of the sort. Instead we find a series of contradictory moves, none of them intelligibly related to her purpose. To begin with Glauce 'at last' hits upon the right plan, rather than which she formulates, belatedly, a general sentiment of *a priori* validity: 'Daughter, I deeme that counsell aye most fit, / That of the time doth dew advauntage take' (52). She does not explain in what way the fact that 'now all Britanie doth burne in armes bright' favours Britomart's chances of finding Artegall in Faeryland.

One would have thought that war is an impediment to free travel. In fact, Glauce changes tack in the next stanza: 'That therefore nought our passage may empeach, / Let us in feigned armes our selves disguize.' Whereupon she makes Britomart wear a disguise that advertises itself as such, giving her the armour of Angela, the famous Saxon queen recently vanquished (58–9). But then, Spenser never tells any story of Britomart passing undetected through the Saxon ranks. Nor does he say that, fortunately, the disguise turned out to have been an unnecessary precaution. He drops the idea of disguise at once and presents Britomart as donning armour out of a desire to embrace the life martial for its own sake, in emulation of the great female warriors Bunduca, Guendolen, Martia, Emmilen, and Angela (54–7). One wonders what contribution Britomart in Angela's armour could make to the military fortunes of the Britons in their resistance against the Saxons; for the poet never tells us. One also wonders how the adoption of 'advent'rous knighthood' as an end in itself could yet be instrumental in the promotion of her marital destiny. True, as a matter of fact Britomart meets Artegall in her knightly capacity, in IV. iv–vi. And, on the premiss that we are reading story, her career would be providential. However, on the same premiss she would have to '*guide* the heavenly causes to their *constant* terme' (25). And Artegall is the opposite of 'constant', stationary (ii. 14); while Britomart complains that 'love my lewd Pilot hath a restlesse mind / And fortune Boteswaine no assurance knowes, / But saile withouten starres' (iv. 9).

Even the palpable continuity between the consultation scene and the departure scene does not quite surface. In the former, Britomart and Glauce 'unto their home retird', away from Faeryland. So the latter, where they sally forth into Faeryland, reflects a change of mind; in failing to mention which it falls short, if only just, of realizing a narrative transition (for the text does not imply the change but pretends that there is no occasion for it). Nor is this discontinuity too minimal to deserve credit. It necessitates symbolic reading, which does indeed show Britomart reversing herself radically. In Book I Merlin identifies Arthur by revealing his parentage (ix. 5) and arms him (vii. 36). In the consultation scene Merlin identifies Britomart, *per contra*, by revealing her progeny and so, one infers, keeps her unarmed. *Ergo* her military ambition in the departure scene is a complete turn-about. She becomes her own mirror image, another Artegall, to signify justice. Arming herself, she obliterates her sex, manifest glory. Angela's armour is merely 'fretted round with gold' (58), like that of Artegall in the mirror. It has a 'brave bauldrick' (59), like Arthur's (I. vii. 29–30) but lacking its central glory, the jewel shining like Hesperus, so that it must be night-Time. Indeed, Glauce arms Britomart 'in th'evening late'. (Similarly, Artegall's quest in aid of Irena takes him westward (V. vi. 7), like a setting sun. It does, of course, allude to Lord Grey's 'pacification' of Ireland. But it cannot *mean* it, because he did not dispose of its Grantorto. Or are we to suppose that Spenser naïvely dreamt he did? On the contrary, the poet evokes England's involvement in Ireland as history's metaphor for justice, Eternity bogged down in Time.) And then, Britomart's 'mighty speare, / Which Bladud made by Magick art of yore' (III. iii. 60), elsewhere specified as 'Hebene' (IV. v. 8, 26; vi. 6), is patently the selfsame spear Timias carries for Arthur (I. vii. 37; II. viii. 17); that is, the spear with which Achilles kills Hector. Dissociating it from the squire, she obscures its preciousness, while clinching her alignment with Artegall *qua* Achilles.

To establish Britomart's full equivalence with Artegall in the departure scene we must emphasize, as we have done so far, her ingloriousness. She would not personify justice, though, if we did not sense her essential glory, despite its invisibility. But then, so we do; for we are not allowed to forget her true sex. Nor is this the only way Spenser conveys it. Just as the armour won from Achilles makes Artegall implicitly Trojan, so the armour of the defeated Angela makes Britomart implicitly Troynovantine. Meaning dictates the counter-productive disguise. Or take Britomart simply as another Angela. As such she is, passively, dead or, actively, *qua* Saxon leader, killing New Trojans. Yet, implicitly, Spenser qualifies. Angela and her Angles (56) suggest 'angels' and thus heaven (one thinks of the celebrated papal pun). Also, the Saxons are pagan invaders. They symbolize Time invading Eternity, a variant of the Faeries, Time stealing Eternity, that specifies the dispossessors' residence as heaven itself. (Red Cross, their Christian kinsman, descended 'from ancient race / Of Saxon kings' or, more specifically, 'from English race' (I. x. 65, 60), conversely symbolizes Eternity invading Time. That is why *qua* Saxon Britomart encounters Red Cross. Their 'friendship' (III. iii. 62), as different virtues, is an aspect of multifarious moral perfection, Arthur. Britomart gives it a particular slant: 'She fond . . . discourses to *dilate* . . . of Art*h*egall.' This does not mean that she started going on about her lover. It means that she focuses her friendship with Red Cross, which *is* 'Arthegall', equivalence with Arthur, as unfolding and delay (of glory); thus defining herself as justice and redefining him as such so as to remind us of his transparency even as she obscures it.) Again, Glauce's decision to take advantage of the time (52), that is, of Time, implies the vantage point of Eternity. This is the opportunity she sees:

> good king Uther now doth make
> Strong warre upon the Paynim brethren, hight
> Octa and Oza, whom he lately brake
> Beside Cayr Verolame, in victorious fight.

A self-contradiction such as this precludes literal reading. Uther could not very well continue to fight those he has already overcome. Anyway, he was poisoned soon after this battle and did not survive.[31] The quotation symbolizes justice as God 'Pendragon', Lord of Hosts, Eternity so militant as to hide its triumph. Also, it indicates the juncture at which Arthur accedes to the throne: Britomart's chance to equal Arthur as justice by taking on his fateful earthly rule *as though* to the exclusion of his heavenly come-back. Yet whereas in the other two scenes of the flashback Glauce and her foster-child repudiate Time, severely or mildly, as not suited to love, here they embrace Time as suitable. Whereas chastity and friendship are partial oneness variously emerging, justice is absolute oneness totally immersed. 'So time their *turne* did fit.' (58.) From the perspective of justice, essentially of Eternity, Time is a 'passage' that 'nought . . . may empeach' (53): it is palpably, though secretly, passing away.

As apparently transitional narrative in its entirety with nothing to connect in reality, the departure scene symbolizes Time's transience. Eleven stanzas long, like the Proem to Book V, which spells out the passage of Time, it presents Time at the eleventh hour.

II Britomart and Arthur

Intent on showing that the flashback constitutes a small-scale counterpart to Books III–V, we seem to have created a problem for ourselves: its polysemy transgresses the rule that each Legend symbolizes its titular virtue only. Or does it? The episode distinguishes itself from the rest of the Britomart fiction not just as a flashback. It is also wholly and exclusively about her, other characters being, unlike anywhere else, totally subordinate and indeed subservient; and moreover concerns her as a woman. Hence it means glorious oneness throughout even as it means three virtues in a row. The latter meaning, while disrupting the former, lets it be. In this situation the polysemy itself symbolizes wholeness in part, chastity; especially since one of the parts corresponds to the whole. The flashback presents Britomart as she looks in the mirror, in both senses of the phrase: we see her reflecting herself as well as her reflection. (In the departure scene the two senses coincide.) Books III–V, which do not flash back, present Britomart, to all intents and purposes a man appearing intermittently on a par with other characters, as her reflection only. They truly reflect her attitudes in the flashback, where she recoils from identity with her image, first violently then gently, before accepting it with a vengeance. To signal identity they feature Britomart herself as her mirror image. To prove it a reflection they reverse her attitudes. She finds herself totally in Book III, as its titular quest hero. She dissociates herself implicitly from Book IV, in that she has nothing to do with its quest hero, Scudamour, when questing, in Canto x. And she dissociates herself explicitly from Book V, in rescuing its quest hero, Artegall, not from defeat inflicted but from defeat self-imposed, the corollary of a victory. And, of course, she becomes less and less prominent. However, for Books III–V to reflect Britomart in the flashback they must also be a 'magnifying' glass that presents her 'Arthegall', like Arthur, as a personification of their virtues emphatically in a row, one by one. To signal her identity as such each does in fact feature her in the Arthurian role of (apparent) rescuer. In Book III she helps out Scudamour in dire straits. In Book IV she vindicates the knights of Maidenhead at Satyrane's tournament in the nick of time. And in Book V she releases Artegall from his paradoxical plight. (We may observe, in anticipation, that this alignment with Arthur implies the illusoriness of her career.) As the remainder of this Section will show, the peculiarities of her Arthurian performances parallel her attitudes to her mirror image in the flashback. Just as there she variously identifies herself with it as though it were somebody else, so in the Books at large she enacts Arthegality not as Arthur but over against an Arthur the peculiarities of whose own, by definition Arthurian, performances match those of hers in reverse.

In Book III Britomart violently contradicts her Arthurian identity. Arthur leaves it to the Outer Books' quest heroes to deal with their cardinal antagonists, the Dragon, Acrasia, Grantorto, and the Blattant Beast. Britomart tackles Scudamour's enemy, Busirane, herself. In so doing she challenges Faery Court, to prove Time an evil spell; whereas Arthur, indulging Time, thinks the world of Faery Court. Structurally, too, she dissociates herself from Arthur as far as possible. His interventions always take place in Canto viii: there he overcomes Orgoglio (I), Cymochles and Pyrochles (II), Corflambo (IV), the Souldan (V), and Disdain (VI). By contrast, Britomart overcomes Busirane in Canto xii, at the outer edge of Book III. And Spenser pointedly removes her from the four central Cantos, where, in the other Books, he locates Arthur's emergence. (She is absent from iv. 46 till ix. 12.) Besides, what with her prominence and her climactic victory over the magician, she resembles Red Cross, Guyon, Artegall, and Calidore, the knights who 'hold up' Arthur. Even her flashback proves a counter-Arthurian protest, when compared with Arthur's in I. ix. The latter immediately follows his intervention in aid of Red Cross, as his own quiet afterthought. The former long precedes her intervention in aid of Scudamour, as the poet's emphatic premiss, interrupting the flow of the apparent narrative. Also, the order of its constituents reverses that of its counterparts. Arthur mentions first his military training, which corresponds to Britomart's arming in the departure scene, then his consultation of Merlin, and lastly his dream vision of Gloriana, which corresponds to Britomart's mirror vision (stanzas 3–4, 5, 9–15 respectively).

Arthur himself, in Book III, denies as vehemently as does Britomart his normal role, but so as to redouble the impact of their opposition. He does not perform any rescue operation, though Florimell's captivity in the cave of Proteus, in his own Canto viii, provides him with a wellnigh typical opportunity. This is not a gratuitous observation. The poet's final apostrophe to her, 'it yrkes me, leave thee in this wofull state' (43), suggests anew the deficiency of the Prince, the vainness of whose concern for her he had established in Cantos i, iv, and v. Now Florimell's captivity parallels Amoret's. (Spenser mentions their predicaments in the same breath in IV. i. 1.) This parallelism focuses the startling contrast between Arthur's miserable non-intervention and Britomart's Arthurian success. Nor is this the only way in which Arthur contradicts his normal role. In no other Book does he appear in the opening Cantos. Again the poet hints that this cannot be a gratuitous matter of fact. Arthur's exit from the fiction occurs at precisely the same point as his earliest entry, in Book VI: Canto v, stanzas 11–12. Moreover, in Book VI he emerges with Timias emphatically regained where in Book III he disappears complaining about Timias lost. And within the opening Cantos Spenser dwells cruelly on that aspect of Arthur which elsewhere he no sooner introduces than dismisses, namely his separation from Gloriana. For in Florimell, the golden representative of Faery Court (i. 15; v. 4, 5), glory's elusiveness highlights itself. Instead of the evening star, regular harbinger of darkness, she resembles a comet that 'importunes death and dolefull drerihed' (i. 16). Arthur chases her 'so long that now the golden Hesperus / Was mounted high in top of heaven sheene' (iv. 51),[32] only to find his pursuit thwarted by murky vapours totally obscuring her as they do Hesperus and the stars it summons. The 'sun of righteousness' goes down cursing Night (55-60), unable to sleep and thus—as stanza 53 *qua* verbal echo of I. ix. 14 suggests—deprived of Gloriana's blissful visitation. Britomart will have nothing to do with Arthur's pursuit (III. i. 19). On the contrary,

> Yet did false Archimage her still pursew . . .
> Now that he had her singled from the crew
> Of courteous knights, the Prince, and Faery gent
> (iv. 45)

—to the bewilderment of story readers, who are bound to protest that there is no Archimago narrative for these lines to refer to. Spenser means that she remains image, 'like Arthur', even as she disowns him. Accordingly Arthur and Britomart alike disappear beyond the fiction's horizon. But whereas he, for once, does not go gentle into that good night but rages against the dying of the light, she vanishes not only at once but tacitly, without a word from the poet.

In Book III Britomart and Arthur almost completely reject typical Arthegality. In Book IV they almost completely accept it. Britomart's aid to the knights of Maidenhead at Satyrane's tournament sums up quite recognizably Arthur's role in *The Faerie Queene* as a whole, his aid to Gloriana's knights considered collectively as jousting at her feast. This summary is mildly adverse in being a unified counterpart to a poem which looks primarily like a set of distinct quests. It is less obvious that Arthur joins the Legends' heroes than that they divide him; but only a little: the work readily dispels the impact of its self-dispersing layout. Hence, though Britomart counters rather than assists Cambel and 'Telamond', the Book's titular heroes, who endorse this layout in their duality and in siding against Satyrane's party, they require only faint opposition. They virtually concede his point by agreeing to fight him in his tournament. They act more manifestly side by side than do Red Cross, Guyon, Scudamour, Artegall, and Calidore; while 'Telamond' infolds a trio. Accordingly Britomart's Arthurian intervention, four Cantos away from Canto viii here as in Book III, occurs not near the outer edge but on the very threshold of the middle four Cantos, as though she were only just checking her emergence as Arthur there.

Arthur himself, in Book IV, welcomes Arthegality with the same minor reservations as Britomart, but again in reverse. Unlike Britomart he does not intervene in a tournament. On the contrary, rescuing Amyas and slaying Corflambo in Canto viii, he suggests his role in single Books rather than his overall performance. But then, Amyas is neither a quest hero nor a titular hero. His interchangeability with Placidas actually aligns him in pointed, if weak, opposition to the titular, infolded, Telamond, so jarringly doubled by Cambel. In championing Amyas Arthur repudiates duality as Britomart does in defeating the titular pair. This can be inferred also from Corflambo's end:

> The while his babling tongue did yet blaspheme
> And curse his God, that did him so confound;
> The whiles his life ran foorth in bloodie streame,
> His soule descended downe into the Stygian reame.
>
> (45.)

This evokes the closing line of Virgil's epic, describing the death of Turnus: 'vitaque cum gemitu fugit indignata sub umbras.' Now the Rutulian king would have been spared had he not reminded Aeneas of having killed his companion Pallas, by wearing his baldric (τελαμών). Thus he fatally rekindles the fury of the Trojan, who imagines himself possessed by the spirit of his dead friend, like another Telamond.[33] Spenser's allusion implies that in slaying Corflambo Arthur puts a stop to his self-division as Aeneas-Turnus, highlighted in the titular self-division of Book IV. Imitating Aeneas' final act he 'ends' *The Faerie Queene*: he proves himself its τέλος, its perfection in one, confirming Britomart's point. Book IV bears out its finality in other ways. Whereas elsewhere Arthur finds his assistance required as soon as he appears above the poem's horizon, here he emerges 'seeking adventures' (vii. 42), as though there were none left. Again, whereas elsewhere he disappears beyond the poem's horizon as soon as he resumes his pursuit of Gloriana, here he stays in full view (ix. 17 ff.), as though she were present on the scene. Of course, the fact that he looks for love and work also qualifies finality. So does the fact that the tournament ends inconclusively and that Amyas is not Placidas and ends up coupled with the wrong girl, Pœana, instead of his own Æmylia.[34] Arthur and Britomart do, after all, have some scope for contrariness. Accordingly while Satyrane's feast disintegrates despite her stance, he positively bungles his job. Spenser neatly clinches their relation in Canto ix, where he meets her as, together with Scudamour, she opposes Druon *cum suis*. He unhesitatingly takes her part. They are alike also in their fundamentally pacific intentions (31, 32, 35). Yet having learnt about the cause of the quarrel, the tournament, Arthur finds against Britomart and proceeds to scold her (37). She does not answer back, though, but, with peace in sight, allows herself to be put in the wrong—as she does structurally by performing her Arthurian intervention on the wrong side of the Book's centre.

In Book V Britomart and Arthur both embrace Arthegality with a vengeance. Their very contrariness realizes, secretly, their utter identity. Britomart substitutes for its quest hero as Arthur does for those of the other Outer Books. But she does not simply emerge at the opportune moment to enjoy a good fight. She is summoned to reactivate Artegall's quest when it ought to be ended already (vi. 3); as indeed it is in a sense: he stays put of his own accord. The complete determination with which she expedites him palpably masks a conviction that really there can be no need for her to intervene at all. She as it were closes her eyes to her own action. As well she may; for in overthrowing Radigund and undoing Artegall's sexual transformation she suppresses womanhood, her own essential glory. Thus she focuses Arthur, who unfolds himself as a matter of course to aid single titular heroes, as de-part-ure from his hidden unity, Gloriana; all the more so in that her irruption is itself interrupted, by the Dolon episode and the Temple of Isis episode. She also highlights his self-contradiction in vanishing from the poem at a loss for his hidden integrity by doing likewise but without searching, to indicate that he does indeed already contain himself. Moreover, intervening in Canto vii, she 'prevents' his interventions in Canto viii, to prove his 'end' by thrusting it even more emphatically 'into the middest'.

Arthur himself, in Book V, does vanish from the fiction searching (xi. 35). However, he lingers on not only far beyond his assistance to Artegall but in a sense till the close of the Book; for what follows his disappearance, Artegall's quest proper, takes place (on literal reading) not after but simultaneously with his own exploits in support of Belge (see x. 17). Now the conclusions of Books are ingathering returns to the Faery Queen. So Arthur's loss is as markedly self-contradictory as Britomart would have it. Reversing her early disappearance after an intervention *preceded* by 'irrelevant' episodes, 'preventing' the Legend's 'end', he proves himself even so entirely synonymous. Again, though like Britomart Arthur does not simply emerge, unlike her he seems to have been expectantly waiting in the wings for an opportunity, to judge from the eagerness with which he rushes in to rid Samient of her pursuers (viii. 5). But then, instead of substituting for a paralysed quest hero, he acts jointly with a resuscitated quest hero; a singularity to which her name draws attention: it means 'going together'. Thus he unfolds himself with abnormal emphasis precisely when, in light of the norm, there is no need for him to intervene at all. Nor does he fail to suppress womanhood in spite of himself; or rather, in reverse, to endorse its own self-suppression. Samient leads him to Mercilla, who is, *qua* virgin queen authorizing the extirpation of public evil, Gloriana verily present. But as far as we can see she does not make love to him, as though there were no question of her being his glory. And he, instead of making himself at home and claiming his reward, begs her humbly to send him abroad for the sake of Belge's twelve dead sons (x. 15); that is, to allow him to enact the twelve titular knights' several commitments to Gloriana's perfection in mortality perfectly, in one, to be sure, yet all the more emphatically unto death.

The dissociation of Mercilla and Arthur is so incongruous as to explode the story. Yet they also leave it mercifully whole by pretending nominally that she is not Gloriana. Indeed, it might seem that this time Spenser's dynamite implodes without affecting the narrative. To show its impact requires more than a casual footnote. Mercilla hides her complete identity with Gloriana as completely as she gives it away, thus letting literalist sceptics go unpunished for believing that she is simply a different person and so naturally does not make love to Arthur. She spares 'Duessa'. However, she also executes her—a paradox incapable of literal resolution. The partisans of duplicity must share her double fate. Arthur is quite capable of loving Gloriana in another character, Florimell. Now his successful pursuit of Samient, who belongs to Mercilla's entourage, into the fiction with Artegall manifestly reverses his vain pursuit of Florimell, who belongs to Gloriana's entourage, out of the fiction with Guyon. Both damsels are fleeing on a palfrey, with streaming hair and eyes cast backward in terror (compare V. vii. 4 and III. i. 15-16). We do not learn, though, that Samient's horse is 'milk-white', spotless, nor that her locks are a glorious yellow. Presumably Spenser merely *covers up* likeness in this respect, for it is Samient's *garments*, 'all to rent', that contrast with Florimell's, 'all . . . wrought of beaten gold'. One cannot but infer that the former is the latter obliterating her glory, while hiding her identity by her name. Mercilla relates to Gloriana as Samient does to Florimell. And Arthur relates to Mercilla as he does to Samient. In both he *obviously* finds Gloriana darkling; fittingly, since mercy is that aspect of justice which highlights its palpable though secret oneness by waiving justice, leaving it 'alone', letting it take care of itself. That is why Mercilla appears as though 'in the cloudes of heaven with power and great glorie', like the Son of Man on the Last Day (V. ix. 27-9),[35] yet also softens 'that Majestie and awe',

> As the bright sunne, what time his fierie teme
> Towards the westerne brim begins to draw,
> Gins to abate the brightnesse of his beme,
> And fervour of his flames somewhat adaw.
>
> (35.)

That is why she tries and executes Duessa, false Una, making 'mercie and trueth . . . mete',[36] yet also will 'not let just vengeance on her light' but weeps and covers her face 'with her purple pall', immediately reminiscent of lack-lustre Prays-desire (50, 28; compare II. ix. 37), as are her angels with their wholly 'purpled wings' (29; contrast IV. x. 42).

III Busirane Revisited

In Books III–V Britomart and Arthur are, as the previous Section has shown, (convergent) Arthegality. But what about Art(h)egall himself? On the strength of his name he must be the prime exponent of Arthegality. And one is led to postulate an alignment with Arthur, and so against Britomart. Yet spelled without the 'h' his name also implies denial of what is manifestly Arthurian in Arthur's Arthegality, namely unfolding of and unfulfilled aspiration to Gloriana. In Book V Spenser favours the shorter spelling to the exclusion of the longer; appropriately, for as justice Artegall is sheer glory concealed in sheer looseness. We have already seen that the knight's own Legend does not allow Arthur a proper intervention and a proper search. We must now add that to forestall Arthur it allows Britomart to reverse Artegall's contrariness to herself in dressing up as a woman. Also, instead of intervening in other knights' quests Artegall actually performs a quest himself; one in which he would have intervened on his own behalf, were it not for 'want of meanes' (v. 42), in other words, for being the 'end'. Superfluously he is his own Arthur. But if he is himself Arthur at any point in his quest, he must be Arthur throughout. He contains the Prince in himself as the Prince contains *The Faerie Queene* in himself, secretly. In Book V Artegall does indeed represent Arthegality 'to perfection'.

In Book IV Spenser uses both spellings. 'Artegall' occurs eleven times, a number signifying Time's transience from the perspective of justice, as we found at the end of Section I. 'Arthegall' occurs four times, the number of the Legend of Friendship, which focuses Arthur as Telamond unfolded.[37] After the knight reveals his face (vi. 25) the poet uses only the shorter spelling; though he does so eight times, the number of Arthur's substitution Canto. To redress the slight imbalance in favour of dissociation from Arthur, he uses the longer spelling four times and the shorter three times before the knight reveals his face. Also, he lets him be known by his disguise as epitomized in his motto, *Salvagesse sans finesse* (iv. 39), whose meaning, commitment to *silva*, woody matter, *without end*, associates him with Arthur; though the appellation 'Salvage Knight' occurs five times, the number of the Legend of Justice.[38] For all his h-less selfhood Artegall flaunts Arthegality. In Book IV he represents it not perfectly but magnificently. His role highlights Arthur's in the poem at large as 'breaking up' Gloriana's feast. He emerges to intervene not in a quest but in the tournament organized by Satyrane, who offers as a prize not Gloriana unspecified but the girdle of her lady Florimell, which tends to untie even as it binds (v. 16–18). While single, he opposes the knights of Maidenhead in their joint triumph on 'the last day' (iv. 37–8). But just when he seems about to prove *perfectly* Arthurian in overthrowing them severally, 'one after other' (41), 'till evening, that the Sunne gan downward bend' (43), Britomart rushes in to defeat him at once (44). Still, he divides her victory by his come-back in Canto vi, if only to reveal her sex and acknowledge her as his glory. Even so they continue in opposition, in that he leaves her against her will. Yet he does so *magnificently*. Although he 'was bound / Upon an hard adventure yet *in quest*' (42), in order to perform it he not only disappears from the fiction, itself a manifestly Arthurian gesture, but almost explicitly admits it to be pageantry by announcing its duration in advance (43).

In Book III Spenser again uses both spellings, but with frequencies that betoken barely discernible Arthegality. Whereas in Book IV 'Artegall' occurs eleven times, to emphasize self-clouding glory as indeed glory by suggesting that the cloud shall be lifted, here it occurs two times, the number of the Legend of Temperance, as though it were nothing but an inglorious cloud. Again, whereas in Book IV 'Arthegall' occurs four times, to signify glory displaying itself broadly if not yet highly, here it occurs five times, as though it eclipsed its self-display completely.[39] Only the necessity to say 'as though', because the frequencies are, after all, properties of Arthegalitarian names, forces us to look for Art(h)egall's Arthegality in a Book which would seem to deny it *a priori*, in that it does not feature Art(h)egall: it presents only his name and his mirror image. Yet what could we say about a character that is not there? Precisely that Arthur's role in the poem as a whole can be summed up as 'aiding titular knights' and 'being not there'. Art(h)egall focuses the former aspect in Book IV and the latter in Book III (thus intimating that these Books are collapsible, as we had already inferred from Scudamour's two 'half-quests' in Section I of Chapter Two). Now one would expect that, just as in Book IV Art(h)egall conjures up a disruptive Arthur to balance the suggestion of his sheer presence at Gloriana's feast, so in Book III he will conjure up an Arthur somehow united with Gloriana to balance the suggestion of his sheer absence. He obliges. Nominal presence characterizes Gloriana generally as it does Art(h)egall in Book III. And since *The Faerie Queene* symbolizes heavenly glory seeing itself as yet indirectly, reflected in Time, what is it but Gloriana *qua* mirror image? Spenser himself reveals the analogy, just about, by explicitly presenting the Faery Queen as such in the Proem to Book III (5). In this Legend Art(h)egall flaunts the other side of Arthegality, Arthur's being 'at one' with Gloriana in being equally lost. In a word he represents it not perfectly, as in Book V, nor magnificently, as in Book IV, but gloriously.

The peculiar lostness of Gloriana is brought out most strikingly in the Busirane Cantos. She must be there, because the magician practises at Faery Court. He masks her. So if Art(h)egall equals Gloriana, the magician ought to mask him too. Spenser does in fact hint that he must be there, through his source, *Orlando Furioso* II. 31–IV. 50. Britomart comes upon Scudamour complaining about Amoret's fate at the hands of Busirane in much the same way that Bradamante comes upon Pinabello complaining about his lady's fate at the hands of Atlante. And just as Bradamante tackles Atlante, so Britomart gets to grips with Busirane. Again, alike victorious, they both spare their antagonists, though both magicians are compelled to destroy their prisons. One notable difference, though, is Bradamante's motivation. She attacks Atlante in order to free her own lover, Ruggiero, whom, as she hears from Pinabello, Atlante has captured too. Now one could, of course, tacitly agree that this difference does not call for comment: Spenser has his own tale to tell. But if so, why should he have gone out of his way to make it so like Ariosto's in other respects? Could the resemblance simply be an involuntary and gratuitous echo, resulting from long familiarity with the Italian romance? Since the poet's use of Homer and Virgil has turned out to be anything but mindless, the odds are that he treats Ariosto with comparable finesse. Surely we must infer that Britomart frees Art(h)egall from Busirane as Bradamante frees Ruggiero from Atlante. Even if we had to say that this achievement is so utterly elusive as not to happen at all, it would be hardly more so than that of her counterpart: no sooner is Ruggiero delivered than he is carried off on Atlante's hippogriff. But we do not have to say quite that. The achievement does happen for those who grasp that Busirane is Art(h)egall in disguise. Britomart's action, as defined by its Ariostan matrix, just about releases his hidden identity. The 1590 ending actually alludes to it, through mentioning her envy of Scudamour and Amoret (46). For the contrast beween their bliss and her deprivation would be far more pointed if Busirane should *be* her lover escaping her than if she should merely be reminded that she has not yet found her man. (That she should need to be reminded of this is odd anyway, though apparently true, to judge from the readiness with which she forgets herself throughout Book III in her zest for irrelevant adventures.) Everything favours the equation. For one thing, it qualifies heavily Britomart's success with Busirane and thus truly aligns her with Scudamour, Amoret, and Cupid, symbols of glory mostly opaque, chastity. For another thing, the imaginative leap necessary parallels that required by the Letter's account of Book III, where Spenser leaves it to his readers to grasp that the complaining groom is Scudamour. Besides, Britomart counters Art(h)egall in disguise in Book V (as a woman) and IV (as salvage knight), so that it is fitting that she should do so in Book III as well, in a disguise even more impenetrable. Considered as their meeting the Busirane episode constitutes an appropriately dark variant of their meeting in IV. vi. Also, if Busirane masks Art(h)egall in this sense, he must mask Gloriana in the same sense. They are indeed gloriously at one—an inference that prepares us for the (unrealized) sexual transformation in V. v. Art(h)egall *qua* female eluding the knight Britomart in the final Cantos equals in reverse Florimell eluding Arthur in the opening Cantos: just as she rushes into darkness, so 'he' has darkness rushing in upon him.

It might seem that in identifying Busirane with Art(h)egall Spenser makes him good at heart, particularly in view of his counterpart in Ariosto. Atlante is Ruggiero's foster-father. He does not object to his marriage as such, out of malice, but obstructs it of necessity, given his anxiety that his charge should not get involved in the war, so contrary a road to happiness, and in particular that he should escape his imminent fate, 'morir cristiano a tradimento'. His ideal for Ruggiero is a life at ease in a pleasantly enchanted castle. Having died through grief at the futility of his protective schemes, he positively paves the way for Ruggiero's union with Bradamante, as a voice from the sepulchre.[40] However, it is not as though Ariosto excuses Atlante on the grounds that *he* means well. Rather, he shows us evil at its most insidious, namely when *it* appears to mean well. For Ruggiero to entrust himself to Atlante's benevolent care and shun the agony of fighting against his lady would have been to forfeit his ultimate bliss. In the first Section of this Chapter we saw how the mirror scene equals its Virgilian source in reverse and imports it whole in part. The same relation obtains between the Busirane episode and its Ariostan source. Spenser shows us good at its most insidious, namely where it appears to mean evil: Art(h)egall *qua* Busirane masking life as departure of ease in a horribly enchanted castle. He does in fact introduce the Ruggiero of his own that he seems to leave out in such a way as to make his episode apparently autonomous, thus 'motivating' Britomart as Ariosto does Bradamante. But through the identity of Busirane and Art(h)egall her preliminary, partial, performance, undoing the magician, is identical with the whole, freeing her love. Seeing it in part, we see their union as opposition.

Spenser's other deviations from Ariosto are of the same kind. Just as he infolds Ruggiero and Atlante by virtually confining Art(h)egall inside Busirane, so he infolds the Italian episode generally by situating his action almost entirely within the magician's domain. Bradamante's clash with Atlante takes place outside his castle. Ariosto has nothing to correspond to Spenser's elaborate description of the interior of Busirane's castle. He does have Bradamante, before she reaches the enchanter, witness, in the cave of Merlin, a prophecy about her descendants, which is structurally central to the episode like the castle interior in its English analogue. Spenser actually imitates the prophecy in Ariosto; but he removes it ostentatiously from its proper place to the centre of the flashback, leaving the tapestries and the Mask as a counter-prophetic gap, insisting as they do on the ultimacy of Time. However, for 'ostentatiously' we may read 'ostensibly'. In spite of Busirane, because of Art(h)egall, tapestries and Mask really symbolize chastity, which does prophesy Eternity, however faintly. Again, Scudamour, one of Gloriana's noble quest heroes, appears to be the antitype of Pinabello, who

> tra sua gente scelerata solo
> Leale esser non volse né cortese,
> Ma ne le vizii abominandi e brutti
> Non pur gli altri adeguò, ma passò tutti.[41]

A deadly enemy to Bradamante's family, he attempts to wreck the rescue operation as soon as he has gathered her identity, trapping her in what fortunately turns out to be Merlin's cavern. Considering Scudamour's moral stature, Spenser cannot but omit Ariosto's story of treachery; or so it seems. In fact the story we are left with is itself one of treachery in reverse, involuntary treachery. Scudamour's predicament presents itself to Britomart as an opportunity to join forces with him as Arthur does with Artegall in Book V: to be Sam-ient; much though he tries to dissuade her (xi. 16–17, 19, 24). Since she insists, he does his best to be Artegall by following her through the flaming porch, only to find 'with huge impatience . . . that he could not pas' (27); that is, that he does not represent Time as passage. Instead he lets her in for Art(h)egall *qua* Busirane, Time pretending it is there to stay. Or take Britomart's freeing of Amoret. This appears to be a Spenserian addition, for Ariosto does not describe Bradamante's freeing of Pinabello's lady. What he does describe is the release of a whole band of knights and ladies, of whom he names four males, at a markedly tetradic point.[42] Spenser's one lady reverses (sexually) part (one instead of four) as whole (being, like Gloriana, the infolded counterpart of a multiplicity of knights). The association of the liberated Amoret with Ariosto's four anticipates the Legend of Friendship, whose number it is, just as does Scudamour's self-release from paralysed heroism into search for 'further aide' (xii. 45).

When Bradamante realizes that Atlante is only an old man, she disdains to take his life, even though he begs her to finish him off now that his plans for Ruggiero are proving hopeless. Let him effect his own 'passage', she says.[43] By contrast, Britomart sees no signs of Busirane being on his way out, and therefore

So mightily she smote him, that to ground
He fell halfe dead; next stroke him should have slaine,
Had not the Lady, which by him stood bound,
Dernely unto her called to abstaine,
From doing him to dy. For else her paine
Should be remedilesse, sith none but hee,
Which wrought it, could the same recure againe.
Therewith she stayd her hand, loth stayd to bee;
For life she him envyde, and long'd revenge to see.

(34.)

Again Spenser imitates Ariosto in reverse, by omitting Bradamante's magnanimity. Yet he equals his model even so. Britomart, while barely yielding to Amoret's anxious request to spare Busirane and, in sheer unbelief that he would heal his victim, holding her sword ready to strike (36), actually 'lets him off' demonstrating his transience. In dispelling his own magic Busirane dispels himself: he just evaporates from the fiction, as none of the other evil powers do, without needing to be killed or bound. Since 'glad of life' (35) he gladly lives out his death, he corresponds to Atlante living glad to die. For Britomart to kill Busirane would have been to belie Amoret, and hence herself as Amoret's champion. Her violent intentions, pointedly aroused by the wound he inflicts upon her (33), which brings home her equivalence to Amoret, parallel her recoil from identity with her mirror image. Love must indeed oppose Time, by its very nature; but that means first of all, in order of presentation, painfully suffer Time in opposition. It is Britomart in Book III, not Scudamour in Book IV, whom Hieatt might have accused of tending to be overbold. The context of their exploits supports this. Whereas Womanhood's rebuke of Scudamour in the Temple of Venus is virtually overruled by the smiles of the goddess, nothing qualifies the inscriptions above the doors in the House of Busirane, enjoining Britomart to 'be bold', certainly, yet also to 'be not too bold' (xi. 54). Hill traces these injunctions to Ovid's myth of Venus and Adonis, as rendered by Golding:

> she warned also thee
> Adonis . . . if thou wooldst have warned bee.
> *Bee bold* on cowards (Venus sayd) for whoso dooth advaunce
> Himselfe against the bold, may hap too meete with sum mischaunce.
> Wherfore I pray thee my sweete boy *forbeare too bold to bee.*[44]

She misses the implication of her discovery, though. The allusion suggests that Britomart is another Adonis; a suggestion she apparently belies by forbearing, if only just (as she should, being another Venus). However, her victorious tolerance of Busirane aligns her precisely with the Adonis of the Garden, 'eterne in mutabilitie', indulging 'wicked Time' (vi. 47, 39), in token of chastity. She represents this same virtue also as mostly Adonis and barely Venus, to highlight Man almost imperceptibly revived out of his death in separateness, due to his wound 'sub inguine' ('in his codds').[45]

IV The Grand Encounter

Just as it is the middle scene of the flashback in particular that seems to link its constituents, so it is the central Book in our triad of Legends in particular that seems to link them together as progressive Britomart-Artegall narrative. Take their first meeting, in Canto iv. Although it could not possibly be called the result of Britomart's search, as an accidental event it follows on naturally enough from her fortuitous career in Book III; while Artegall's emergence might be said to follow on by default: since Book III does not describe his previous career, the question of sequence does not arise. Only when we grasp, with appropriate difficulty, that Britomart rescues Artegall out of Busirane does their subsequent clash reveal its incongruity. Free, he ought to have been Satyrane's partisan, not his opponent. And it is Book III that makes for this conspicuous illogicality. It requires considerable effort to see that the perspective of Book IV has its own, inconspicuous, illogicality. True, Britomart and Artegall both appear as bolts out of the blue, rushing in from nowhere and for no given reason. However, one feels entitled to infer that Britomart somehow got wind of Satyrane's proclamation (ii. 26) and held herself in knightly duty bound to procure Florimell's girdle for 'his' Amoret. Surely the poet need not spell out everything? But then, in Canto v she allows the false Florimell to snatch it from Amoret without protest (19-20); which argues little sense of public honour. Also, her last-minute entry looks peculiar. One would have expected her to participate from the start, like the other knights. If, for some reason, she could not make it in time, this explanation should be in the text: we cannot just invent it. This applies to Artegall as well. Besides, he does not even have a lady of his own to vindicate. We must read symbolically. That both Artegall and Britomart turn up at the last moment to perform extremely similar actions highlights friendship as the virtue to end all virtues, virtue coming into its own. That they do so in opposition reminds us that 'yet the end is not', as Merlin had said (III. iii. 50)—or, as Spenser himself comments here, 'so nought may be esteemed happie till the end' (IV. iv. 43). But to qualify as a separate allegory the tournament scene must be discontinuous at both ends. And who could deny that it leads up to the judgement scene in Canto v? Even that scene itself does not wind up the story but remains open-ended. As soon as she senses that the knights are going to fall out among themselves, Britomart 'upon her first adventure forth did ride, / To seeke her lov'd' (29). Does this not imply that her involvement with Satyrane is, as its unsatisfactory outcome now reminds her, a distraction from her search? Again, how can we explain Artegall's attempt at revenge in Canto vi if not with reference to his defeat at her hands in Canto iv and the judges' confirmation of her victory in

Canto v, considered as previous events? Moreover, in Britomart's recognition of Artegall Spenser would seem to be making explicit its temporal link with the flashback itself:

> When Britomart with sharpe avizefull eye
> Beheld the lovely face of Artegall . . .
> She gan eftsoones it to her mind to call,
> To be the same which in her fathers hall
> Long since in that enchaunted glasse she saw.
>
> (26.)

To answer the first query we should ponder the conditions of the

> solemne feast, with publike turneying,
> To which all knights with them their Ladies are to bring.
>
> And of them all she that is fayrest found,
> Shall have that golden girdle for reward,
> And of those Knights who is most stout on ground,
> Shall to that fairest Ladie be prefard.
>
> (ii. 26–7.)

This is odd. One can see that every knight would wish himself to be acknowledged as the strongest and his lady as the fairest. But usually, by romance convention, a knight's strength is regarded as itself the measure of his lady's beauty.[46] Not so at Satyrane's festival, where the two are to be assessed independently. The knights are as ready to present their ladies for inspection at the beauty contest (v. 10–11) as they are to join in the tournament. This rules out that the latter precedes the former. No knight, once beaten, could wish his lady to be chosen in the certain knowledge that as her champion he will be superseded. No knight, coming out on top, would run the risk of having to abandon his own lady. Nor, for that matter, could the ladies' desire to win the girdle be totally unaffected, positively or negatively, by their feelings about the victorious knight. Yet nothing suggests that it is not. Actually, one wonders why they consent to having the victor imposed on them at all. According to the code of chivalry to ladies 'the world this franchise ever yeelded, / That of their loves choise they might freedom clame' (ix. 37). Moreover, they have prior commitments, which they could not ignore without dishonour. As a two-stage event Satyrane's festival is a monstrous absurdity. Nobody could want to take part in it unless they should all know that the strongest knight already serves the fairest lady, so that there will be no embarrassing adjustment in the event. But they could not possibly know this if it should be the case. And, in fact, it is not: false Florimell outshines even Amoret (v. 13–14). Nor does this complete the list of incongruities. How can you allot a girdle that has itself the power to decide who shall wear it (16–19)? And why does Blandamour, 'who thought he had the trew / And very Florimell' (13), not at once present her to Satyrane, claim the girdle for her as of right, and insist that he should cancel both tournament and beauty contest? To judge from the universal failure to question her identity, his demand would certainly have been met. The festival ought not to have happened. Its outcome, false Florimell's free choice of the non-combatant Braggadochio, is not only hilariously funny but, on the face of it, a supremely just denunciation of the whole enterprise.

Canto v does not follow on from Canto iv. The ladies, in their eagerness for the girdle, are not pitted against each other as rival persons. Even as a multitude of competitors they are at one in their manifestly celestial beauty, which the poet cannot describe for want of '*golden* pen' (12). Thus they stand for friendship as almost transparent glory; as they do in their patently just aspiration to the golden, circular prize, attribute of 'Dame Venus . . . What time she usd to live *in wively sort*' (3): Venus Androgyne, symbolic of Eternity. Of course it will not fit any one of them separately (17). Even Amoret can wear it only 'at last' (19). Yet this uncomfortable fact is nothing worse than a mortifying joke (18), to complement Busirane's abduction of Amoret *qua* mad prank and Merlin's feigned misunderstanding of Glauce in the flashback. Their inferiority to false Florimell conveys the same qualification. For they are inferior. Her artificiality must not be taken as a suggestion that she is a show-piece of cosmetics, unattractive to the truly discerning Lewisian eye, attuned to natural beauty. '*All* that her saw with wonder ravisht weare' (14), not excluding Britomart. Her preference for Amoret's 'virtuous government' implies no negation of the other's 'beauties wonderment' (20) nor a suspicion of vice. Like Scudamour's tacit razing of the Island Paradise in the Temple of Venus episode, it intimates that even as friendship love, though virtually heaven, remains still virtue. Florimell is fake in that she pretends to be unqualified glory. She is too beautiful to be true—whence the Homeric simile of the 'guilefull *Gold*smith' (15). She 'shone as *Phebes* light, / Amongst the lesser starres in evening cleare' (14), both like and unlike Gloriana *qua* Hesperus at the centre of Arthur's τελαμών (I. vii. 30), drowning them in her own light rather than vanishing in their favour. That is why all take her for the real thing, true Florimell, 'yet thought that Florimell was not so faire as shee' (IV. v. 14)—an illogicality which will duly embarrass literal readers. Similarly, ignoring the rules of Satyrane's festival with apparent justice, she symbolizes love as though already beyond virtue militant. Not that we should not despise Braggadochio and side with those prepared for a trial of strength. Significantly, however, their efforts are gratuitous: Britomart and Triamond, the jousters with the greatest prominence in Book IV, need not fight for a reward they claim to possess already in their own Amoret and Canacee (20–1). By way of complementary metaphor, the poet sends Britomart on her search for Artegall again only to stress that in their very clash 'he was unto her selfe most nie' (29), instead of yielding to the 'neede, / [Her] hard adventures and strange haps to tell', 'here' and 'now' (28).

Canto vi does not follow on from Canto v any more than Canto v follows on from Canto iv. Artegall's revenge may seem to make perfect sense as narrative. He has a motive for his action. However, both motive and action are ignoble. Since the judges decided correctly that he did not win in the tournament and therefore does not deserve the prize, he has no just cause for complaint. His grudge is most unknightly. And in seeking private satisfaction, by ambushing Britomart, rather than arguing his case, such as it is, publicly, he himself commits the 'foule despight' of which he so unjustifiably holds her guilty (vi. 5). Can this be our patron of justice, fitting partner for blameless Britomart? Can it be that her progress towards marital felicity turns upon the spiteful treachery of her destined husband? Furthermore, considering his recent experience of Britomart's effortless superiority in battle, it is strange that Artegall never forms a realistic estimate of his chances of success; still more so that he suddenly proves to be more than a match for her (16–18). Indeed, his base, imprudent attack would seem useless as an attempt to find compensation for his loss 'both of victors meede, / And eke of honour' (v. 9): there are no spectators to witness his come-back, while Britomart does not have her prize. Ironically, he would have gained it if he had not left the judgement scene in high dudgeon (21). His grievance is largely imaginary. And then, Britomart presumably recognizes the Salvage Knight as the first opponent she overthrew in the tournament, since he still wears his distinctive disguise (vi. 5). Knowing that he was not there to receive false Florimell, she could easily guess the reason for his hostility. Why, then, does she not beg for a parley, to put him in the picture? It is not as though, taken completely by surprise, she has no opportunity. Artegall allows Scudamour, who has meanwhile joined him, to attack her first (9–10). And even Scudamour's attack hardly qualifies as a blind onslaught, which leaves her no option:

> soone as she him saw approaching neare
> With so fell rage, her selfe she lightly gan
> To dight, to welcome him, well as she can.
>
> (10.)

If she has time to prepare herself, she must have time to eschew the clash, in a lance fight on horseback. Her failure to do so passes credibility, if she should recognize Scudamour; as she must, since Artegall does too (3). After all, Scudamour is her protégé, on whose behalf she has rescued Amoret from Busirane and for whom she is now searching. Since she was 'stonisht sore' on finding him absent after her defeat of the magician (III. xii. 45), she ought to be totally bewildered by his turning against her, and desperate to stop him. Instead she wipes him out with careless indifference in less than a stanza. Nor does she, subsequently, demand an explanation for his double folly. On the contrary, he, without courting forgiveness at all, demands news of Amoret, 'without offence';

that is, well aware of being offensive (IV. vi. 34). It is Artegall who 'pardon her besought his errour frayle, / That had done outrage in so high degree' (22), prompted by her sex—strangely, since inability to see through her disguise would be the one thing for which he need not blame himself. Equally strangely, Britomart continues severe, instead of thankfully accepting his apologies for her own sake, survival with honour. Worse, she tries hard to keep up a pretence of severity even after she has discovered that the Salvage Knight is none other than her own Artegall (27, 29, 32). One should think that she, who has allegedly been seeking him for so long, ought to be even more anxious to desist, aghast at the nearly fatal manner in which Providence has brought them together and oblivious of his mean revenge. True, Spenser does not ascribe her stance to lingering anger on that account. He provides a more absurd alternative. She keeps him at arm's length as an importunate suitor, 'full of wrath for *that late stroke*', which revealed her sex, and 'threatning to strike, *unlesse he would withstand*' (23).

Artegall's revenge does not express personal spite. Complementing the spuriousness of Florimell and Britomart's renunciation of her, he highlights these as the need for virtue militant, as befits the patron of justice, glory suppressed. His dishonourableness is this meaning almost completely translated into story: near-exemplary fiction, which makes him symbolic of friendship as well. Further evidence of this other meaning readily emerges. In 'getting even' with Britomart, he mirrors her manifestly rather than obscurely, so that her identification outweighs her repudiation. The grand encounter stresses this aspect even more than their encounter in the tournament: there Spenser does not so much advertise their similarity in opposition directly as prevent Artegall's defeat, which belies it, from having any serious impact, by keeping the scene minimally short, making no mention of his mortification, and ignoring the dramatic irony of the clash instead of marking it rhetorically as in Canto vi (16–17). Since the episodes are polarized synonyms even so, we need not postulate any sudden increase in Artegall's strength and skill or, lame alternative, attribute the more successful result to (providential) luck. Again, his attack on Britomart to deprive her of the lady-prize she has already ceded matches her gratuitous participation in the festival, in reverse. Certainly, he does not know that Florimell has been assigned to him, or he would not have fought. But his ignorance is not contingent. It corresponds to his unawareness of his British nationality (III. iii. 26). Britomart enlightens him on his terms. She fights back in order to be revealed as near glory through his stroke 'toward th'end' (IV. vi. 18). 'Her ventayle shard away . . . her *angels* face, unseene afore, / *Like to the ruddie morne* appeared in sight' (19); as when Merlin sees through her disguise (III. iii. 20). This analogy draws attention to Artegall's typical 'dimness'. Like Merlin he should have 'descryde . . . her selfe' without exposing it. That is why he craves pardon. However, in his apologetic worship (IV. vi. 22) he overadjusts, treating Britomart as heaven itself, as though he identified her with false Florimell. As friendship she represents only the dawn of Eternity. Her long locks resembling sunbeams (III. ix. 20), the glory of her sex,[47] are compared to the product of an honest rather than a cheating goldsmith yet also said to have 'loosd their wonted band' (IV. vi. 20)—a 'realistic detail' signifying glory transparent but still 'apart'. Hence her insistence that he should continue fighting. His determined submission, with his helmet covering his face, mirrors 'beyond recognition' her determined militancy, with her face revealed; so that her attitude is one of violent repudiation. But this is only a fleeting reminiscence of Book III, like Merlin's pretended failure to see Glauce's point (III. iii. 17). Artegall submits only to have his beaver raised (IV. vi. 25). This prompts her to relent almost completely, so that he becomes recognizably like Britomart with 'her ventayle shard away' (19). True, he replicates even so his appearance in Ryence's mirror, with his 'ventayle lifted up' (III. ii. 24). Actually, it is to ensure this perception that Spenser makes her remember her experience 'in her fathers hall / Long since' (IV. vi. 26). The implication, that she has forgotten all about it, invalidates literal reading: the notion of a progressive search hinges on the assumption that she has been treasuring his picture in her mind all along. The poet's reference back explodes sequentiality even as it seems to establish it. It marries the Middle Books into separateness, like the wedding of Scudamour and Amoret. Britomart's distant memory of Artegall as herself in reverse is a thematic symbol; complemented by mild repudiation of him.

Britomart and Artegall remain contrary. Although she allows him to woo her and consents to marry him, they hold back (41); significantly, because there is nothing in the story to prevent the immediate consummation of their love. To be sure, Britomart still has to fulfil her vow to Scudamour to seek and revenge Amoret (38), while Artegall still has to get his quest in aid of Irena out of the way (42). But these tasks cannot be regarded as prior commitments. Neither appears to be in a hurry to undertake them, for they do not set out until after 'they had long time there taken rest'. Yet neither, as far as we can tell, experiences any conflict of love versus duty. Artegall seems keen 'to follow that, which he did long propound'. At least, he expresses no regret on having to leave Britomart. And she, instead of appreciating and easing by her acquiescence any emotional dilemma, mindful of her own, is utterly reluctant to let him go and clings to him a long part of the way (44–6), apparently oblivious of Scudamour, nor reminded of him by the more dutiful Artegall. The tasks do not *cause* the wedding's postponement: like the wedding they are themselves postponed, as though they were negligible, in token of friendship, the end even as the end is not yet. For Artegall to get back to work is not to defer the end but, on the contrary, to realize it, though in hiding, as justice. He de-parts only to go it alone, all one, secretly precipitating Eternity. It is Britomart who wants '*the time* for to delay' (45). In accompanying him she identifies herself with his task yet forestalls his de-part-ure, so that they are manifestly at one in opposition, again in token of friendship. So far from forsaking Scudamour in this way, she 'forsakes' Artegall by trying to maintain with him the same relationship in which she finds herself with Scudamour himself when forced to let Artegall go 'at last' (46) into Book V: togetherness in adventures the need for which she barely admits. This insistence to find Scudamour in Artegall compensates for her insistence in Book III to find Artegall in Scudamour, yet also parallels it: in both cases she seeks to deny the 'questing' identity, in vain. But while Scudamour frustrates her almost from the start, Artegall frustrates her only towards the end, in accordance with the shift from chastity to friendship. Correspondingly, whereas in Book III she returns from an Artegall who virtually eludes her to a Scudamour absent in reproachful despair, having gained Amoret only just 'with proofe of last extremity' (III. xi. 18), here she returns from an Artegall who can hardly get away from her to a Scudamour present in reproachful hope, having lost Amoret only just through 'fearelesse' over-confidence (IV. vi. 35–6).

For his part, Scudamour, who in the Busirane episode had almost completely failed to be another Artegall to Britomart, here almost completely succeeds. While in both cases he involuntarily betrays her as such, the betrayal, maximal there, is minimal here. Not only are Scudamour and Britomart virtually Sam-ient from the end of Canto vi, with Amoret to all intents and purposes their common cause and Scudamour so obviously fit that Britomart hardly stands in for him. At the beginning of the Canto we actually seem to see him lapsing casually from manifest equality with Britomart to side with an Artegall who also equals Britomart manifestly, though as yet in opposition. Confronted by Artegall, he 'forth issewed / To have rencountred him in equall race' (3), like herself later on. Artegall has second thoughts. As he 'vewed / The armes he bore, his speare he gan abase, / And voide his course', to submit and crave pardon. But since this change of mind resembles his later reaction to the revelation of Britomart's sex, it seems only to confirm Scudamour as another Britomart. Yet Scudamour's response seems to suggest also that he is not. Although he does observe that 'small harme it were / For any knight, upon a ventrous knight / Without displeasance for to prove his spere' (4), he accepts Artegall's submission, unlike Britomart. But then, Artegall submits to Britomart as though she were full glory, in that he 'of his wonder made religion, / Weening some heavenly goddesse he did see' (22); whereas he submits to Scudamour because of his shield, to judge from the fact that he addresses him by name, 'Ah gentle Scudamour' (3). That is, he recognizes him as near glory, in virtue of the major emblem of friendship. Accordingly he wishes to be known 'magnificently', as Salvage Knight (4). Since he thus symbolizes the virtue of Book IV himself, its quest hero changes sides vacuously. Even so he betrays Britomart; for he does not align himself with Artegall's true identity. We see this betrayal, slight considering Artegall's (successful) determination to show himself Britomart's equal, also in the fact that Scudamour, while joining with the Arthur of Satyrane's feast in the same cause as though they were Sam-ient, begs to stand in for him, rather, when it comes to the crunch (9) and, through his defeat by Britomart (10), puts Artegall in a position to substitute for him and so confirms him in his 'magnificent' role.

Nevertheless, the main thing is that here Artegall and Britomart clearly come together via Scudamour as they do not in Book III. Indeed, it may seem that both the knight of justice and the knight of friendship make amends for their shortcomings as Artegall when, after the revelation of Britomart's sex, they jointly worship 'that peerelesse patterne of Dame *natures* pride, / And heavenly *image* of perfection' as though it were 'some celestiall vision' (24)—a worship in Scudamour hardly intelligible, one must say, in narrative terms, as a response to the discovery that Britomart is not a rival male: it suggests unfaithfulness to Amoret, rather. He exults in his companion's adoring humility, utter height in utter depth symbolic of justice, and so calls him by his true name (without showing the ignorance or at least surprise one would expect on literal reading): 'Certes Sir Artegall, / I joy to see you lout so low on ground' (28). But of course the sheer visibility of Britomart's glory disqualifies their worship as an allegory of justice. Her excitement on hearing her love's name (29) should not deceive us into thinking that Scudamour identifies him for her. After all, she has already identified him herself (26). As we have seen, though, her distant memory of him as a mirror image makes him symbolic of friendship. Scudamour conveys his true meaning; which, to be sure, she cannot share in Book IV. However, in this very act he stands in for Artegall, thus testifying again to his 'magnificent' leanings. Moreover, he manœuvres Britomart, vacuously, into his likeness. Speaking to her about her liberation of Amoret and addresssing her as 'Sir' for the purpose, he treats her as an Arthur to take over from rather than join: 'That where ye left, I may her seeke' (34). And when he hears of Amoret's loss, he 'dies' (37), so as to prompt Britomart's offer to substitute for him (38). True, he recovers himself to the extent of accompanying Britomart. She does not need to rescue Amoret for him, as in Book III. Yet neither do they jointly rescue Amoret, as Arthur and Artegall do Samient in Book V. Instead they are forestalled by Arthur, who himself has been forestalled by Timias, who in his turn has been half forestalled by Amoret herself. We are to infer that Amoret is almost as safe in the very midst of danger as she herself assumes when she 'of nought affeard, / Walkt through the wood, for pleasure, or for need' (vii. 4)—a thumb-nail allegory, this, of love, even while of necessity still confined to *silva*, already enjoying itself to the full: naturally over-confident friendship; not, as some would have it, a delicate intimation that Amoret wants to do a wee-wee.[48]

V Radigund

If the illusion of sequential Britomart–Artegall narrative is powerful as between Books III and IV, it is even more so as between Books IV and V. For Spenser reintroduces her in Book V awaiting 'the utmost date, assynde / For his returne' from his quest in aid of Irena (vi. 3), in accordance with his promise, on leaving her in Book IV, to be back in three months' time (vi. 43). Yet he suggests this palpable continuity in Book IV only to hide it completely in Book V, in token of justice. Book IV makes Artegall fall in love at some point during his quest, in saying that he 'all this while was bound / Upon an hard adventure . . . which he did long propound' (42). But in Book V, which makes him undertake this task as soon as Gloriana has chosen him (i. 3–4, 13), he nowhere temporarily abandons it in order to participate in Satyrane's tournament. Nor are there any signs that he treasures the thought of Britomart. We never once find him fondly recalling his first meeting with her or eagerly anticipating the projected consummation of their love. For instance, the equanimity with which he bears Envy and Detraction, towards the end of the Book, could so easily have been made convincing by a reference to the prospect of soon being united with Britomart. It is not. Even her intervention on his behalf in Book V itself, compelling testimony, one would have thought, to active persistence in her care for him, elicits no response whatsoever, whether gratitude or embarrassment. He allows her to scold and rearm him like a senseless doll (vii. 40–1), without either attempting to justify himself or else penitently concurring with her censure. He seems to accept her authority over him as a matter of course, rather than because of any previous commitment, subject to the strains and stresses of contingent existence. Who shall say whether he even recognizes her? He certainly leaves her, to resume his quest, with utter indifference. Britomart, to be sure, manifests jealous concern; not, however, on account of his curious blankness as to their common past and future, which she does nothing to remedy. She takes him to task for his ungainly condition *per se*, not for his fall for Radigund's beauty, which, incompatible as it is with his solemn vows of love to herself (IV. vi. 41), one would assume to be his real crime. Similarly, she does not exact the promise of his return that he so readily offered of his own accord in Book IV. Though pained by their separation, she finds consolation in the 'hope of his successe', 'seeing his honor, which she tendred chiefe, / Consisted much in that adventures priefe' (V, vii. 44); not, to judge from the actual text, in any expectation of a speedy reunion, as Book IV would lead one to think. The fact that she feels comforted at all, set against Artegall's drastic change in attitude towards her, makes her present plight unintelligible as a prolongation of that in Book IV. More is meant than meets the eye when Spenser calls his departure 'her *new* cause of griefe'.

The novelty of Britomart's situation in Book V consists in a self-reversal that aligns her fully with Artegall. Instead of opposing each other in their very equality, as in Book IV, they coincide, though separate—a meaningful paradox. Artegall's unawareness of Britomart and her failure to assert herself over against him as the object of his commitment alike imply the complete coalescence which, as distinct characters, they belie. In their hidden indistinguishability they stand for Eternity itself immersed in Time, justice.

Accordingly they are not as good as married, as in Book IV, but actually married as obscurely as possible. With studied casualness the poet calls Artegall Britomart's 'Lord' (vi. 18; vii. 40, 45) as well as her knight and her love. In its context, depicting his domination by women, this quite special title, which expresses a husband's authority over his wife on the model of Christ's headship of the Church, looks heavily ironical. But then, so it does in the biblical passage that establishes it. Sarah calls Abraham 'my lord' when dismissing as laughable the idea that, in their old age, he could still be the channel for the fulfilment of God's promise to them, offspring.[49] Yet he is. 'Lord' symbolizes heaven in spite of the evidence; indeed, disdaining evidence. Christ Himself is 'Lord' on the strength of His wilful abdication from divinity.[50] Spenser does not use the title, with male chauvinism, to criticize Artegall literally for failing to 'be a man'. We must abandon the prevailing conception of the episode as an *exemplum* of the iniquity of female supremacy corrected, as though he were endorsing women's natural and proper, as well as divinely ordained, deference to the male.[51] It seems to have escaped our exemplary interpreters' notice that, on this view, he would be undermining his own case. For he has a man emancipated with mindless passivity at the behest of a woman celebrated for the masculinity supposedly denounced in Radigund. Similarly, his community of Amazons reforms itself vacuously in their enthusiastic embrace of a male magistracy for the sake of the woman who introduces it and hence must be the ultimate authority: 'All they as a Goddesse her adoring, / Her wisedome did admire, and hearkned to her loring', not to that of Artegall (vii. 42-3). The knight's submissive attitude to Britomart, his marriage partner, would exemplify the evil rather than its correction. After all, he does not obey Radigund through inclination (v. 22, 23, 26). Spenser's alleged blast against the monstrous regiment of women explodes itself. Artegall's lordship in subordination highlights the paradox of justice, glory's self-denial. Britomart affirms this with a vengeance. What grates on her is not his (glorious) effeminacy but the spuriousness of his androgyny. So far from recalling him to his manhood for its own sake, as his true self, she makes him hide rather than compromise 'das ewig Weibliche' in him; that is, she forces him to model himself on her (with vacuous force). Gloriana treats him likewise: she occasions his return to Faery Court in disgrace rather than in glory precisely when he has restored Irena, everlasting peace. Neither of his ladies will allow him, the perfect end, to have done manifestly; just as, despite having been palpably lifted by 'the *heavens* . . . to lawfull soveraintie', they foster their own glory as virtue on earth, like '*vertuous* women . . . borne to base humilitie' (25).

Adopting this symbolic interpretation, we can account for Spenser's Homeric simile comparing Britomart, as she comes upon Artegall in his degradation, with Penelope receiving back the long lost and hardly recognizable Ulysses (vii. 39). To literal readers this comparison could not be more inept. Artegall, so far from being another Ulysses finally returning to his homeland long after the completion of the Greeks' punitive expedition against Troy, gets caught up on his way out to vindicate Irena. And Britomart, so far from being another Penelope incredulous on finding herself reunited after all with Ulysses, whom she had passively waited for without real hope, having long given him up for dead, actively intervenes to send Artegall, whose identity she never questions, off on his mission again. Even the immediate ground for the comparison proves perverse: Ulysses, difficult to identify because of his 'many scarres and many hoary heares', offers precisely the 'dreadfull manly looke' (40) that Artegall does not and, having just killed Penelope's wooers, could not possibly prompt Britomart's complaint about Artegall, 'where be / Those mighty palmes, the which ye wont t'embrew / In bloud of Kings'. We must take the simile allegorically. It instructs us to regard what appears to be an intermediate stage of a progressing narrative as a symbol of the end spiting itself into the midst, glory doing justice to itself, as Penelope scorns (ἀτιμάζει) the be-all and end-all of her life, her very own Ulysses in rags.[52]

Let us consider Radigund, beginning with her name. According to Aptekar 'the whole Radigund episode is illuminated by the fact that one of Radigund's namesakes, Saint Radigund, was remarkable for her insistence on remaining a virgin after her marriage: from an anti-Catholic viewpoint, a notable example of wifely disobedience'.[53] Really? Even rabid Protestants cannot have been unaware that Catholics cherish wifely obedience as much as they do themselves. True, they regard virginity as a supreme value. But this leads them to exalt celibacy rather than to cultivate unconsummated marriages. Spenser's supposed polemic would be as pointless as its target is untypical. Worse, it would be grossly misdirected. St. Radigund's behaviour, so far from exemplifying female 'maistrye' in the cause of a pseudo-ideal, finds its explanation in her forced marriage to Clotair I, who had conquered her country and put her brother to death.[54] To refuse coition in such circumstances is to refuse to make a mockery of holy matrimony; an altogether laudable decision from any point of view. Anyway, Spenser's indictment fails to suggest its object. His Radigund, unmarried, lustful, and committed to the subjugation of men on principle, qualifies not even as a caricature of her canonized counterpart. Aptekar's analogy illuminates with darkness visible. But then, *The Faerie Queene* consists not of variously plain or far-fetched analogies but of dark conceits. In calling his Amazon Radigund Spenser models her symbolically on a historical, real-life, virgin wife, to suggest Eternity as manifestly at odds with itself. Thus she contrasts within equivalence with Britomart as Eternity in hidden agreement with itself. We see this polarization in Radigund's Amazonian flaunting of her sex as against Britomart's wilful resort to masculinity; and in Radigund's disastrous reign as queen as against Britomart's beneficent rule 'as Princess' (vii. 42; as 'Arthegall' she parallels *Prince* Arthur). The poet's choice of name makes Radigund also, symbolically, a Frankish queen. As ruler of a race of invaders she is frankly, openly, what Britomart is in virtue of her disguise as 'Angela, the Saxon Queene' (III. iii. 58). Significantly, the Franks of Radigund's time were already manifestly settled. To judge from Gregory of Tours, though, they were usually embroiled in internecine strife. Their illustrious age of Charlemagne was still to come. By contrast, Angela's Saxons were imperceptibly but single-mindedly settling.

Sir Terpin says that Radigund behaves as she does

for the sake of Bellodant the bold,
To whom she bore most fervent love of late,
And wooed him by all the waies she could:
But when she saw at last, that he ne would
For ought or nought be wonne unto her will,
She turn'd her love to hatred manifold.

(V. iv. 30.)

This does not explain her as a person, though. Perhaps the phenomenon of frustrated love developing into a compulsion to unman the sex is intelligible to psycho-analysts. But Spenser's conspicuous failure to offer any psychological rationalization at all hardly suggests profound insights unverbalized only for want of our modern science of the mind. His characters are personifications. Radigund loves Bellodant by definition. As an Amazon, woman yet warrior, she equals Bellodant, both 'hating war' and 'giving war', the paradox of justice in Time as militant peace. She also hates him by definition. For all their equality he will not be transformed into womanhood 'at last', even though he represents the end of Time. Radigund does not change from love to hate. Her 'hatred manifold' *is* her love 'turn'd': intolerance of multiplicity and craving for eternal peace are two sides of the same coin. Naturally this hatred expresses itself in defiance of 'all the brave Knights, that hold of Maidenhead' (29), who, after all, unfold as men the woman Gloriana.

The introductory description of Radigund in Canto v (1-4) identifies another counterpart; as Aptekar correctly notes, only to press yet again for a false analogy. 'Radigund resembles the disguised Venus, and, even more, the hunt- and love-ready Dido who, coming out, splendidly dressed, at dawn, attended by a great throng, was soon to try to deflect Aeneas from the course of his duty.'[55] The suggestion that Radigund deflects Artegall from the course of his duty is specious. Spenser certainly defines Artegall's submission to her as a predicament. Yet there is no hint that he feels restive because of his duty to Irena; as, for literal readers, he ought to, since his predicament results from his own choice, not from *force majeure.* Radigund deflects Artegall not from any course of action but from masculinity. Her obstructive passion concerns Artegall in female trappings. Thus she contrasts with Dido, who, maintaining a precarious foothold in hostile country, is moved by the heroism of Aeneas and yields to her passion for him when her sister Anna conjures up the military glory the Trojan hero and his band would bring to the colony of Tyrian exiles: 'Teucrum comitantibus armis, / Punica se quantis attollet gloria rebus.'[56] The point at which Spenser aligns Radigund with Dido heightens our sense of their dissimilarity. Radigund comes out not to engage in a friendly hunt with a stranded voyager, as yet dependent on her protection, of whom she is already enamoured but to decide in single combat the fate of Sir Terpin's formidable avenger, who has already inflicted great ruin on her state and for whom at this juncture she cannot be supposed to feel anything but hatred. Once again the parallelism subverts itself literally. To appreciate it as a conceit we should take our cue from what it actually conveys, namely Radigund as Dido *qua* Venus or, to be more specific, *qua* Venus in the guise of a votaress of Diana.[57] The end term, Venus, is far more prominent than the middle term, Dido; an impression reinforced by Radigund's unmistakable similarity to Belphœbe (II. iii. 26–7), herself modelled primarily on Virgil's Venus.[58] Hence Radigund is first and foremost a symbol of heavenly love. As we shall see, her identification as Dido actually confirms this, even while alluding to the necessity for her to represent her realm militantly, as she does in her battle with Artegall.

In the event Dido does not instate Aeneas as her champion. She wants to make love, nor war. Yet it would be a very insensitive reader of the *Aeneid* indeed who can remain content to sum her up as a temptress seducing him from his proper course. True, Renaissance readers perceived the characters of classical epic as images of virtue and vice. But this does not imply any reduction to semi-abstractions, whose 'ideal' morality, instead of being enacted within a nexus of personal relationships, to some extent absolves them from it. Virgil goes out of his way to present Dido's frenzy and self-immolation so as to arouse pity and terror in genuinely tragic fashion. No one could possibly feel the kind of righteous satisfaction at her fate that is prompted by the collapse of suprapersonal embodiments of evil as found in romance or fairy tale. Moreover, the Latin poet carefully refrains from describing the condition of Aeneas, as though to forestall our measuring his 'degradation' and censuring Dido's influence accordingly. Who shall say whether he is another Rinaldo basking voluptuously in Armida's embraces or rather another homesick Ulysses wistfully longing to be released from the no longer pleasing Calypso?[59] We learn only that he readily falls for her and as readily abandons her at the summons of Jove's messenger. To be sure, rumour has it that 'nunc hiemem inter se luxu, quam longa, fovere / regnorum immemores turpique cupidine captos'. But then, rumour 'pariter facta atque infecta canebat': Virgil will not commit himself. Dido is definitely a person and more certainly spellbound than spellbinding. Hence it would be arbitrary to insist on Aeneas' duty to Italy without even considering whether he might not have incurred a duty to Dido. In fact, the notion of being in duty bound to live up to your *fatum*, the ruling principle in Virgil's universe, barely makes sense. Now Aeneas' self-defence—'nec coniugis umquam / praetendi taedas'—does not stand up at all well, morally, against Dido's withering accusation that he has abused her hospitality and affection: 'perfide, perfide.'[60] Convinced that their union could only be temporary, he ought not to have consented to it at all. 'I told you so' is a rotten excuse. However, the mere thought of Aeneas the villain is so patently damaging to his epic stature and hence so prejudicial to Virgil's sanity as to discredit the narrowly moral approach *a priori*. It is not as though Aeneas swerves from his duty, or even from his fate (how could he?). On the contrary, he already tastes the consummation of his destiny. It is not some cruelly irrelevant quirk of fortune but purposive fate which brings Aeneas and Dido together, the selfsame fate which cannot but part them, falling over itself to fulfil what cannot yet be fulfilled, the promise of New Troy. Already Juno and Venus, still implacable enemies, are apparently acting in collusion over Carthage ('quin potius pacem aeternam pactosque hymenaeos / exercemus?'—'perge, sequar'); as one day, according to Jupiter's prophecy, they will both whole-heartedly favour the Roman 'imperium sine fine' in which 'claudentur Belli portae'. Already Aeneas finds himself within the rising walls of a city which, centred as it is around a temple where the glory and pathos of Troy in its downfall are most feelingly depicted ('sunt hic etiam sua praemia laudi, / sunt lacrimae rerum'), emanates the very spirit of New Troy. Here he is welcomed with striking prevenient grace, hardly matched in Italy itself, into a situation lacking manifest divine deterrents: Iarbas is only a very minor Turnus. Here he is given ample opportunity to expatiate fondly on the Trojans' hardships: 'renovare dolorem', yes, but surely in the sense so poignantly anticipated once when he was in dire distress, 'forsan et haec olim meminisse iuvabit', as though from the vantage-point of a destiny already secured.[61] It is this understanding of Virgil that informs Spenser's conceit. Radigund relates to Gloriana as Dido and Carthage do to Lavinia and Rome. She symbolizes glory only too obviously, confounding itself.

The marked contextual difference between the Venerean appearances of Dido and Radigund precludes any literal analogy. Spenser evokes Virgil's context for thematic purposes. The hunting scene leads up to Dido's consummation of her love unsealed by marriage. This condition amounts to a contradiction in terms (for marriage is legalized cohabitation, not merely the formal sanction). As such it symbolizes Eternity manifestly at odds with itself, like the condition of virgin wife which Radigund inherits in virtue of her name. Spenser implicitly demands its transfer from Dido to Radigund. He makes Artegall's clash with and submission to Radigund a replica of his grand encounter with Britomart in Book IV. His behaviour in the two episodes is the same, both in its outward course and in its aim, to prove a match for would-be infolders of the Order of Maidenhead. Now Britomart 'yeelded her consent / To be his love, and take him for her Lord, / Till they with mariage meet might finish that accord' (IV. vi. 41). The conjunction 'till' conveys primarily that they are not yet married. However, it entails logically that they live together as though they were, like Aeneas and Dido. Given the compelling parallelism of the two episodes, one must infer that the same applies to Artegall and Radigund. Spenser clinches the inference by comparing

Artegall, towards the close of the scene, with Hercules as 'for Iolas sake' he not only 'did apply / His mightie hands, the distaffe vile to hold' but also 'forgetting warres . . . onely joyed / In combats of sweet love, and with his mistresse toyed' (V. v. 24). Of course, applied to the literal narrative this comparison is false: we are about to get an account of Radigund's unsuccessful wooing. We could dismiss it as mindless nonsense, in the 'charitable' belief that, if Homer himself sometimes nods, a lesser Homer must be allowed to suffer from constitutional drowsiness. This would be rash, though. Since the Legend of Justice links Artegall with Hercules at the very outset (i. 2–3), the comparison cannot be simply local decoration; especially in view of Artegall's marked connection with Arthur, himself a twelve-laboured Hercules. The Greek hero's readiness to make love when committed to war symbolizes the (unduly revealed) presence of the end in the midst. We had better accept the comparison as an apt conceit—and embrace the corollary: the internal discontinuity of the Radigund episode and hence that of the Artegall story as a whole.

But surely Radigund's lack of success in love makes sense only if we read sequentially, attributing to Artegall a prior commitment to Britomart? For it can hardly be due to disenchantment with Radigund. If her charms are powerful enough to turn him into a willing victim of her loathsome practices in the very heat of his vengeance, they must be impressive indeed. In fact, when Clarinda urges him to woo her mistress, he responds so enthusiastically (v. 40–1) that we can only conclude that Britomart does not count for anything as a restraining influence. Nor does he merely fake love in order to obtain his release. Clarinda initially approaches him as though she would be a compassionate accomplice in such treachery, only to elicit solemn protestations of his readiness to continue in captivity forever (36–8). Are we to say that these cannot be genuine because he is nevertheless roused by the hope of liberty? More probably he envisages not escape but freedom as Radigund's lover, exactly like Radigund herself (32–3). After all, if Clarinda's suggestion were that Radigund, once blinded by love, would naturally create opportunities for him to give her the slip, it would not only be untrue as a matter of fact but even more transparently illogical than Radigund's expectation that a loosening of his bonds will prompt sexual passion. Can we possibly be meant to consider Artegall stupid as well as insincere? Can we possibly give credence to a Clarinda of such self-defeating clumsiness in double perfidy? We must treat the fiction as allegory. Radigund is not a bisexual woman lusting after a male transvestite. She personifies Eternity in Time recognizing itself in Time as Eternity, personified in Artegall, who, even as Bello-dant, proves himself to be Bell-odant, throwing away his sword (13), and who, as man, would precipitate himself as woman. As always in Spenser, love symbolizes equivalence.. Hence it is mutual. Artegall credits Radigund with abundant favour (42). The heavy irony of this does not cancel out the straightforward meaning. She reveals him to himself as gloriously like her. He would court her as a matter of duty (41; an absurdity, in terms of story, conveying a conceptual imperative). Now this love frustrates itself: it repolarizes Radigund and Artegall sexually, thus destroying its ground. He rightly pleads that 'want of meanes hath bene mine onely let' (42), as Spenser brings home in the ensuing scene. Clarinda, intermediary or 'means' between Radigund and Artegall, embodies the impossibility of mediation precisely through her equivalence, in her own love for Artegall, both to her mistress and to him. One senses Radigund's misgivings when enlisting her services: 'Now is *the time*, that *I untimely* must / Thereof make tryall' (29). Considering this, and the fact that there are no narrative circumstances to make it necessary for Radigund to woo Artegall by proxy, the scene can only be an allegory. It highlights justice as Eternity thwarted. Let us not deprive it of its point by insisting that Artegall must be pretending all along. True, we have Spenser's word for it that 'yet never meant he in his noble mind, / To his owne absent love to be untrew' (56; and compare vi. 2). This does not mean, though, that he really cherishes Britomart, not Radigund. It means that his committed and confident captivity in incommunicable aspiration to Radigund *is*, only too manifestly, his love for Britomart as she effaces herself, by way of complementary metaphor. That explains why to Britomart the very spectacle that confirms her worst suspicions also allays them: she

> then too well beleev'd, that which tofore
> Jealous suspect as true untruely drad,
> Which vaine conceipt now nourishing no more,
> She sought with ruth to salve his sad misfortunes sore.
>
> (vii. 38.)

Spenser's narrative would suggest that Britomart offers Artegall something rather more substantial than the pity of this quotation's last line. But the narrative is illusory. She cannot remedy the paradoxicality of justice; she can only anoint its soreness, administer a pain-killer, in not allowing it to manifest itself.

The preceding pages more than imply that Britomart's two meetings with Artegall, in Books IV and V, cannot be successive events. Let us finally dispose of the most obvious objection to this contention, namely that Spenser suggests an interval of three months (IV. vi. 43). It is a little strange that Artegall knows in advance the duration of his quest and that Britomart does not start worrying until after this time (V. vi. 3). It is most odd that she should be uncertain about her time reckoning; unbelievable that she should feign such uncertainty; preposterous that she should substitute days for hours and months for weeks (5). And it is strictly impossible that her desperate anxiety should at once be caused by the arrival of Talus with his bad news 'in untimely houre, ere it was sought' (3) yet also long precede this arrival 'at last' (6–8). Britomart's confusion in her very certainty concerns not a particular period of time but Time, temporality, which in justice expires 'already' in principle but manifestly 'not yet'. Significantly, she suffers this perplexity as woman, thus paralleling the predicament of Artegall. However, covering it as man, she 'streight her selfe did dight, and armor don' (17); in rather extravagant haste, literal readers are bound to think, with Radigund so far to seek and with no less a scourge of villainy than Talus to safe-conduct her.

EPILOGUE

The temptation is great to write a peroration ringing with triumphant QEDs. I shall resist it; not to retract or even just qualify my thesis at the last minute, but to end with a properly Spenserian anticlimax. The preceding argument, in putting *The Faerie Queene* on the map, may lead readers to expect that, on returning to the poem, they will find it readily falling into place. Such optimism must be forestalled. Exposed anew to its sheer copiousness, they are likely to be overwhelmed and to conclude, regretfully, that the argument is as inadequate as it is selective. After all, vast stretches have been left out of consideration. And the episodes actually discussed will inevitably seem to belie their conceptual interpretations when again confronted in all their density and opulence. The poem demands great faith. But perhaps it would be unrealistic to think that readers will feel prompted to return to the poem in the first place. While assenting to my thesis, they might decline to put their belief to the test, deciding that they have no time for a huge cryptogram, whose every rift is loaded with ore of 'conceitful thought'. The poem demands great patience. Long by any standard, it aggravates its length in that it is too arresting to be 'read' in the usual sense of the word. My thesis does not seem calculated to win an audience for it. Indeed, it may well alienate a good many of its former champions, whose free-ranging exploits it checks with a forbidding claim to exclusive truth. Worse, in presenting Spenser's fiction as utterly determined by his doctrine, itself certainly no longer common ground and possibly unpalatable, I have allowed no scope for enjoying the poem purely 'as literature' and thus, to many, justified its removal from the canon. *The Faerie Queene* is a *σκάνδαλον*, like the Cross of Christ. Only if we let it crucify us shall we behold its glory.

APPENDIX

A
Letter of the Authors expounding his whole intention in the course of this worke: which for that it giveth great light to the Reader, for the better understanding is hereunto annexed.

To the Right noble, and Valorous, Sir Walter Raleigh knight, Lo. Wardein of the Stanneryes, and her Majesties liefe-tenaunt of the County of Cornewayll.

SIr knowing how doubtfully all Allegories may be construed, and this booke of mine, which I have entituled the Faery Queene, being a continued Allegory, or darke conceit, I have thought good aswell for avoyding of gealous opinions and misconstructions, as also for your better light in reading therof, (being so by you commanded,) to discover unto you the general intention and meaning, which in the whole course thereof I have fashioned, without expressing of any particular purposes or by-accidents therein occasioned. The generall end therefore of all the booke is to fashion a gentleman or noble person in vertuous and gentle discipline: Which for that I conceived shoulde be most plausible and pleasing, being coloured with an historicall fiction, the which the most part of men delight to read, rather for variety of matter, then for profite of the ensample: I chose the historye of king Arthure, as most fitte for the excellency of his person, being made famous by many mens former workes, and also furthest from the daunger of envy, and suspition of present time. In which I have followed all the antique Poets historicall, first Homere, who in the Persons of Agamemnon and Ulysses hath ensampled a good governour and a vertuous man, the one in his Ilias, the other in his Odysseis: then Virgil, whose like intention was to doe in the person of Aeneas: after him Ariosto comprised them both in his Orlando: and lately Tasso dissevered them againe, and formed both parts in two persons, namely that part which they in Philosophy call Ethice, or vertues of a private man, coloured in his Rinaldo: The other named Politice in his Godfredo. By ensample of which excellente Poets, I labour to pourtraict in Arthure, before he was king, the image of a brave knight, perfected in the twelve private morall vertues, as Aristotle hath devised, the which is the purpose of these first twelve bookes: which if I finde to be well accepted, I may be perhaps encoraged, to frame the other part of pollliticke vertues in his person, after that hee came to be king. To some I know this Methode will seeme displeasaunt, which had rather have good discipline delivered plainly in way of precepts, or sermoned at large, as they use, then thus clowdily enwrapped in Allegoricall devises. But such, me seeme, should be satisfide with the use of these dayes, seeing all things accounted by their showes, and nothing esteemed of, that is not delightfull and pleasing to commune sence. For this cause is Xenophon preferred before Plato, for that the one in the exquisite depth of his judgement, formed a Commune welth such as it should be, but the other in the person of Cyrus and the Persians fashioned a governement such as might best be: So much more profitable and gratious is doctrine by ensample, then by rule. So have I laboured to doe in the person of Arthure: whome I conceive after his long education by Timon, to whom he was by Merlin delivered to be brought up, so soone as he was borne of the Lady Igrayne, to have seene in a dream or vision the Faery Queen, with whose excellent beauty ravished, he awaking resolved to seeke her out, and so being by Merlin armed, and by Timon throughly instructed, he went to seeke her forth in Faerye land. In that Faery Queene I meane glory in my generall intention, but in my particular I conceive the most excellent and glorious person of our soveraine the Queene, and her kingdome in Faery land. And yet in some places els, I doe otherwise shadow her. For considering she beareth two persons, the one of a most royall Queene or Empresse, the other of a most vertuous and beautifull Lady, this latter part in some places I doe expresse in Belphœbe, fashioning her name according to your owne excellent conceipt of Cynthia, (Phœbe and Cynthia being both names of Diana.) So in the person of Prince Arthure I sette forth magnificence in particular, which vertue for that (according to Aristotle and the rest) it is the perfection of all the rest, and conteineth in it them all, therefore in the whole course I mention the deedes of Arthure applyable to that vertue, which I write of in that booke. But of the xii. other vertues, I make xii. other knights the patrones, for the more variety of the history: Of which these three bookes contayn three, The first of the knight of the Redcrosse, in whome I expresse Holynes: The seconde of Sir Guyon, in whome I sette forth Temperaunce: The third of Britomartis a Lady knight, in whome I picture Chastity. But because the beginning of the whole worke seemeth abrupte and as depending upon other antecedents, it needs that ye know the occasion of these three knights severall adventures. For the Methode of a Poet historical is not such, as of an Historiographer. For an Historiographer discourseth of affayres orderly as they were donne, accounting as well the times as the actions, but a Poet thrusteth into the middest, even where it most concerneth him, and there recoursing to the thinges forepaste, and divining of thinges to come, maketh a pleasing Analysis of all. The beginning therefore of my history, if it were to be told by an Historiographer, should be the twelfth booke, which is the last, where I devise that the Faery Queene kept her Annuall feaste xii. dayes, uppon which xii. severall dayes, the occasions of the xii. severall adventures hapned, which being undertaken by xii. severall knights, are in these xii. books severally handled and discoursed. The first was this. In the beginning of the feast, there presented him selfe a tall clownishe younge man, who falling before the Queen of Faries desired a boone (as the manner then was) which during that feast she might not refuse: which was that hee might have the atchievement of any adventure, which during that feaste should happen, that being graunted, he rested him on the floore, unfitte through his rusticity for a better place. Soone after entred a faire Ladye in mourning weedes, riding on a white Asse, with a dwarfe behind her leading a warlike steed, that bore the Armes of a knight, and his speare in the dwarfes hand. Shee falling before the Queene of Faeries, complayned that her father and mother an ancient King and Queene, had bene by an huge dragon many years shut up in a brasen Castle, who thence suffred them not to yssew: and therefore besought the Faery Queene to assygne her some one of her knights to take on him that exployt. Presently that clownish person upstarting, desired that adventure: whereat the Queene much wondering, and the Lady much gainesaying, yet he earnestly importuned his desire. In the end the Lady told him that unlesse that armour which she brought, would serve him (that is the armour of a Christian man specified by Saint Paul v. Ephes.) that he could not succeed in that enterprise, which being forthwith put upon him with dewe furnitures thereunto, he seemed the goodliest man in al that company, and was well liked of the Lady. And eftesoones taking on him knighthood, and mounting on that straunge Courser, he went forth with her on that adventure: where beginneth the first booke, vz.

A gentle knight was pricking on the playne. &c.

The second day ther came in a Palmer bearing an Infant with bloody hands, whose Parents he complained to have bene slayn by an Enchaunteresse called Acrasia: and therfore craved of the Faery Queene, to appoint him some knight, to performe that adventure, which being assigned to Sir Guyon, he presently went forth with that same Palmer: which is the beginning of the second booke and the whole subject thereof. The third day there came in, a Groome who complained before the Faery Queene, that a vile Enchaunter called Busirane had in hand a most faire Lady called Amoretta, whom he kept in most grievous torment, because she would not yield him the pleasure of her body. Whereupon Sir Scudamour the lover of that Lady presently tooke on him that adventure. But being unable to performe it by reason of the hard Enchauntments, after long sorrow, in the end met with Britomartis, who succoured him, and reskewed his love.

But by occasion hereof, many other adventures are intermedled, but rather as Accidents, then intendments. As the love of Britomart, the overthrow of Marinell, the misery of Florimell, the vertuousnes of Belphœbe, the lasciviousnes of Hellenora, and many the like.

Thus much Sir, I have briefly ovreronne to direct your understanding to the wel-head of the History, that from thence gathering the whole intention of the conceit, ye may as in a handfull gripe al the discourse, which otherwise may happily seeme tedious and confused. So humbly craving the continuaunce of your honorable favour towards me, and th'eternall establishment of your happines, I humbly take leave.

23. January. 1589
Yours most humbly affectionate.
Ed. Spenser.

ABBREVIATIONS

Variorum	*The Faerie Queene*, Vols. I–VI of *The Works of Edmund Spenser: A Variorum Edition*, edited by Edwin Greenlaw, Charles Grosvenor Osgood, Frederick Morgan Padelford, Ray Heffner (Baltimore, 1932–8)
OED	*The Oxford English Dictionary*, 12 vols. and Supplement/ Bibliography (Oxford, 1933; repr. 1961)
CamJ	*Cambridge Journal*
ELH	*Journal of English Literary History*
ELN	*English Language Notes*
HLQ	*Huntington Library Quarterly*
JWCI	*Journal of the Warburg and Courtauld Institute*
MLN	*Modern Language Notes*
MLR	*Modern Language Review*
PMLA	*Publications of the Modern Language Association of America*
SP	*Studies in Philology*
TLS	*The Times Literary Supplement*
UTQ	*University of Toronto Quarterly*

NOTES

ONE

1. *Edmund Spenser*, Writers and their Work, 258 (Harlow, 1977), p. 26; *Reading Spenser: An Introduction to 'The Faerie Queene'* (New York, 1968), pp. 10, 29.

2. Not that this is the 'whole point' of the technique. On *entrelacement* in general see Eugène Vinaver, *The Rise of Romance* (Oxford, 1971), especially Chapter V. For an admiring account of Ariosto's skilful handling of its see *Orlando Furioso (The Frenzy of Orlando): A Romantic Epic by Ludovico Ariosto*, translated by Barbara Reynolds, 2 vols. (Harmondsworth, 1975–7), II, 7–18.

3. *The Evolution of 'The Faerie Queene'* (Chicago, 1942).

4. References in this form are to the Letter to Ralegh as reproduced in the Appendix. This, and all other Spenser quotations, are from *Poetical Works*, edited by J. C. Smith and E. de Selincourt (Oxford, 1912; repr. 1975). The distribution of i/j and u/v has been normalized. Proper names are not printed in italics.

5. e.g. A. C. Hamilton, *The Structure of Allegory in 'The Faerie Queene'* (Oxford, 1961), pp. 1–43; Thomas P. Roche, Jr., *The Kindly Flame: A Study of the Third and Fourth Books of Spenser's 'Faerie Queene'* (Princeton, 1964), pp. 3–31; Rosemary Freeman, *'The Faerie Queene': A Companion for Readers* (London, 1970), pp. 59–83; John Erskine Hankins, *Source and Meaning in Spenser's Allegory: A Study of 'The Faerie Queene'* (Oxford, 1971), pp. 17–33.

6. See Alastair Fowler, *Spenser and the Numbers of Time* (London, 1964), pp. 148–55, 182–91.

7. See *Edmund Spenser: A Critical Anthology*, edited by Paul J. Alpers (Harmondsworth, 1969), p. 19.

8. *A Preface to 'The Faerie Queene'* (London, 1962), pp. 95–9, 131–7.

9. *An Experiment in Criticism* (Cambridge, 1961), pp. 40–4.

10. Freeman, p. 45; Humphrey Tonkin, *Spenser's Courteous Pastoral: Book Six of the 'Faerie Queene'* (Oxford, 1972), p. 26.

11. *The Allegory of Love: A Study in Medieval Tradition* (Oxford, 1936; corr. repr. 1938), p. 358.

12. See the Preface to his edition, as reprinted in *The Prince of Poets: Essays on Edmund Spenser*, edited by John R. Elliott, Jr. (New York and London, 1968), pp. 196–202.

13. *English Literature in the Sixteenth Century, Excluding Drama* (Oxford, 1954), p. 389.

14. Letter VIII, from *Letters on Chivalry*, as reprinted in *English Critical Essays: Sixteenth, Seventeenth and Eighteenth Centuries*, edited by Edmund D. Jones, The World's Classics, 240 (London, 1922; reset 1947), pp. 319, 325.

15. e.g. Harry Berger, Jr., *The Allegorical Temper: Vision and Reality in Book II of Spenser's 'Faerie Queene'*, Yale Studies in English, 137 (New Haven and London, 1957); Angus Fletcher, *The Prophetic Moment: An Essay on Spenser* (Chicago and London, 1971); Isabel G. MacCaffrey, *Spenser's Allegory: The Anatomy of Imagination* (Princeton, 1976); James Nohrnberg, *The Analogy of 'The Faerie Queene'* (Princeton, 1976).

16. Sidney's term; see *An Apology for Poetry; or, The Defence of Poesy*, edited by Geoffrey Shepherd (London and elsewhere, 1965), p. 101.

17. See Bennett, pp. 24–38.

18. Alpers, *Anthology*, p. 20.

19. Robert Lacey, *Sir Walter Ralegh* (London, 1973; repr. 1975), pp. 149–260.

20. This is really an imponderable matter. Spenser did not withdraw his laudatory allusion to the author of *Cynthia* in the Proem to Book III, which might be considered more offensive.

21. ' "In These XII Books Severally Handled and Discoursed" ', *ELH*, 19 (1952), 165–72 (pp. 165, 171).

22. *English Literature*, p. 379.

23. *Spenser's Images of Life*, edited by Alastair Fowler (Cambridge, 1967), pp. 137–40 (p. 139).

24. *Structure*, p. 52.

25. 'Spenser's Letter to Ralegh—A Reply', *MLN*, 75 (1960), 195–7.

26. Chapter Two of *Allegorical Imagery: Some Mediaeval Books and Their Posterity* (Princeton, 1966).

27. p. 136, n. 49; pp. 351–2, n. 12.

28. *The Poetry of Edmund Spenser: A Study* (New York and London, 1963; repr. 1971), pp. 116–23.

29. The *OED* does not instance this passage.

30. e.g. Quintilian, *Institutio Oratoria* VIII. vi. 44–53; George Puttenham, *The Arte of English Poesie*, edited by Gladys Doidge Willcock and Alice Walker (Cambridge, 1936), pp. 186–8.

31. *Structure*, p. 29.

32. *Images*, p. 138 (and see *Nicomachean Ethics* 1123b). The idea is not original with Lewis. As early as the late seventeenth century we find Dryden, perhaps not inadvertently, speaking of 'magnanimity, which is the character of Prince Arthur' (Alpers, *Anthology*, p. 73).

33. *Images*, pp. 138, 137.

34. Hankins, Chapter I, especially pp. 3–5.

35. 'Spenser's Letter to Raleigh and the Averroistic *Poetics*', *ELN*, 14 (1976–7), 246–9 (pp. 247, 248).

36. *Discourses on the Heroic Poem*, translated by Mariella Cavalchini and Irene Samuel (Oxford, 1973), pp. 43–4; and see also the Introduction, p. xxviii.

37. Sidney, *Apology*, p. 109 (a close rendering of *Poetics* 1451b).

38. *Allegorical Imagery*, pp. 57, 77.

39. See Hugh MacLachlan, ' "In the Person of Prince Arthur" ': Spenserian *Magnificence* and the Ciceronian Tradition', *UTQ*, 46 (1976–7), 125–46 (especially Section I and pp. 135–6).

40. *Allegorical Imagery*, p. 60.

41. *OED* s.v. Perfect *a.* B I 4; 3, 5.

42. Alastair Fowler, 'Emanations of glory: Neoplatonic order in Spenser's *Faerie Queen*', in *A Theatre for Spenserians*, Papers of the International Spenser Colloquium, Fredericton, New Brunswick, October 1969, edited by Judith M. Kennedy and James A. Reither (Toronto, Buffalo, and Manchester, 1973), pp. 53–82 (p. 76).

43. *Pagan Mysteries in the Renaissance* (London, 1958), p. 39.

44. Galatians 5: 22–3 and Romans 13: 9, *The Authorised Version of the English Bible, 1611*, edited by William Aldis Wright, 5 vols. (Cambridge, 1909), V, 423 and 358.

45. *Theologisches Wörterbuch zum neuen Testament*, Volume VIII, edited by Gerhard Friedrich (Stuttgart, 1969), p. 71, §3.

46. Hankins, pp. 35, 54.

47. *English Literature*, pp. 382–3.

48. 'Emanations', p. 75.

49. *OED* s.v. Glory *sb.* 5. (2b is also relevant, as will soon appear.)

50. I Peter 1: 21. Unless annotated otherwise all biblical quotations are from *The Geneva Bible: A Facsimile of the 1560 edition*, introduced by Lloyd E. Berry (Madison, Milwaukee, and London, 1969).

51. I Corinthians 15: 43 (σπείρεται ἐν ἀτιμίᾳ, ἐγείρεται ἐν δόξῃ).

52. Colossians 1: 19; 2: 9.

53. I Corinthians 6: 20; II Corinthians 4: 7.

54. Philippians 1: 20.

55. *Theologisches Wörterbuch zum neuen Testament*, Volume II, edited by Gerhard Kittel (Stuttgart, 1935; repr. 1950), p. 395, lines 16–18.

56. Colossians 1: 28.

57. John 19: 30.

58. For glory as 'riches' see Romans 10: 23 and Philippians 4: 19. The 'earthen vessels' of II Corinthians 4: 7 contain it as a 'treasure'. II Peter 1: 17 actually uses the collocation μεγαλοπρεποῦς δόξης, to refer to God acknowledging Jesus as His Son (that is, as His Self-giving).

59. I Timothy 6: 18-19.

60. Edmund Spenser, *The Faerie Queene*, edited by A. C. Hamilton, Longman Annotated English Poets (London and New York, 1977), p. 734, note on 58. 3-7.

61. *OED* s.v. † Dilate *v.*[1] Obs.; for an illuminating parallel see *Amoretti* LXVI.

62. *Pace* Sherman Hawkins, 'Mutabilitie and the Cycle of the Months', in *Form and Convention in the Poetry of Edmund Spenser*, Selected Papers from the English Institute, edited by William Nelson (New York and London, 1961), p. 98.

63. *Edmund Spenser*, pp. 44, 45.

64. See John 14: 6.

65. Shelley, *Adonais*, stanza 52.

66. Ephesians 5: 16; Colossians 4: 5.

67. II Timothy 4: 7-8; I Peter 5: 4.

68. Matthew 6: 4, 6, 18.

69. *ELH*, 16 (1949), 194-228 (pp. 199, 225).

70. 'Spenser's Pluralistic Universe: The View from the Mount of Contemplation (*F.Q.* I. x)', in *Contemporary Thought on Edmund Spenser: With a Bibliography of Criticism of 'The Faerie Queene', 1900-1970*, edited by Richard C. Frushell and Bernard J. Vondersmith (Carbondale and Edwardsville, London and Amsterdam, 1975), pp. 121-49.

71. In spite of Virgil K. Whitaker, *The Religious Basis of Spenser's Thought*, Stanford University Publications, University Series, Language and Literature, Volume VII, Number 3 (Stanford and London, 1950), Chapter IV.

72. G. R. Elton, *Reformation Europe 1517-1559* (Glasgow, 1963; repr. July 1976), pp. 215-16, 219, 218 (n. 4). The printer's device for the 1596 *Faerie Queene* is singularly apt: ANCHORA SPEI.

73. A. G. Dickens, *The English Reformation* (London, 1964), p. 288.

74. Spenser, *Poetical Works*, Introduction, p. xxvi.

75. Alpers rightly draws attention to *The Faerie Queene* as rhetoric but wrongly supposes that in doing so he obviates the problems raised by its narrative (*The Poetry of 'The Faerie Queene'* (Princeton, 1967), Chapter One).

76. For an application to literal reading see Sidney on the *Aeneid* (*Apology*, pp. 119-20, 124-5).

77. *Pace* Nelson, *Poetry*, p. 130.

78. The point seems to have escaped Alpers (*Poetry*, pp. 335-8), Evans (*Spenser's Anatomy of Heroism: A Commentary on 'The Faerie Queene'* (Cambridge, 1970), pp. 92-3), Freeman (pp. 59-67), Hamilton (*Structure*, pp. 29-43), Nelson (*Poetry*, p. 173), to mention only a few.

79. John 14: 6, 17.

80. *Poetry*, pp. 133–5.

81. 'The Dragon's Spark and Sting and the Structure of Red Cross's Dragon-Fight: *The Faerie Queene*, 1. xi–xii', as reprinted in *Essential Articles for the Study of Edmund Spenser*, edited by A. C. Hamilton (Hamden, Conn., 1972), pp. 425–46 (especially p. 443).

82. e.g. Hough, pp. 161–6; Alpers, *Poetry*, p. 306.

83. 'C. S. Lewis and Spenser: Nature, Art and the Bower of Bliss', *CamJ*, 2 (1948–9), 420–34. Lewis and Brooke are conveniently juxtaposed in Hamilton, *Essential Articles*, pp. 3–12, 13–28.

84. Perhaps not accidentally, the idea that Acrasia does not stand for moral intemperance finds support in a biblical text whose reference seems as specifically sexual as Spenser's episode. In I Corinthians 7: 5 St. Paul counsels against prolonged abstention from intercourse in order that 'Satan tempt you not for your incontinencie' (*διὰ τὴν ἀκρασίαν ὑμῶν*). We may safely assume that the apostle's acceptance of this *ἀκρασία* is no pandering to vice. Calvin glosses the word as 'carnis nostrae infirmitatem' (*Opera*, Volume 49, column 405); that is, surely, our natural constitution, a liability ever since the Fall. Although both envisage marital love-making as the remedy against sexual laxity in particular, their terms are so unspecific as to suggest that the fulfilment it brings tempers the passions generally. Acrasia's sexiness reflects the key role of sex in moral temperance.

85. Lewis, *English Literature*, p. 382; Tuve, *Allegorical Imagery*, p. 137; Tonkin, p. 74; MacCaffrey, p. 85.

86. In spite of Lewis, *Images*, p. 138; Freeman, p. 157; Douglas Brooks-Davies, *Spenser's 'Faerie Queene': A Critical Commentary on Books I and II* (Manchester, 1977), p. 166.

87. e.g. Woodhouse, pp. 209–12; Hamilton, *Structure*, pp. 77–9, 98–9; Tuve, *Allegorical Imagery*, pp. 135–8 ('Magnificentia always comes in when the hero is "used up" '); Evans, pp. 13–14, 105, 133, 200; Tonkin, p. 74.

88. As Thomas Warton notes (Alpers, *Anthology*, pp. 101–2).

89. Cain, in the wake of Fletcher, invokes the 'taboo of the ruler' (*Praise in 'The Faerie Queene'* (Lincoln, Nebr. and London, 1978), p. 112). While not demonstrably wrong, this smacks of *lucus a non lucendo*.

90. Lewis, Tuve, and many 'myth' critics are influentially silent or negative about the historical allegory. O'Connell spurns it in favour of his own discovery, the historical dimension (*Mirror and Veil: The Historical Dimension of Spenser's 'Faerie Queene'* (Chapel Hill, 1977), pp. 13, 125–6, 156).

91. Lewis, *Allegory of Love*, p. 349.

92. I argue the necessity of this type of reading at length in 'Spenser

and History: A Case Study of the Belge Episode' (unpublished article).

93. Nelson, *Poetry*, p. 124.

94. 'Ye reigne as Kings without us, and wolde to God ye did reigne' (I Corinthians 4: 8). 'They shal reigne for evermore' (Revelation 22: 5).

95. Cain, pp. 51-4, 184.

96. I Corinthians 11: 7.

97. 'Pluralistic Universe', especially pp. 132-3. The New Jerusalem is not, as she says, egalitarian: 'sam', in the preceding stanza, means 'together', not 'equal'.

98. Cain, p. 113.

99. From the last verse of 'Wachet Auf', the well-known hymn of Spenser's German contemporary Philipp Nicolai (1556-1608); compare I Corinthians 2: 9.

100. Revelation 21: 10-22.

101. Kaske, 'Pluralistic Universe', p. 132.

102. 'Open thou my lippes, ô Lord, and my mouth shal shewe forthe thy praise' (Psalm 51: 15).

103. These terms, *per se* less specific, can be similarly focused through context; as in the Magnificat, and in 'the shepherds returned, glorifying and praising God' (Luke 1: 46; 2: 20).

104. Brooks-Davies, p. 167.

105. Ripa describes *Honore* thus: 'Giovane bello, vestito di Porpora, & coronato d'Alloro, con' un' asta nella mano destra, & nella sinistra con un Cornucopia, pieno di frutti, fiori, & fronde' (*Iconologia*, Facsimile of the Roman edition of 1603, introduced by Erna Mandowsky (Hildesheim and New York, 1970), p. 202).

106. *OED* s.v. Pall *sb.*[1] II 5 and 6b.

107. John 19: 2.

108. *OED* s.v. Pall *sb.*[1] I 4.

109. Brooks-Davies, p. 166.

110. Servius, *Commentarii in Virgilium*, edited by H. Albertus Lion, 2 vols. (Göttingen, 1826), I, 467 (on *Aeneid* VIII. 276) and II, 146 (on *Eclogues* VII. 61).

111. See n. 51.

112. Compare John 8: 49 and 50; or 12: 23 and 26.

113. *Poetical Works*, Critical Appendix, p. 645. 'The corrections of F.E. are frequently ignored by 1596', as the editors observe *ad* I. i. 12 (p. 644). This increases one's suspicion that many of the F.E. are pseudo-faults. Recognition in 1596 need not be a guarantee of genuineness.

114. *Images*, p. 137; and compare John Hughes, in Alpers, *Anthology*, p. 94. Murrin offers an unsatisfactory but thought-provoking explanation in 'The Rhetoric of Fairyland', in *The Rhetoric of Renaissance Poetry: From Wyatt to Milton*, edited by Thomas O. Sloan and

Raymond B. Waddington (Berkeley, Los Angeles, and London, 1974), pp. 73–95 (especially pp. 91–5).

115. *OED* s.v. Pendragon[1].

116. e.g. John 14: 9.

117. II. x. 46; III. ix. 38, 45, 51; IV. xi. 28.

118. *Aeneid* VII. 646.

119. *Aeneid* VIII. 620, 440, 419; VII. 785–6; XII. 90–1 (and see *Variorum* I, 251–2; II, 274).

120. *Aeneid* VI. 89, and compare IX. 742.

121. *Iliad* VI. 466–71.

122. Ephesians 6: 17; I Thessalonians 5: 8.

123. Ecclesiastes 12: 5 and marginal gloss.

124. *Iliad* XXII. 315–16, 134–5, 317–18; see Michael Peter Leslie, 'Martial and Chivalric Symbolism in Spenser's *The Faerie Queene*' (Ph.D. dissertation, University of Edinburgh, 1981), pp. 78–80.

125. *Iliad* XVI. 133–4, 140–4; XXII. 359–60.

126. I Corinthians 15: 55.

127. Romans 13: 12.

128. Malachi 4: 2.

129. 'Neoplatonism in the Poetry of Spenser', a review of Robert Ellrodt's book with the same title (Geneva, 1960), in *Studies in Medieval and Renaissance Literature*, collected by Walter Hooper (Cambridge, 1966), pp. 149–63 (p. 159).

130. Keats, 'Ode to a Nightingale', lines 79–80.

131. Galatians 4: 4; Ephesians 1: 10; also Mark 1: 15 and I Peter 1: 20.

132. 'Emanations', p. 74.

133. I. ix. 20; III. v. 12; IV. ix. 17; V. xi. 35; VI. viii. 30.

134. Compare Romans 8: 22 and Mark 13: 8.

135. *Poetical Works*, Critical Appendix, p. 648.

136. Dryden, and Hurd (implicitly): Alpers, *Anthology*, pp. 74, 118; Upton: Elliott, p. 199. Modern readers, taught not to speculate about the unwritten, usually do not commit themselves—but see Donald Cheney, *Spenser's Image of Nature: Wild Man and Shepherd in 'The Faerie Queene'*, Yale Studies in English, 161 (New Haven and London, 1966), pp. 174, 192; Hankins, p. 52; Roche, p. 50 (with significant hesitation).

137. *Aeneid* VII. 71–80 (79–80).

138. Exodus 3: 2; Acts 2: 3.

139. Priscilla Bawcutt, *Gavin Douglas: A Critical Study* (Edinburgh, 1976), p. 104. Vegio's dates are 1407–58.

140. Elizabeth did visit her subjects sexually in dreams, witness Simon Forman (A. L. Rowse, *The Elizabethan Renaissance: The Life of the Society* (London, 1971; repr. 1974), pp. 170–1). But they would

not have dreamt of publishing the fact, least of all in works dedicated to her. The public cult of the Queen was either pseudo-erotic ('the marriage of Elizabeth and England') or, when overtly erotic, decidedly Petrarchan (see Frances A. Yates, 'The Triumph of Chastity', in *Astraea: The Imperial Theme in the Sixteenth Century* (London, 1975; repr. Harmondsworth, 1977), pp. 112–20, 215–16). Presumably she did not will these phantom visits, let alone support them bodily.

141. Compare Nelson, *Poetry*, pp. 121–3, on Spenser's use of 'fashion'.

142. Keats, 'Ode to a Nightingale', lines 74, 70.

143. Angus Fletcher, *Allegory: The Theory of a Symbolic Mode* (Ithaca and New York, 1964), pp. 25–69.

144. *The Statesman's Manual*, December 1816; reprinted in *Imagination in Coleridge*, edited by John Spencer Hill (London and Basingstoke, 1978), pp. 151–2.

145. *Images*, p. 137.

146. e.g. Gavin Douglas, *Eneados*, I Prologue, lines 325–32 (see Bawcutt, p. 84). Compare Nohrnberg, pp. 22–34.

147. Owen, ' "In These XII Books . . ." ', p. 167.

148. See Philippians 2: 12 (*Authorised Version*, V, 439; the *Geneva Bible* shuns 'work', probably to forestall popish misconstructions).

149. 'Elizabethan Chivalry and the Faerie Queene's Annual Feast', *MLN*, 50 (1935), 158–61 (p. 158).

150. 'Elizabethan Chivalry: The Romance of the Accession Day Tilts', *JWCI*, 20 (1957), 4–25.

151. Lewis, *Allegory of Love*, p. 359.

152. Bennett, p. 28.

153. Owen, ' "In These XII Books . . ." ', p. 167.

154. Compare 'clowdily enwrapped in Allegoricall *devises*' (L 34–5).

155. *Pace* Arthur Colby Sprague, 'Gloriana's Annual Feast', *TLS*, 27 April 1933, p. 295.

156. *OED* s.v. Magnificence 4b.

157. Revelation 19: 7, 9.

158. O'Connell, p. 191; Robin Headlam Wells, 'Semper Eadem: Spenser's "Legend of Constancie" ', *MLR*, 73 (1978), 250–5.

159. 'Emanations', pp. 74–5.

160. II Corinthians 3: 18.

161. Bennett, p. 31.

162. ' "In These XII Books . . ." ', p. 166.

163. See Sprague. George B. Parks, in his rejoinder ('Gloriana's Annual Feast', *TLS*, 29 June 1933, p. 447), rightly rejects Sprague's contention that Spenser means twelve New Year Day feasts.

164. i.e. Ephesians 6: 10–17.

165. See verse 12.

166. *Martin Luthers Geistliche Lieder*, edited by Albert Leitzmann, *Kleine Texte für theologische Vorlesungen und Übungen*, series editor Hans Lietzmann, 24/25 (Bonn, 1907), p. 18.

167. Alpers quotes from the second edition, of 1627 (*Anthology*, pp. 54–5).

168. *Poetry*, pp. 172–3.

169. Compare Nelson, *Poetry*, pp. 158–9.

170. I Corinthians 15: 42.

171. Salter echoes Romans 8: 37.

172. e.g. Tintoretto's 'Resurrection' in the Ashmolean Museum, Oxford; or Piero della Francesca's, reproduced in Peter and Linda Murray, *The Art of the Renaissance* (London, 1963; repr. 1974), p. 127, Plate 101.

173. *Images*, p. 138.

174. The connection between *tempus* and temperance can be inferred from one of the virtue's traditional attributes, the hourglass (see Guy de Tervarent, *Attributs et symboles dans l'art profane, 1450–1600: dictionnaire d'un langage perdu*, Travaux d'humanisme et renaissance, 29, 3 vols. (Geneva, 1958–64), I, column 220, s.v. Horloge I). Both are 'moderate', measured and measuring.

175. *Aeneid* II. 3–5.

176. *Poetry*, p. 142.

177. On this see also A. D. S. Fowler, 'The Image of Mortality: *The Faerie Queene*, II. i–ii', *HLQ*, 24 (1960–1), 91–110 (pp. 98–100)—a fine introduction to Book II, though unnecessarily concerned with baptism (con-fusion of tenor and vehicle?).

178. *Poetical Works*, p. 628: Gabriel Harvey echoing what Spenser himself had 'flatly professed'.

179. *OED* s.v. Palmer *sb.*[1].

180. Alpers, *Anthology*, p. 93.

181. Hankins, pp. 46–50. This theory was originally put forward by Rathborne in *The Meaning of Spenser's Fairyland*, Columbia University Studies in English and Comparative Literature, 131 (New York, 1937).

182. See especially Berger, pp. 89–114, 161–76; also Roche, pp. 31–50; and Cheney, *Image of Nature*, pp. 8–9.

183. Keith Thomas, *Religion and the Decline of Magic: Studies in Popular Beliefs in Sixteenth- and Seventeenth-Century England* (London, 1971; repr. Harmondsworth, 1978), p. 731.

184. 'The Red Crosse Knight and Mediaeval Demon Stories', *PMLA*, 44 (1929), 706–14 (p. 706).

185. Revelation 21: 2, 10; 4, 8; 11.

186. Philippians 2: 5–7.

187. Romans 8: 14–18; for 'sonne and heire' also Galatians 4: 1–7.

188. See Selden's 'Illustration' to Drayton, *Polyolbion* X. 14,

quoted in *Variorum* I, 265-6; *The Works of Sir Thomas Malory*, edited by Eugène Vinaver, second edition, 3 vols. (Oxford, 1967), I, 38, line 35; C. G. Osgood in *Variorum* III, 224-5.

189. Shakespeare, *The Merry Wives of Windsor* V. v. 48 (quoted from Thomas, p. 734).

190. Bennett, pp. 8-9.

191. Hankins, pp. 201-4.

192. Bennett, pp. 11-23 (p. 18).

193. 'Spenser *ludens*', in Kennedy and Reither, *Theatre*, pp. 83-100 (pp. 95-6, 83, 96).

194. 'Emanations', pp. 81-2, n. 60.

195. *The Works of Geoffrey Chaucer*, edited by F. N. Robinson, second edition (London, 1957), p. 167, line 930; p. 164, lines 703-4.

TWO

1. Colossians 3: 14 (*σύνδεσμος τῆς τελειότητος*). See Calvin *ad locum*: 'vocat vinculum perfectionis: quo significat, virtutum omnium chorum sub ea contineri' (*Opera*, Volume 52, column 123).

2. Matthew 13: 10; I Timothy 1: 5.

3. Matthew 19: 19; Romans 13: 9; John 17: 23 (*τετελειωμένοι εἰς ἕν*).

4. —and, as Michael Leslie informs me, 'baldric' (*Iliad* XVIII. 480). Arthur's baldric (I. vii. 29) makes him 'the perfection of all the rest' (L 60-1) even as it equates him with Telamond in particular.

5. Ephesians 4: 13, 16; and compare Romans 12: 4-5.

6. I Corinthians 13: 10.

7. 'On Murder Considered as One of the Fine Arts', in *Selected English Essays*, chosen and arranged by W. Peacock, The World's Classics, 32 (London, 1903; repr. 1930), pp. 303-53 (p. 351).

8. e.g. C. S. Lewis, for whom Arthur represents the Eros religion, as we saw in Section III of Chapter One; and Enid Welsford, *Spenser: Fowre Hymnes: Epithalamion: A Study of Edmund Spenser's Doctrine of Love* (Oxford, 1967), Introduction, pp. 10-11, 87-8, *et passim*.

9. Romans 13: 8; and, by implication, Luke 10: 36-7.

10. Viktor Warnach, *Agape: Die Liebe als Grundmotiv der neutestamentlichen Theologie* (Düsseldorf, 1951), p. 6.

11. Ephesians 5: 31-2 (*μυστήριον*—whence 'those *mysterious* parts', Milton's periphrasis for the sexual organs, *Paradise Lost* IV. 312).

12. I Corinthians 15: 28.

13. Psalm 85: 10.

14. Philippians 4: 7.

15. Roche, pp. 72-88, 117-28, 128-33, 133-6, 116, 103.

16. *Images*, pp. 60, 36.

17. Though not printed till 1590; see Alfred Harbage, *Annals of English Drama 975–1700: An Analytical Record of All Plays, Extant or Lost, Chronologically Arranged and Indexed by Authors, Titles, Dramatic Companies, &c.*, revised by S. Schoenbaum (London, 1964), pp. 52–3. Compare *II Tamburlaine* IV. iii. 116–24 and *FQ* I. vii. 32.

18. See *Elizabethan Critical Essays*, edited by G. Gregory Smith, 2 vols. (Oxford, 1904), I, 305. Fraunce quotes *FQ* II. iv. 35.

19. Bryskett says that the poet circulated 'parcels' of his unpublished work among friends (Spenser, *Poetical Works*, Introduction, p. xxvii).

20. See his first Letter to Harvey, *Poetical Works*, p. 612.

21. Roche, pp. 73, 74–5, 76, 75. The play is listed as by Fletcher only in Harbage, pp. 118–19.

22. See E. B. Fowler, *Spenser and the Courts of Love*, as quoted in *Variorum* IV, 165–6. He also says: 'That lovers used the disguise afforded by the masque, not only to meet their ladies, but also to steal them away is a matter of common knowledge to students of Shakespeare. . . . In the last act of *Merry Wives* Fenton, the favored lover, circumvents the scheming parents and steals Nan Page during the performance of a fairy anti-masque.' But this is not Nan's wedding mask. Nor does Fenton organize it.

23. Roche, pp. 133, 83, 80–1, 77, 83.

24. *Triumphal Forms: Structural Patterns in Elizabethan Poetry* (Cambridge, 1970), p. 53. Compare Nohrnberg, p. 475 and nn. 94, 95.

25. Hankins, p. 162.

26. 'Scudamour's Practice of *Maistrye* upon Amoret', *PMLA*, 77 (1962), 509–10.

27. Roche, p. 129, n. 42.

28. *Images*, pp. 28–9.

29. *English Literature*, p. 388.

30. Roche, pp. 83–4.

31. Painters traditionally used it for the 'glories' of saints.

32. *Numbers of Time*, pp. 139–41.

33. Compare I. x. 40 and II. ix. 47.

34. Roche, p. 116.

35. Hamilton, *Essential Articles*, p. 14.

36. *Allegory of Love*, p. 342; *Images*, p. 33.

37. Nohrnberg's summary of the myth (p. 476).

38. *Numbers of Time*, p. 149; *Triumphal Forms*, pp. 52–3 (the Ovidian reference is to *Amores* I. ii, from which I go on to quote lines 31–2, 36–7, 35).

39. Cheney, too, stresses the union's ambiguity in 'Spenser's Hermaphrodite and the 1590 *Faerie Queene*', *PMLA*, 87 (1972), 192–200.

40. Alpers, *Anthology*, pp. 109–10.
41. Alpers, *Anthology*, p. 147.
42. See Collier's delightful story, printed in *Variorum* IV, 198.
43. *Inferno* V. 121–3.
44. *Variorum* IV, 215–16.
45. *Allegory of Love*, pp. 117, 118, 118, 119. Probably no single post-Lewis reading holds the field today. Yet there is plenty of sense in John V. Fleming, *The 'Roman de la Rose': A Study in Allegory and Iconography* (Princeton, 1969).
46. *Allegory of Love*, Appendix II, pp. 364–6.
47. In his catalogue of 'The Defects of our Modern Poets in their Allegories, Instanced from Spenser's *Faerie Queene*' (Alpers, *Anthology*, p. 100).
48. Roche, p. 129, n. 42; p. 133.
49. Roche, pp. 129, 131.
50. *Images*, p. 45.
51. *Allegory of Love*, p. 339.
52. e.g. Ephesians 5: 25 and Colossians 3: 19.
53. See Galatians 3: 28.
54. stanzas 21–38 (18) / *39* / stanzas 40–57 (18)

THREE

1. *Variorum* III, 334.
2. *Images*, pp. 113, 105.
3. *Poetry*, p. 393; also 183–4.
4. Richard Ellmann, *James Joyce* (London, 1959; repr. 1966), p. 164.
5. *Poetry*, p. 232.
6. MacCaffrey, pp. 299–300.
7. *Faerie Queene*, p. 320, note on 18. 8.
8. In its original sense the word means 'announcement of an event or occurrence' and sometimes the 'event, incident, occurrence' itself (*OED* s.v. 'Tiding' *sb.* 2, 1).
9. *Variorum* III, 334.
10. Hankins, p. 40.
11. *The Shorter Poems of Gavin Douglas*, edited by P. J. Bawcutt, The Scottish Text Society, Fourth Series, Vol. III (Edinburgh and London, 1967), pp. 96 (lines 1492, 1493, 1495–7) and 200 (notes).
12. I Corinthians 13: 12.
13. Or incest; one thinks of Nohrnberg's splendidly wrong-headed psycho-sexual lucubrations (pp. 432–3, 442–52).
14. Kathleen Williams, *Spenser's 'Faerie Queene': The World of Glass* (London, 1966), p. 133.

15. 'quid facundia posset, / re patuit, fortisque viri tulit arma disertus' (Ovid, *Metamorphoses* XIII. 382–3).

16. *Inferno* I. 101; and see Leslie, pp. 89–94.

17. Sidney has 'the hate-spott Ermelin' (*Poems from 'The Old Arcadia'* 62, line 116) and 'spotlesse Ermine' (*Astrophil and Stella* 86, line 5). See *The Poems of Sir Philip Sidney*, edited by William A. Ringler, Jr. (Oxford, 1962; repr. 1971), pp. 89, 212.

18. For this spelling of 'Ptolemy' see also V Proem 7.

19. One thinks of Giordano Bruno. Spenser seems to be alluding to such speculation in II Proem 3.

20. Matthew 5: 16, 14.

21. *Ciris* 328–9.

22. Not from γλαυχη, which does not exist (Hamilton, *Faerie Queene*, p. 322, note on 30. 2).

23. Chaucer, *The Parliament of Fowls*, line 343 (*Works*, p. 314); and compare *FQ* I. ix. 33 and, especially, II. xii. 36.

24. 'Six Knights at Castle Joyous', *SP*, 56 (1959), 583–99.

25. *UTQ*, 30 (1961), 109–27.

26. Although there was a historical Arthgal of Warwick (according to Geoffrey of Monmouth, that is), he was not a brother of Cador and a son of Gorlois like Spenser's Artegall, as Hamilton inadvertently suggests (*Faerie Queene*, p. 530, note on 3. 2; p. 330, note on 26. 2).

27. See Carrie A. Harper, *The Sources of the British Chronicle History in Spenser's 'Faerie Queene'* (Philadelphia, 1910); relevant extracts in *Variorum* III, 228–34.

28. Matthew 24: 6–8.

29. ἀρχὴ ὠδίνων; compare Romans 8: 22 (συνωδίνει).

30. *The History of the Kings of Britain*, translated by Lewis Thorpe (Harmondsworth, 1966; repr. 1978), pp. 261–3.

31. Geoffrey, pp. 209–12.

32. A fine astronomical howler, to explode the story, meaning glory radically at odds with itself, chastity.

33. *Aeneid* XII. 952; 942 ('balteus et notis . . . cingula bullis'), and compare Chapter Two, n. 4; 948–9 ('Pallas te hoc volnere, Pallas / immolat').

34. For this apparently mindless incongruity, so easily corrected, is not Spenser's mistake but a significantly gentle explosive. Amyas, the squire of low degree, cannot marry Æmylia, 'daughter unto a Lord of high degree' (vii. 15), because depth and height, Time and Eternity, are not quite compatible under the rubric of friendship. But Pœana will do almost as well, as Amyas' contentment implies. Like her father, Corflambo, she represents the disjunction of 'Telamond', togetherness: as *poena*, penalty; but far more emphatically as Paean, hymn of

triumph to Apollo, the sun of righteousness, as though virtue's battle were already over.

35. Matthew 24: 30.

36. Psalm 85: 10 (the same verse in which justice and peace kiss).

37. 'Artegall': iv. Argument, 44; vi. 11 / vi. 26, 28, 29, 31, 32, 39, 40, 42. 'Arthegall': iv. 42; v. 9; vi. Argument, 18.

38. v. 8, 21; vi. 4, 5, 9 (not counting iv. 42 and vi. 31, where the appellation is not in italics).

39. 'Artegall': ii. Argument; iii. Argument. 'Arthegall': ii. 8, 9, 25; iii. 26, 62.

40. *Orlando Furioso* IV. 29–32, XXXVI. 64–6.

41. *Orlando Furioso* II. 58.

42. Gradasso, Sacripante, Prasildo, Iroldo (IV. 40).

43. *Orlando Furioso* IV. 27, 28, 36.

44. 'Britomart and *Be Bold, Be Not Too Bold*', *ELH*, 38 (1971), 173–87 (p. 174); *Metamorphoses* X. 626–30 (542–5 in the Latin).

45. *Metamorphoses* X. 715 (839).

46. e.g. Sidney's story of Phalantus, in Book I of *The Countesse of Pembrokes Arcadia*, edited by Albert Feuillerat (Cambridge, 1912; repr. 1969), pp. 96–7.

47. 'But if a woman have long heere, it is a praise (*δόξα*) unto her' (I Corinthians 11: 15). Britomart is too precisely meaningful to qualify as an archetypal blonde.

48. Nelson, 'Spenser *ludens*', p. 93.

49. Genesis 18: 12; and, for its normative status, I Peter 3: 6.

50. Philippians 2: 5–11.

51. He does take for granted the propriety of woman's subordination to man; not, however, as an admission of inferiority but as a token disavowal of glorious equality, symbolizing justice: men and women are equal, but some (women) are more equal than others (men). While using the 'hierarchy' of the sexes as a ready-made symbol, the poet did not, of course, suppose that it is thus symbolic outside his poem. However, his use of it does testify to his proper appreciation of its rationale in the real world. God ordained female obedience *after* the Fall (Genesis 3: 16). He did so not to punish women nor to show that He has greater confidence in men but to 'save' the disgrace of humanity, which now cannot but flounder in its way through life, by relieving the glorious sex of direct responsibility. (That is why, in the end, He took upon Himself the sins of the whole world in a male redeemer.)

52. *Odyssey* XXIII. 116.

53. *Icons of Justice: Iconography & Thematic Imagery in Book V of 'The Faerie Queene'* (New York and London, 1969), p. 97.

54. Hankins, p. 153, n. 2.

55. Aptekar, p. 187; *Aeneid* IV. 136–42.

56. *Aeneid* IV. 48–9.

57. With *Aeneid* IV. 136–42 compare I. 314–20 (Venus) and 496–501 (Dido).

58. *FQ* II. iii. 31, in translating part of the last passage referred to in the previous note, makes Belphœbe another Dido as well, presumably not only so that she may 'shadow' Queen Elizabeth through Dido's alternative name 'Elissa' (*Aeneid* IV. 335, 610) but also to align her even more closely with Radigund. The stanza goes on to compare her with 'that famous Queene / Of Amazons, whom Pyrrhus did destroy'; that is, Penthesilea. Radigund, too, is another Penthesilea, being killed by Britomart, as Artegall's wife and full counterpart another Achilles: according to the ancients, as against Dares and the romance tradition, Penthesilea was slain by Achilles rather than by Pyrrhus (see Jortin and Upton in *Variorum* II, 218–19).

59. *Gerusalemme Liberata* XVI. 17–27; *Odyssey* V. 151–8.

60. *Aeneid* IV. 193–4, 190, 338–9, 305, 366.

61. *Aeneid* IV. 99–100, 114; I. 279, 294, 461–2; II. 3; I. 203.

BIBLIOGRAPHY

NB Classical authors have not been listed. Quotations and translations are in all cases from the editions in the Loeb series.

Alpers, Paul J. *The Poetry of 'The Faerie Queene'* (Princeton, 1967).

——, ed. *Edmund Spenser: A Critical Anthology* (Harmondsworth, 1969).

Aptekar, Jane. *Icons of Justice: Iconography & Thematic Imagery in Book V of 'The Faerie Queene'* (New York and London, 1969).

Ariosto, Ludovico. *Orlando Furioso*, ed. Nicola Zingarelli (Milan, 1934).

——. *Orlando Furioso (The Frenzy of Orlando): A Romantic Epic by Ludovico Ariosto*, trans. Barbara Reynolds, 2 vols. (Harmondsworth, 1975–7).

Bawcutt, Priscilla J. *Gavin Douglas: A Critical Study* (Edinburgh, 1976).

Bennett, Josephine Waters. *The Evolution of 'The Faerie Queene'* (Chicago, 1942).

Berger, Harry, Jr. *The Allegorical Temper: Vision and Reality in Book II of Spenser's 'Faerie Queene'*, Yale Studies in English, 137 (New Haven and London, 1957).

Bible. *The Authorised Version of the English Bible, 1611*, ed. William Aldis Wright, 5 vols. (Cambridge, 1909).

——. Η ΚΑΙΝΗ ΔΙΑΘΗΚΗ, ed. British and Foreign Bible Society, second edition (London, 1958).

——. *The Geneva Bible: A Facsimile of the 1560 edition*, introd. Lloyd E. Berry (Madison, Milwaukee, and London, 1969).

Brooke, N. S. 'C. S. Lewis and Spenser: Nature, Art and the Bower of Bliss', *CamJ*, 2 (1948–9), 420–34.

Brooks-Davies, Douglas. *Spenser's 'Faerie Queene': A Critical Commentary on Books I and II* (Manchester, 1977).

Cain, Thomas H. *Praise in 'The Faerie Queene'* (Lincoln, Nebr. and London, 1978).

Calvin. *Ioannis Calvini Opera Quae Supersunt Omnia*, ed. Guilielmus Baum, Eduardus Cunitz, Eduardus Reuss, 59 vols. (Brunswick, last two vols. Berlin, 1863–1900). *Corpus Reformatorum* XXIX–LXXXVII.

Chaucer. *The Works of Geoffrey Chaucer*, ed. F. N. Robinson, second edition (London, 1957).

Cheney, Donald. *Spenser's Image of Nature: Wild Man and Shepherd in 'The Faerie Queene'*, Yale Studies in English, 161 (New Haven and London, 1966).

Cheney, Donald. 'Spenser's Hermaphrodite and the 1590 *Faerie Queene*', *PMLA*, 87 (1972), 192-200.

Coleridge. See Hill, ed.

De Quincey, Thomas. 'On Murder Considered as One of the Fine Arts', in *Selected English Essays*, arr. W. Peacock, The World's Classics, 32 (London, 1903; repr. 1930), pp. 303-53.

Dickens, A. G. *The English Reformation* (London, 1964).

Douglas. *The Shorter Poems of Gavin Douglas*, ed. P. J. Bawcutt, The Scottish Text Society, Fourth Series, Vol. III (Edinburgh and London, 1967).

Elizabethan Critical Essays. See Smith.

Elliott, John R., Jr., ed. *The Prince of Poets: Essays on Edmund Spenser* (New York and London, 1968).

Ellmann, Richard. *James Joyce* (London, 1959; repr. 1966).

Ellrodt, Robert. *Neoplatonism in the Poetry of Spenser*, Travaux d'humanisme et renaissance, 35 (Geneva, 1960).

Elton, G. R. *Reformation Europe 1517–1559* (Glasgow, 1963; repr. July 1976).

English Critical Essays. See Jones.

Evans, Maurice. *Spenser's Anatomy of Heroism: A Commentary on 'The Faerie Queene'* (Cambridge, 1970).

Fleming, John V. *The 'Roman de la Rose': A Study in Allegory and Iconography* (Princeton, 1969).

Fletcher, Angus. *Allegory: The Theory of a Symbolic Mode* (Ithaca and New York, 1964).

——. *The Prophetic Moment: An Essay on Spenser* (Chicago and London, 1971).

Fowler, Alastair D. S. 'Six Knights at Castle Joyous', *SP*, 56 (1959), 583–99.

——. 'The Image of Mortality: *The Faerie Queene*, II. i–ii', *HLQ*, 24 (1960–1), 91–110.

——. *Spenser and the Numbers of Time* (London, 1964).

——. *Triumphal Forms: Structural Patterns in Elizabethan Poetry* (Cambridge, 1970).

——. 'Emanations of glory: Neoplatonic order in Spenser's *Faerie Queen*', in *Theatre* (see Kennedy), pp. 53–82.

——. *Edmund Spenser*, Writers and their Work, 258 (Harlow, 1977).

Freeman, Rosemary. *'The Faerie Queene': A Companion for Readers* (London, 1970).

Friedrich, Gerhard, ed. *Theologisches Wörterbuch zum neuen Testament*, Vol. VIII (Stuttgart, 1969).

Frye, Northrop. 'The Structure of Imagery in *The Faerie Queene*', *UTQ*, 30 (1961), 109-27.

Geoffrey of Monmouth. See Monmouth.

Hamilton, A. C. *The Structure of Allegory in 'The Faerie Queene'* (Oxford, 1961).

——, ed. *Essential Articles for the Study of Edmund Spenser* (Hamden, Conn., 1972).

——. See Spenser.

Hankins, John Erskine. *Source and Meaning in Spenser's Allegory: A Study of 'The Faerie Queene'* (Oxford, 1971).

Harbage, Alfred. *Annals of English Drama 975–1700: An Analytical Record of All Plays, Extant or Lost, Chronologically Arranged and Indexed by Authors, Titles, Dramatic Companies, &c.*, rev. S. Schoenbaum (London, 1964).

Harper, Carrie A. *The Sources of the British Chronicle History in Spenser's 'Faerie Queene'* (Philadelphia, 1910).

Hawkins, Sherman. 'Mutabilitie and the Cycle of the Months', in *Form and Convention in the Poetry of Edmund Spenser*, Selected Papers from the English Institute, ed. William Nelson (New York and London, 1961), pp. 76–102.

Hieatt, A. Kent. 'Scudamour's Practice of *Maistrye* upon Amoret', *PMLA*, 77 (1962), 509–10.

Hill, Iris Tillman. 'Britomart and *Be Bold, Be Not Too Bold*', *ELH*, 38 (1971), 173–87.

Hill, John Spencer, ed. *Imagination in Coleridge* (London and Basingstoke, 1978).

Hough, Graham. *A Preface to 'The Faerie Queene'* (London, 1962).

Jones, Edmund D., ed. *English Critical Essays: Sixteenth, Seventeenth and Eighteenth Centuries*, The World's Classics, 240 (London, 1922; reset 1947).

Kaske, Carol V. 'The Dragon's Spark and Sting and the Structure of Red Cross's Dragon-Fight: *The Faerie Queene*, I. xi–xii', repr. in Hamilton, *Essential Articles*, pp. 425–46.

——. 'Spenser's Pluralistic Universe: The View from the Mount of Contemplation (*F.Q.* I. x)', in *Contemporary Thought on Edmund Spenser: With a Bibliography of Criticism of 'The Faerie Queene', 1900–1970*, ed. Richard C. Frushell and Bernard J. Vondersmith (Carbondale and Edwardsville, London and Amsterdam, 1975), pp. 121–49.

Kennedy, Judith M., and James A. Reither, eds. *A Theatre for Spenserians*, Papers of the International Spenser Colloquium, Fredericton, New Brunswick, October 1969 (Toronto, Buffalo, and Manchester, 1973).

Kittel, Gerhard, ed. *Theologisches Wörterbuch zum neuen Testament*, Vol. II (Stuttgart, 1935; repr. 1950).

Kouwenhoven, Jan Karel. 'Spenser and History: A Case Study of the Belge Episode' (unpublished article).

Lacey, Robert. *Sir Walter Ralegh* (London, 1973; repr. 1975).

Leslie, Michael Peter. 'Martial and Chivalric Symbolism in Spenser's *The Faerie Queene*' (Ph.D. dissertation, University of Edinburgh, 1981).

Lewis, C. S. *The Allegory of Love: A Study in Medieval Tradition* (Oxford, 1936; corr. repr. 1938).

——. *English Literature in the Sixteenth Century, Excluding Drama* (Oxford, 1954).

——. *An Experiment in Criticism* (Cambridge, 1961).

——. *Studies in Medieval and Renaissance Literature*, coll. Walter Hooper (Cambridge, 1966).

——. *Spenser's Images of Life*, ed. Alastair Fowler (Cambridge, 1967).

Luther. *Martin Luthers Geistliche Lieder*, ed. Albert Leitzmann, *Kleine Texte für theologische Vorlesungen und Übungen*, series ed. Hans Lietzmann, 24/25 (Bonn, 1907).

MacCaffrey, Isabel G. *Spenser's Allegory: The Anatomy of Imagination* (Princeton, 1976).

MacLachlan, Hugh. '"In the Person of Prince Arthur": Spenserian *Magnificence* and the Ciceronian Tradition', *UTQ*, 46 (1976–7), 125–46.

Malory. *The Works of Sir Thomas Malory*, ed. Eugène Vinaver, second edition, 3 vols. (Oxford, 1967).

Mills, Jerry Leath. 'Spenser's Letter to Raleigh and the Averroistic *Poetics*', *ELN*, 14 (1976–7), 246–9.

Monmouth, Geoffrey of. *The History of the Kings of Britain*, trans. Lewis Thorpe (Harmondsworth, 1966; repr. 1978).

Murray, Peter and Linda. *The Art of the Renaissance* (London, 1963; repr. 1974).

Murrin, Michael. 'The Rhetoric of Fairyland', in *The Rhetoric of Renaissance Poetry: From Wyatt to Milton*, ed. Thomas O. Sloan and Raymond B. Waddington (Berkeley, Los Angeles, and London, 1974), pp. 73–95.

Nelson, William. *The Poetry of Edmund Spenser: A Study* (New York and London, 1963; repr. 1971).

——. 'Spenser *ludens*', in *Theatre* (see Kennedy), pp. 83–100.

Nohrnberg, James. *The Analogy of 'The Faerie Queene'* (Princeton, 1976).

O'Connell, Michael. *Mirror and Veil: The Historical Dimension of Spenser's 'Faerie Queene'* (Chapel Hill, 1977).

Owen, W. J. B. '"In These XII Books Severally Handled and Discoursed"', *ELH*, 19 (1952), 165–72.

——. 'Spenser's Letter to Ralegh—A Reply', *MLN*, 75 (1960), 195–7.

Parks, George B. 'Gloriana's Annual Feast', *TLS*, 29 June 1933, p. 447.

Puttenham, George. *The Arte of English Poesie*, ed. Gladys Doidge Willcock and Alice Walker (Cambridge, 1936).

Rathborne, I. E. *The Meaning of Spenser's Fairyland*, Columbia University Studies in English and Comparative Literature, 131 (New York, 1937).

Ripa, Cesare. *Iconologia*, facsimile of the Roman edn. of 1603, introd. Erna Mandowsky (Hildesheim and New York, 1970).

Roche, Thomas P., Jr. *The Kindly Flame: A Study of the Third and Fourth Books of Spenser's 'Faerie Queene'* (Princeton, 1964).

Rowse, A. L. *The Elizabethan Renaissance: The Life of the Society* (London, 1971; repr. 1974).

Sale, Roger. *Reading Spenser: An Introduction to 'The Faerie Queene'* (New York, 1968).

Schulze, Ivan L. 'Elizabethan Chivalry and the Faerie Queene's Annual Feast', *MLN*, 50 (1935), 158–61.

Servius. *Commentarii in Virgilium*, ed. H. Albertus Lion, 2 vols. (Göttingen, 1826).

Sidney. *The Countesse of Pembrokes Arcadia*, ed. Albert Feuillerat (Cambridge, 1912; repr. 1969).

——. *The Poems of Sir Philip Sidney*, ed. William A. Ringler, Jr. (Oxford, 1962; repr. 1971).

——. *An Apology for Poetry; or, The Defence of Poesy*, ed. Geoffrey Shepherd (London and elsewhere, 1965).

Smith, G. Gregory, ed. *Elizabethan Critical Essays*, 2 vols. (Oxford, 1904).

Spenser. *Poetical Works*, ed. J. C. Smith and E. de Selincourt (Oxford, 1912; repr. 1975).

——. *The Faerie Queene*, Vols. I–VI of *The Works of Edmund Spenser: A Variorum Edition*, ed. Edwin Greenlaw, Charles Grosvenor Osgood, Frederick Morgan Padelford, Ray Heffner (Baltimore, 1932–8).

——. *The Faerie Queene*, ed. A. C. Hamilton, Longman Annotated English Poets (London and New York, 1977).

Sprague, Arthur Colby. 'Gloriana's Annual Feast', *TLS*, 27 April 1933, p. 295.

Tasso, Torquato. *Discourses on the Heroic Poem*, trans. Mariella Cavalchini and Irene Samuel (Oxford, 1973).

Tervarent, Guy de. *Attributs et symboles dans l'art profane, 1450–1600: dictionnaire d'un langage perdu*, Travaux d'humanisme et renaissance, 29, 3 vols. (Geneva, 1958–64).

Theologisches Wörterbuch. See Friedrich and Kittel.

Thomas, Keith. *Religion and the Decline of Magic: Studies in Popular Beliefs in Sixteenth- and Seventeenth-Century England* (London, 1971; repr. Harmondsworth, 1978).

Tonkin, Humphrey. *Spenser's Courteous Pastoral: Book Six of the 'Faerie Queene'* (Oxford, 1972).

Tuve, Rosemond. 'The Red Crosse Knight and Mediaeval Demon Stories', *PMLA*, 44 (1929), 706–14.

——. *Allegorical Imagery: Some Mediaeval Books and Their Posterity* (Princeton, 1966).

Vinaver, Eugène. *The Rise of Romance* (Oxford, 1971).

Warnach, Viktor. *Agape: Die Liebe als Grundmotiv der neutestamentlichen Theologie* (Düsseldorf, 1951).

Wells, Robin Headlam. 'Semper Eadem: Spenser's "Legend of Constancie" ', *MLR*, 73 (1978), 250–5.

Welsford, Enid. *Spenser: Fowre Hymnes: Epithalamion: A Study of Edmund Spenser's Doctrine of Love* (Oxford, 1967).

Whitaker, Virgil K. *The Religious Basis of Spenser's Thought*, Stanford University Publications, University Series, Language and Literature, Volume VII, Number 3 (Stanford and London, 1950).

Williams, Kathleen. *Spenser's 'Faerie Queene': The World of Glass* (London, 1966).

Wind, Edgar. *Pagan Mysteries in the Renaissance* (London, 1958).

Woodhouse, A. S. P. 'Nature and Grace in *The Faerie Queene*', *ELH*, 16 (1949), 194–228.

Yates, Frances A. 'Elizabethan Chivalry: The Romance of the Accession Day Tilts', *JWCI*, 20 (1957), 4–25.

——. *Astraea: The Imperial Theme in the Sixteenth Century* (London, 1975; repr. Harmondsworth, 1977).

INDEX

NB Superscript numbers refer to Notes developing or introducing topics, or identifying critics quoted or alluded to but not mentioned by name in the text. Italic type, in long character entries, indicates pages relating the character to its conceptual meaning.